WHAT OTHERS A
ABOUT THIS I

This book from start to finish demonstrates   ѡ ѡ ᴇᴇᴇᴇr of God can work
through a person willing to leave everything and follow God's calling. It also
shows the need and importance of prayer support to bring vision to reality. The
reader is compelled to desire the same power of God in their own life.

– Sid Cordle MBE, London, England

Anne's book is truly an inspirational read, with all the amazing stories of healings and people giving their lives to Jesus. But I found the nuggets of wisdom
she shares here and there even more challenging, as they come out of life
spent in obedience to Jesus and a heart full of love for God and His kingdom. I
have met Anne several times and she is, like most Finns, very straightforward
and frank in her approach, thus releasing others in the freedom of the truth and
grace of Jesus. But everything comes with a twinkle in her eye that lightens the
heart. I recommend her book with all my heart.

– Eva Sarsa, House Church leader, Helsinki, Finland

If you enjoyed Jackie Pullinger's 'Chasing the Dragon' you are in for another
treat. Anne Miettinen is a Finnish servant of God from the same mould as Jackie Pullinger. This is an inspiring book packed full of God's amazing miracles, as
He responds to the desperate needs of some of the poorest people in the world
and the simple obedience of one of His servants. Again and again God releases
His dazzling miracles in the heart of darkness as His servants obediently follow
where He leads. In fact, there are so many miracles in this book that you almost
begin to take them for granted.

This book has a completely 'real' feel to it – nothing hidden. It could be sub-titled,
'The Cost of Miracles', because it reveals the price some were willing to pay to
carry God's love into dark places, where most of us would be fearful to go.

This is an amazing testimony of God's work in and through an extraordinary
lady from Finland as she brings God's love and hope to the slum-dwellers of the
Philippines. We highly recommend it.

– Vic & Di Whittaker, Open Kingdom, Sheffield, England

I love the way it is written, Anne has a wonderful sense of humour but more than
that I can feel the anointing on it.

– Jacqui Shuttleworth, Sheffield, England

This is a faith stirring, awe inspiring book, encouraging you to believe God for the impossible! In her daily life, Anne Miettinen truly participates with heaven's objective to bring His Kingdom down to earth. With so much need in this world, we would all benefit from a dose of Anne's love for God, love for the lost and radical child-like faith in her loving Father, who truly is a God of miracles! Enjoy as you read this heavenly nugget!

– **Heidi Tiplady**, Bushfire Ministries International, Sheffield, England

Miracles
in the
Philippines' Slums

Anne Miettinen

HIMbooks

Sheffield, England

Published by HIMbooks Ltd, Sheffield, England.
Email: info@himbooks.com
Website: http://www.himbooks.com

Unless otherwise indicated, scriptures are quoted from The Holy Bible, New Century Version®, copyright © 2005 by Thomas Nelson, Inc. Used by permission.

10 9 8 7 6 5 4 3 2 1

ISBN 978-0-9562211-0-0

Printed and bound in England by WFO Print.
Website: http://www.wfo-print.com

Cover design by Bankart Design.
Email: bankartdesign@telkomsa.net

The names of some people appearing in this book have been changed to protect their privacy and security.

The front cover shows Bea Jimenez from Aroma village in Mamburao. The photograph was taken in December 2007, and Bea is starting at Aroma school in 2009.

THANKS

Special thanks to all my intercessors and friends who prayed over this book.

I would like to acknowledge our school children in the Philippines, as you revolutionised my life, you represent real live heroes.

I gratefully acknowledge Bob and Hilkka for their endless editing, typesetting and motivating me to go outside the limits of my comfort zone, to bring this book to fruition.

I am especially grateful to my husband Erno and our grown up children, Chris and Emilie, who understand the calling of the Lord in my life. Your support and encouragement have given me strength in this ministry, and without it I would not be what I am today.

Thank you to those who were with me over the years, for being patient with me.

Most of all, I am grateful to God for empowering me to continue.

I believe this book will bless many.

Anne

CONTENTS

PART ONE.
INTRODUCTION

1. Anne

2. Feeding the children

3. A new school in the slums

CHAPTER 1
WHY BOTHER?

I was at Manila airport in the Philippines, on my way back home to Brisbane, feeling exhausted and very run down after another mission trip. I visited the ladies room and was standing by the wash basins, digging into the depths of my worn-out handbag in the hope of finding just one last paracetamol that might be hiding there. I wanted to try and relieve a throbbing headache before getting on the Qantas plane for the seven hour flight back home. Manila's steamy, hot weather and the long trip to the airport in a totally overcrowded bus had again taken its toll and messed up my head to the point of exploding.

I was seriously questioning myself and my motives for this lifestyle: "What on earth am I doing here? I must be suffering from some sort of advanced dementia to be pushing myself voluntarily into these types of situations yet again. Wouldn't it be much better to stay in Australia and do what I am best at, illustrating books and doing my art-work? That is my profession, for goodness' sake. I could live a nice comfortable life; at peace in my own sweet home … nobody and nothing would bother me. I'm over sixty years old after all! And yet here I am again after a month of hopping from one island to another in the Philippines, wandering like a vagabond in slums and squatter areas, with cockroaches, ants, rats and the like for company."

I looked at myself in the mirror: my eyes had big dark rings round them, in sharp contrast to the rather deathly pallor of my exhausted face staring back at me. I looked scary! I could easily understand why the little kids so often seemed to be frightened when they first saw this albino, perhaps the first white-skinned person they had seen in their lives. My accidental mistake of using whitening soap instead of normal soap for this whole month-long visit in the islands didn't exactly help either: it had taken off any last vestiges of tan that my Finnish skin ever managed to get. How could I possibly know that people in this country like to use that sort of product?

There I was in the middle of my desperate thoughts, when the washroom door opened and in walked a young Filipina lady who parked herself next to me in front of the mirror, to repair her make-up. I find all Filipinas very beautiful and this one was no exception. Out of curiosity the young lady glanced towards me, clearly wanting to say something. Well, I wasn't really in the frame of mind to start any sort of polite conversation at that moment, as I was quite enjoying my own pity-party and didn't want anyone to interrupt it.

But Filipino people often love to talk and they usually want to know everything about everything. They are also very open and friendly, totally without my Finnish "personal space" mentality. I normally really like their personalities and attitudes … but I definitely did not want that sort of interaction now.

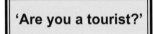
'Are you a tourist?'

They will speak openly and from their hearts: if you have a pimple on your face, they want so lovingly to bring it to your attention, apparently unaware that you might already know about it and might not want to be reminded about it again.

I was just about to leave the ladies room, when the question came: "Why are you here in the Philippines? Are you a tourist?"

I guess I could not avoid answering. "Well, no, actually, this is a working trip," I replied, immediately wishing I hadn't said that. It just slipped out of my mouth. I noticed the surprised look on her face, as no westerner ever comes there to work.

"You're doing work here?" she asked. "What sort of work is that?" This was really annoyingly awkward, it was not her business what I am doing or not doing, said my Finnish mind. But before I could manage to control my words, I had already given her a short summary of what I did in the Philippines. These people have such an innocence and openness; it is difficult to keep any secrets from them.

I told her I had set up schools for kids who have no chance of going to school as they live in squatter areas, on beaches, in slums … we give them pre-

4

school education so that they then will be accepted into the mainstream school system. All these schools are free and we arrange medical missions to them, in the rainy season we pay for rice distribution to their families …

The woman stared back at me, apparently deeply moved, and her make-up problems forgotten. Without any warning she came over and hugged me warmly, saying: "Please, we really need your kind of people, don't stop what you are doing." She continued tearfully, "You have such a good heart … you do not know how much what you are doing means to me." She spluttered something, pressed her handbag close to her chest, turned around and ran out through the door and into the airport concourse.

4. Children from the Mangyan tribe

I was speechless. I just stood gazing at the door, amazed at her words. But then I grabbed my hand luggage and went out after her, hoping to find her and ask a bit about her own life, but she had disappeared completely. I walked around the big airport departure hall a couple of times but could not find any sign of her amongst the crowds of people. How had she been able to disappear so quickly? She was like a heavenly messenger sent to me just at the right time.

Her words had a profound effect on me. Don't get me wrong, I really do enjoy and love what I do, but sometimes little things creep in one by one and manage to pull me down, sometimes to the extent that I end up questioning my own sanity. I had never ever wanted to do charity work in my life, and never planned to work with children. It was certainly not on my career path – this work just found me and took me over. I often say to my friends that I did an accidental landing in my "heavenly plane" – but it came down in just the right place at just the right time and I found my destiny.

I'm not a melancholy sort of person, I don't cry easily and normally I do not take to heart what other people say. But someone's sarcastic words a little while before had somehow stuck in my mind and hurt deeply: "What you're trying to do is just a waste of time – are you aiming to be some kind of Mother Theresa? Leave those kids alone, there are too many squatter people anyway, and it's their own fault …" That is why the lady in the toilet and her sudden outburst was a real encouragement for me, a real word from God. But perhaps you might want to know something about how I came to be there in the first place.

5. *Life in the slum*

6. *Visiting a slum village*

CHAPTER 2
WHO IS ANNE MIETTINEN?

I was born in the chaos following the Second World War, along with millions of other babies, whose fathers returned from the front, each with the same mission: to be fruitful and multiply and fill the earth, all at the same time. Thus there were always too many of us, too many of the same age children, and I just had to learn to push forward in my overcrowded age group. I tried my best to be born somewhat before my proper time was due, to get ahead of the traffic jam for entry into this world. So my father had to literally kick my mum to the maternity hospital along the cold and icy road in January by "kick-sledge". The same vehicle brought me and mum home in great style.

7. Kick-sledge

From that time onwards the course of my life was far from average. Readers may be interested to know that I share my age group with Bill Clinton and with members of the Abba pop group; whether that is honourable or dishonourable company I cannot comment. But at least they handled the politics and the show business side of life respectively, leaving me to focus on areas where there was less of a traffic jam of talent. I concentrated on trying to find my identity – who I actually am.

My mother's ancestors were German Jews and my father's roots were also in Germany. For some peculiar reason these parents of mine decided to choose Finland as their new home country. And that is where I had the honour to be born – I was very grateful that they didn't continue going any further north!

Mother wanted me to become an economist, while my father hoped I would choose a career where I could make a decent living and hence become independent as soon as possible. To my parents' lifelong regret, but to the salvation of the Finnish economy, I decided to be an artist.

I was one of the few non-radical young people of the 1960's, avoiding carefully the communist ideology of my Finnish art school and finding my way into the advertising and graphic design area – because my hungry body wanted food! I also managed to wander around several countries to check out whether they would be potential candidates as my new home country. France felt the most homely to me and I spent time in its artistic environs on several occasions. But trips within Europe did not ease my feelings of rootlessness, so I decided to go even further afield – to Israel.

> **my hungry body wanted food**

For some strange reason when the ship arrived at the harbour of Haifa I felt like I was home. However, at that stage my concept of "home" was fairly wide-ranging, and included wherever my suitcase happened to be at the time.

The first people that I got to know in Israel were a group of young Moroccans and as I picked up their pronunciation, my own command of the Hebrew language developed with a strange accent. This caused great amusement among the local people as my albino appearance was a total contrast to my spoken Hebrew. I didn't let that put me off as I had always felt myself to be a sort of unique compound of many different elements.

I quickly got acquainted with the artistic community in my new home country and through these contacts I found work again, doing what I was best at. The biggest masterpiece that I produced was a set of wall paintings at a big night club in the town of Bersheva, a project that also included creating sixty stained glass windows. My career was just starting to become successful, when one day this exhibition of the work of my dreams was destroyed at a stroke: someone threw a grenade into the building.

Was I upset about the building? Not at all; but I was devastated about the destruction of my masterpieces! After that I was determined to produce something more resilient that would not be so easily destroyed. Now totally disillusioned and fed up with the whole of Bersheva, I joined the first caravan that happened to pass by, or in other words I caught the bus going to Jerusalem.

There I started to study the Torah in Rabanut (where the orthodox Rabbis minister) under the guidance of Rabbi Kahanan and his wife. I used my Finnish *sisu*[1] to dig diligently into the rules and regulations of Judaism, trying to understand the strict time regulations for eating sausage and milk, and why one was not allowed to carry scissors on the Sabbath or to press a light switch. It was the last of these that was to be my undoing.

I had deliberately chosen accommodation in the orthodox quarter to make sure that I would really learn all the possible different regulations with all their intricate twists and turns. One evening I blundered home in the darkness and climbed up the outside stairs up to my room. I opened the door and then stumbled over something … I tried to stop myself from falling over anything else and fumbled for the light switch ... and the light came on! Within a few moments that part

the light came on!

of the suburb was wide awake and my eviction from this orthodox area was so speedy that I only just managed to grab my suitcase. Within minutes I was homeless and I had to sleep on a park bench.

Seeking to learn from my first mistake, I moved to study under a more highly esteemed Rabbi elsewhere. But unfortunately he was more interested in the student than in teaching, so in my embarrassment I gave up studying the Torah at that time, hoping to continue at some time in the future. I decided to travel to Finland for a holiday, and that started a whole new chapter of my life story.

When I arrived in Finland, my finances were so much in the red that I did not have the wherewithal to buy a flight to return to Israel. So out of necessity I hired myself to an advertising agency as an artist. I was quickly promoted to be the manager of their graphic design team, and during that period of my life I got to know a building engineer called Erno Miettinen and we got married.

My health was not good at that time. I struggled with severe migraine headaches which got worse and worse, to the point where I was given morphine injections and ergotamine pills. I also suffered from frequent stomach problems which meant I had to keep to a special diet, as well as haemophilia which I had inherited from my mother. I needed to stay far away from sharp knives: mother had learned to sew and close her own wounds, but my skills as a skin seamstress were much more limited.

---

1   *Sisu* is a Finnish word meaning determination, guts and stamina

One day someone brought a pile of pictures and a magazine article about a Pentecostal pastor to my office desk. I read the text telling about this man who was causing quite a hullabaloo by praying for sick people who then got well. I wondered if such things were possible but then quickly decided not to believe it. I wasn't going to bother about going along to his meetings unless they were held in our immediate neighbourhood. However that is exactly what happened, because one day this very same pastor held a big meeting in the assembly hall of the school next to our home.

At that time I used to buy science fiction books as gifts to my husband who was keen on this type of reading material. I accidentally chose a religious book amongst the sci-fi ones – 'The Late, Great Planet Earth' by Hal Lindsey – and Erno read it. Without my knowing it, he got quite absorbed in its theories about the end-time prophecies in the Bible and how they linked to current world events. He now wanted to unravel what this was all about and told me that out of curiosity he wanted to go to this local meeting to see what was going on. I wasn't interested in doing so but felt I should go along and support him, or at least make sure that he wasn't going to be brainwashed or get involved in some sort of cult.

> **I accidentally chose a religious book**

So we went along together and managed to arrive at the meeting an hour late, but in God's perfect timing, just as the pastor started his sermon. I listened with great interest as he told fascinating stories of his experiences in an absolutely captivating way: I decided to ask him to become a copywriter in my advertising office, as I felt that his place certainly wasn't in a church. Why did he waste his time doing these sorts of things?

My interesting train of thought on such business opportunities was interrupted by the nasty tightening feeling in my head, so familiar to me. That meant that the migraine was starting. I opened my handbag and tried to find my medicines but then realized that I had left them at home. The headache quickly got worse and soon I was in such a bad state that I did not hear or see anything of what was happening on the platform. I just wanted to go home, but when I told Erno he didn't move an inch or seem to pay any attention to my agony.

Suddenly he nudged me and said, "Put up your hand!" and without thinking I did so. Erno was an atheist and I guessed that they must have asked from the platform something like: "Who here does not believe in this poppycock?" I even looked around the room and saw many others raising their hands, so there were obviously quite a few other wise people here as well.

Then I got a very strange sensation – a warm wave passed over me from my head to my feet and I felt suddenly light and free from the heaviness of the migraine. The only thing I could compare it to was the feeling I'd got from the morphine injections – as if I was in a cloud. Yet this felt so different; the morphine always came with unpleasant sensations too. Did they have some sort of laughing gas being pumped around the hall? Or was it a weird mass hypnosis sensation? Whatever it was, I had this amazingly funny floating feeling.

Erno interrupted this lovely sensation as he abruptly stood up. I grabbed his arm – ah, finally he must have understood that we needed to leave this place and go home! But to my surprise he didn't walk towards the exit doors at the side of the hall but instead he headed to the front. "OK," I thought, "What a wise move – we're going to leave through the emergency exit. That's where all these other people must be going too." We made our way forward along the side aisle in the middle of a crowd of others who had obviously had enough of this meeting, just like me. But then my husband surprised me again, turning to the right at the end of the aisle and stopping in front of the platform. All the other people were gathered around me and so I was stuck there, still wondering why nobody walked out through the exit door. Were we just waiting for somebody to open the door? Was it locked?

The pastor bent down towards our group gathered in front of the stage and said in quiet voice: "You have come here to make a very important decision. You have given your lives to Jesus …" Those words hit me like a hammer and I panicked: "What? I certainly didn't come here for that! I was only trying to find the way out!" I tried to shrink and make myself as invisible as possible. My husband sometimes had a strange sense of humour and I imagined that

> **What? I certainly didn't come here for that!**

he was now doing all this as some sort of weird joke, but I really didn't see anything humorous in this at all …. We were going to have a serious talk about this at home!

We walked home in silence and I was still in the middle of this euphoric, cloudy feeling which I could not explain. Whether or not it was laughing gas I didn't know, but it certainly felt very nice. As was my normal routine when migraine symptoms came, I went for my medicines. I walked into the kitchen, over to the medicine cabinet and took out my migraine pills. At that moment I clearly heard a voice saying, "What are you doing here?" I rushed into the lounge where Erno was sitting down and told him in no uncertain terms: "I can do whatever I want in my own home!"

Erno was astonished: "What do you mean? I didn't say a thing!" I went on to give him a serious lecture about the fact that he had no right at all to boss me about or to tell me what I could or could not do. He got even more surprised as he listened to me and he insisted that he had not made any attempt at all to tell me what to do. That made me angry: "Now he won't even admit to what he's said!"

I disappeared back into the kitchen and picked up the medicines again. Just as I was about to take the pills, I heard the same voice again: "What are you doing here?" This time it seemed to come from behind the window, but that was totally impossible as we lived in a very tall building, on the eighth floor. Could that be the voice of God? Was such a thing possible? In any case I decided to obey because there was such authority in that voice and I surely didn't dare to touch the medicines any more. At that moment I recognised that I was free from migraine, and as time went on I discovered that I had been healed from all my other sicknesses as well.

The stories from that magazine article started to fit together in my mind; so they were all true after all. I decided to believe in Jesus even though I did not really know what it meant. In fact I had already become a believer somewhat "accidentally", or at least in a way differing from all the possible textbook approaches to getting saved. I took a Bible off the bookshelf and thumbed through, hoping to figure out what this was all about. It opened at Matthew 15:30, saying:

Great crowds came to Jesus, bringing with them the lame, the blind, the crippled, those who could not speak, and many others. They put them at Jesus' feet, and he healed them.

"Ah ha!" I thought to myself, "So it's that simple." On my next working day I decided to preach my first sermon at our office. We had an open plan layout, and although I had repeatedly asked and hoped for an office of my own, I had never got one. I could see now what a blessing that was. So on Monday morning after my team had settled down behind their desks, I stood up and asked for their attention as I had something very important to tell them. Some of my colleagues were still rather fuzzy-headed after their weekend activities, so my congregation was not as attentive as they could have been. Nevertheless I told them of how I had become a believer and that I had been healed of all my sicknesses. A deep hush descended on the office. Then someone called out, "So what?" So I drew my sermon to a close by stating with conviction: "Well if you don't become believers, you will all go to hell!"

> **I decided to preach my first sermon at our office**

12

My colleagues gaped at me with astonished looks and then one asked, "Did you have something else you want to say?" "No, not now," I replied, "but tomorrow I will tell you more." I went back to my desk fretting that my first preaching engagement had been so short, but I didn't know what else to say and the team hadn't seemed keen on listening either.

> **My colleagues gaped at me**

At midday my desk phone rang and I was invited to pay a visit to the manager of the company. He started off by saying how grateful he was for the long hours that I had been working recently. He told me that he guessed that I was probably quite stressed after such long days, so he felt that it would be a good idea if I now took a couple of weeks holiday! I was really surprised and told him that I felt absolutely fine, and in fact I was actually doing better than ever before, because I had been healed. My boss interrupted me, "Yes, yes I believe that, but I would still want you to take a bit of a break now after all this stressful workload." My dear workmates had probably had something to do with this. Probably one of them had complained that this workaholic had gone crazy and was now pushing her team to hell.

My two weeks holiday gave me a great opportunity to look into spiritual matters but I couldn't help wondering how amazing it was that I get awarded extra holiday when I am healthy – something that never seemed possible previously when I was almost dying in the office with a migraine attack!

I used my holiday profitably: if I had been healed then other people were going to get healed as well when I prayed for them. I started asking my acquaintances and even total strangers if they were ill and if I could pray for them to be healed. For some reason the answer was always no, but I prayed anyway and a couple of people got healed immediately. I had nobody around telling me whether I could do this or not, as I hadn't yet been in contact with any other believers. I didn't understand the importance of gradual and slow development into our spiritual gifting so I just shot forwards like a rocket, through reading the book of Acts.

After my fortnight's holiday I returned to the office, and I saw to my amazement at the end of the open plan area a new little room that had been constructed. My desk was nowhere to be found, until I peered inside the new room – there it was with all my working materials. One of my colleagues kindly informed me that I had been given the special privilege of an office of my own. Of course this is something that I had always wanted, but not right now when I had prepared the gospel sermon of the century to deliver to my fellow workers. The Lord certainly works in mysterious ways …

At around the time that we got saved, Erno and I had been building our own house in Espoo close to Helsinki. As it was still under construction, my husband decided it would be better to leave out a few of the inner walls so that we could have plenty of space to hold meetings at home. Maybe that would be the task given to us by the Lord, to give others what we had received.

At the same time we also found the local Pentecostal church in Espoo and became members. When our house was ready, we opened it for our church to use for young people's meetings. Soon we had as many as three meetings during the week and people started to come from all over Finland, from different churches. Many were filled with the Holy Spirit and healed.

Later I founded a graphic design company and started to do illustration work for different publishers. I felt that God's destiny for my life was to work as an illustrator, doing commissions for Christian companies. I ended up illustrating books from across the whole spectrum – both spiritual and worldly books. At one stage I was asked to create an advertising video about the same pastor in whose meeting I "accidentally" got saved, and I was delighted to be given the opportunity to get to know him better.

A turning point came as a result of a meeting that my husband and I attended in Central Finland. It was a gathering which included many evangelists and believers from different congregations. At the end of the meeting an evangelist from the Free Church came over to me and started to prophesy: "The Lord is going to send you to preach the gospel in a country far away. The people living there have dark skins, wide noses and curly hair." I got scared, "Africa!

> **The Lord is going to send you to preach the gospel in a country far away**

There is no way that I am going there!" I knew that it was vital to get out of this call to Africa and quickly! I had known that a move away from Finland was on the cards – but we were definitely not moving to Africa. So I started frantically planning a Jonah-style escape route.

Shortly after this fateful prophecy I bumped into a friend in Helsinki city centre whom I had not seen for ages. I asked her about what she had been doing and she told me that they were about to become emigrants, and they were leaving on the next day to Australia. As we parted, she shouted to me over her shoulder, "Why don't you come after us!" That was it, Australia! Certainly far enough away from Africa. This lady had told me that she had relatives in Australia who sponsored them, but I didn't know anyone there. The big emigrant years were already over and the state of Australia wasn't trying to win more European immigrants.

I strolled on further in the city centre, my thoughts in turmoil. I happened to stop in front of a boutique window with a beautiful apricot colour dress on display that caught my attention. I found it very difficult to concentrate on anything else but how to avoid Africa. My pondering and planning was interrupted by a shop assistant who ran from the clothes boutique to where I was standing. "Are you Anne?" she asked. When I owned up to bearing that name she asked whether I remembered her from years ago – it turned out that we had worked together in the same office some time before. We exchanged news about our lives and families and then she said, "You are still young – why don't you go to Australia?" I burst out laughing and wondered how on earth that had come into her mind.

Here within a space of ten minutes was the second person telling me about Australia. But how could we go there as we didn't have a sponsor. She said, "My sister is married to an Australian and lives in Sydney. I will call her and they will be able to sponsor you!" We swopped telephone numbers, but I really didn't believe what this lady had said. Who would take on two total strangers as their responsibility?

However, that same evening my friend called me and cheerfully reported that her sister had indeed promised to sponsor us. She even explained what information we would need to take to the Australian Information Office and how to complete application forms for immigration.

Things were looking good for this modern-day Jonah: I would soon be able to get the ticket to travel in completely the opposite direction to Nineveh, or rather Africa. There was only one hindrance remaining – my husband. How could I plant the idea of moving to Australia into his mind?

> **Things were looking good for this modern-day Jonah**

The Lord had arranged it already in His own way. Erno worked in an engineering office that had several foreign projects underway and that evening he came home depressed, telling me that it looked like he might be sent to Iran for a year to look after projects there. He did not want to go but neither did anyone else in his office – nobody was volunteering to spend a year in Iran.

So now it was clear, we would emigrate to Australia. Within a year of sending in our immigration forms, we were accepted for entry to the country and so we had to sell our house, close down my business and many other things. Christmas was close; who would buy our house at that time of the year? We put a tiny advertisement in the 'Properties For Sale' section of the newspaper even though our house was not even totally ready yet and the peculiar huge open room was not exactly a selling point. The first people that came to look at the house were a husband and wife. The lady looked around and immediately said, "We'll take this." So easy and now everything was clear. We didn't have anyone else responding to the advert but they were not needed – we had our buyers.

Our move happened really quickly, immediately after the house sale was properly finalised and ready. We were in a hurry to go before the big fish ordained by God would come and swallow us up. Before we left, my friend who had so kindly arranged our sponsorship through her sister in Australia, came to visit me. She had a parcel in her hand: "I had a feeling that I should give you a leaving present." I opened the packet and there inside was that wonderful apricot colour dress that I had been admiring in her boutique window. I had not said a word to this lady about the dress, but the Lord wanted to encourage and cheer me up, so it seemed.

> **in a hurry to go before the big fish ordained by God would come ...**

Finland was left behind and we travelled to Thailand en route to our new home country. We decided to take a week's holiday there before embarking on the last leg of the trip. At the end of the week we went to Bangkok airport and checked in for the flight. As we came to board the plane, the air hostess stopped us at the entrance to the economy class cabin and guided us back out again. I whispered to Erno, "I don't understand, is this as far as we're going to get?" The prospect of Jonah's whale was still at the forefront of my mind.

Without any explanation we were guided to a different entrance, up some other steps and straight into business class. We were astonished and wondered what kind of mistake this was, because we only had economy tickets. We were on the upper deck and were almost the only passengers there, except for a couple of other people. For some reason we got VIP treatment – either the cabin staff mistook us for someone else or the Lord had decided to give us a nice surprise even in this.

Finally we stepped onto Australian soil at Sydney airport. The first person who came towards us was a dark skinned, wide-nosed and frizzy haired man. I was shocked and wondered how this could be: was this really Sydney or had we somehow after all landed in Africa? Our sponsors had come to pick us up from the airport so I asked them about this dark skinned guy who clearly appeared just like the person in the prophesy. Our new friends explained to me that the Aborigines were the original inhabitants of Australia .... We had accidentally come to the right country.

We settled down to live on the edge of Sydney and soon started to feel very lonely. I had got used to an active social life in Finland and now I was spending my days alone as Erno had found a job immediately. After a couple of weeks of not coping with quiet suburban life, I started to pray and ask the Lord to give me people with whom I could at least have a conversation, as the Australians seemed to have such an accent that I could not figure out what they were saying.

> **We had accidentally come to the right country**

In prayer I felt the Lord urging me to go to the railway station near us, so I took my bag and ran over there. The platform was empty – what a disappointment! I had assumed that there would have been a ready-made social community waiting for me. The next train stopped and just as I was about to step in I heard a clear "Kymenlaakso" accent from behind me. Kymenlaakso is a province in south-eastern Finland. Wow, Finnish people! I turned around and saw two ladies talking so I went over and joined them. I heard that they were on their way to Liverpool, a suburb in the south west of the city, so I decided to travel there too. During the trip I managed to talk them round to inviting me to visit them in the near future.

It was the next Saturday that we went over to see them. There were six adult children, some of whom had come over to visit their elderly parents who owned the house. The father looked ill, sitting quietly in the rocking chair listening to others talking around him. I sat down beside him and asked what was wrong. He told me that he had leukaemia and had only three months left to live – the doctors had apparently done everything they could to help him. I asked him if he believed in Jesus and that resulted in a torrent of words flooding from his mouth. But after he had finished I said I would still pray for his healing.

The family were watching what was going on with great interest and one of them sceptically commented, "Oh, you are Christians! There are only two types of Finnish people here: those in the Finnish Association and others that are Pentecostal Christians. We like to stay away from both of them." I quickly understood that this invitation to visit might be the last. But during the following week I got a phone call from the daughter, saying that her father had been healed, and his blood tests were absolutely normal: a miracle had taken place!

This was followed by a chain reaction, with all of the family members one after another becoming believers. The first was the eldest daughter and her husband and after that the other sons and daughters of the healed man. This was the start of my evangelistic mission in Australia, which has continued now for about thirty years.

Both of our children were born while we were living in Sydney – Chris in 1983 and Emilie in 1985. Both are committed Christians and have been on mission trips with me: Christopher in the Philippines and Emilie in Papua New Guinea. Chris studied Multimedia and Business and he has his own company, called Wisdomspiral. He currently creates Christian interactive games for children. Emilie is continuing her studies to become a psychologist. The Lord has blessed me with a wonderful family who have given me support and encouragement all the way through.

After five years in Sydney, we felt that the Lord was calling us to move north to Queensland and the city of Brisbane where we acquired an art and picture framing shop. I also worked as an artist, arranged exhibitions, and illustrated books alongside my spiritual work, until the year 2001. That was when the Lord moved me out of secular employment to be a full-time evangelist, and He started opening up to me a mission field in the Asia-Pacific Islands. That work is what I want to tell you about in this book. I want to show how the Lord can use an ordinary person who is willing to let Him work through them, and how He uses very simple methods to open doors for us.

8. One of Anne's paintings, printed as a card

PART TWO.
MINDORO ISLAND

9. On Pastor Sonio's motorbike

10. The Philippines

CHAPTER 3
WILL WE, WON'T WE?

STARTING STEPS

I had a friend who was an evangelist and had done mission trips to India over a period of more than thirty years. Let's call him Mr Tala. Like me he was born in Finland but we had met in our new home city Brisbane. There he was a well-known builder but he ran home meetings mainly reaching out to Finnish migrants. Although Mr Tala's heart was very much for India and its people, one day he asked me if I would come to the Philippines with him. I initially declined because I felt no call at all in that direction. But he was persistent and he kept asking me over and over again, until I finally swallowed the hook in February 2006. At that time for some peculiar reason I heard myself saying, "Yes, I'll come with you."

He was delighted and told me, "It will be a month long trip to Western Mindoro Island. We will hold big meetings in Mindoro where nothing like that has ever happened before, because no one wants to go to these islands. The first meeting will be held in the city of Sablayan. Rather dazed, I wondered what had happened, as my mouth had said yes while my mind was firmly of the opposite opinion. Anyway I decided to ask my son Chris to travel with me and after some persuasion he agreed. So I ordered the tickets.

TRAVEL TROUBLES

In March 2006, one month before we were due to travel, something unforeseen happened: 500 soldiers of the New People's Army (NPA), who are communist terrorists, attacked Mindoro Island and murdered many politicians and civilians. The Philippines government responded by sending troops to the island. Travelling to or from Mindoro was forbidden and all foreigners and political leaders were evacuated. Pastor Edwin Sonio, who was our contact person in the island, told us that we could not travel there as the situation was far too dangerous and the war could easily last for months or even longer. You'll be hearing a lot more about Edwin later.

Many thoughts ran around in my mind … why should I choose to push myself into this sort of chaos? I cancelled the tickets. My son Chris was disappointed and suggested that we should travel to Manila instead of Mindoro. On reflection I felt that this idea of his was a good one so I called the travel agency again: "We'll travel to the Philippines after all but we just want tickets to Manila, please." So that went ahead and soon we had arranged meetings in Manila.

However a short time before we were due to leave on the trip, it all changed again. Our contact person telephoned: "Have you looked at the news, Anne? There are big riots in Manila and they are trying to overthrow the president. The army has surrounded the city and there is a curfew that may last a long time … we cannot hold the meetings there now."

Again I telephoned the travel company: "Cancel the trip, there is war in Manila." The travel agent Jorge Noval was an acquaintance of mine and a believer. Jorge sighed: "OK, we'll try and make the cancellation and hope that Qantas accepts it." I wrote to my intercessors back in Finland (let's call them Hilja and Paula): "I can't travel to the Philippines, the whole country is in a mess." They quickly emailed back: "Have you thought carefully about this decision?" They both had felt an urging from the Lord in prayer: "Anne is going to Philippines" and they both had seen the same thing in a vision.

> **Cancel the trip, there is war in Manila**

I had met Paula for the first time in 2003 in Finland. It was at a meeting of a couple of hundred people where I had been speaking and most of them had come forward to the prayer queue afterwards. I prayed for Paula and passed on, when suddenly I felt the Holy Spirit say some surprising words to me: "You will get to know this person better."

22

I did not know who this lady was, but a month later at the second prophetic seminar that I held in Finland, I saw her again and had opportunity to chat to her between some of the meeting sessions. I was still wondering what the Lord had meant by His words, as many long-lasting friendships started through this seminar.

However the Lord had his own plans: while I was in Finland during the following summer, Paula and Hilja attended another meeting of mine and Paula approached me afterwards. She explained to me a vision that God had given Hilja about the work I was at that time doing in Papua New Guinea. This vision proved to be a very accurate insight into some problems we were currently facing there.

Later Hilja told me that she felt that God had set her to be an intercessor for me and my missionary work. I was really amazed as such intercessors certainly do not 'grow on trees': normally they take much seeking out, and yet here was a lady with obvious prophetic insight who was volunteering! Hilja at that time was already over seventy years old. Paula joined Hilja in this intercessory role as the Lord had already spoken to her about Australia and someone who would come into her life from there. These words had come to her in the mid-1980s.

Both ladies started to receive visions about my work which proved similar and accurate. Paula also acted as the messenger to and from me, wherever I might be, as she had email facilities at home. During the next few years, we developed a good working relationship.

PROPHETIC ENCOURAGEMENT

In their vision Hilja and Paula saw angels forming two long lines with green palm leaves in their hands, holding them up to make a tunnel through which our group could walk safely. As we continued walking so the angelic tunnel was continuing. Hilja also saw rams with big horns pushing blockages away from the road ahead of us.

Paula said, "You will see God doing great deeds and marvel at what happens. In the meetings in Manila there will be a big golden fiery ball, rolling around in the midst of the people."

They also saw more about Mindoro: there was a platform with big soldier angels guarding the rear. Green grass started growing upon the platform and Hilja saw several glowing golden garlands made of red, yellow and orange-coloured flowers hanging in the air everywhere that we prayed for people. The garlands were suspended ready to descend upon the right people. The vision was accompanied with the word: "This is the first fruit of the work that the Lord is doing in the Philippines and it will continue in Europe. Even though the trip will be difficult, it will be the gateway to the new thing ahead of you."

At the same time the Lord showed me in a dream certain details of what would happen on the trip. Next morning I weighed it up. Was I really going to push myself into this mess? But I knew that I did not dare to stay at home after these sorts of prophetic messages. So I decided to go to Manila, but only that far, because the road to Mindoro was not open. I called my friend Jorge again: "Sorry, but I have decided to travel to Manila after all, so could you please book me tickets again?" He called me back within a few minutes saying: "The tickets are okay." It was odd that he didn't even sound angry about these changes.

CHANGES OF PLAN

A few days before our trip to Manila, Pastor Sonio called from Sablayan: "You must come to Mindoro now, because we've been promised that soldiers will be posted around the city venue to keep it safe, and anyway all the advertisements have been published about the meetings. The army has gained the upper hand from the terrorists, who have been pushed back to the mountains."

Oh my goodness! So it was all up in the air again. Now we would be going to Mindoro after all so was there any chance of changing the air tickets again? I would have to make yet another call to Jorge – would he again be so kind and change the tickets so we could travel to Mindoro after going to Manila. How on earth would I explain this to him, and what about Qantas? Would we ever be able to get the tickets at such short notice?

I called Jorge and he immediately burst out laughing. I could not see anything remotely amusing in this situation, in fact to me it was rather humiliating. "So, can you get the tickets for us or not, Jorge?" I asked. "In fact, Anne," he replied, "I never cancelled your original tickets. They are still here in my drawer. I got a bit stressed though, after you told me that you would never travel to the Philippines. I thought I might have to pay for the tickets myself if you weren't going to change your mind." As I voiced my amazement about why he had done this, he answered, "It was a prophetic word. The Lord said to me earlier 'Anne will travel to the Philippines'. I couldn't contradict God

> **everyone apart from me knew this trip was coming**

but I couldn't change your mind either." So, it looked like everyone apart from me knew this trip was coming! Here was another lesson for me in not putting my trust just in the things that we can see.

ATOLLS

More than ten years earlier I had seen a vision, which finally now started to open up to me. Often the Lord talks to us in symbolic language, hiding things if the time is not yet right for the vision to come true. Only at the time of fulfilment do the pieces of the puzzle start to fall into place, to show us that the direction is right.

In that vision I was standing on a map of Australia. As I looked towards the Pacific Islands they came closer. I then looked in the other direction, from Darwin on the northern coast of Australia upwards, past Indonesia. I saw islands that were like loose pieces but they moved towards each other and then became connected. I saw myself jumping from one piece to another and a word appeared in the sky: "atolls". On every piece that I stepped, a different island was formed and the Lord showed through symbols what I did in different islands. He showed me details of the national dress of the people living there. The vision ended and I kept wondering what that word atolls might mean. It was only when I came to the Philippines that I understood how the Lord had showed me not only the Pacific islands but also Asia as a clear route to the Philippines. I just didn't have the illumination in my brain cells yet, to understand the meaning of all of this.

11. View from Mount Moriah

12. Taguig street

CHAPTER 4
ON THE WAY TO MINDORO

MANILA MEETINGS

So at the beginning of April 2006, our little team - Mr Tala, Chris and I - climbed aboard the Qantas plane at Brisbane Airportand the seven-hour trip to the Philippines began.

We arrived at the Ninoy Aquino International Airport in Manila on Saturday morning 8 April. Mr Tala had arranged for us to stay at a mission centre in a suburb of the city called Taguig, on the shores of Laguna de Bay, the largest lake in the Philippines. Taguig has seen a lot of development since its origins as a fishing community but it also contains the biggest slum area in Manila. Our accommodation was at Mount Moriah Christian Academy, a school and church centre right in the middle of it all. We planned to stay three nights there before taking a plane to Mindoro.

The first meeting in Manila was held in the "God Is Good" church and the Holy Spirit came powerfully. Hilja's and Paula's vision came true in front of our eyes. Invisible golden garlands descended upon people who then fell like stones under the power of God. All the Manila meetings were really in God's timing.

We had some time to take in the sights and sounds of the city and my son Chris' practical skills with handling the currency and such practical matters helped me a lot. He was an instant hit with the young people that we met, although his height towered above theirs. His ready sense of humour quickly broke the ice and would prove invaluable in de-stressing some crisis situations that we would find ourselves in, later in the trip.

13. *Three-wheelers*

On the last evening before travelling to Mindoro, we held a meeting in the rubbish tip of Manila. There are one million people living in that tip area; they are born there and they die there. It was shocking to see people digging for something to eat from the rotting food leftovers or trying to find some metal scraps that they could exchange for a few pesos.

The rains had soaked the rubbish to a sticky, thick mud, which sucked the feet in. The smell was strange. "Is it here that you mean me to minister, Lord, or is this just a one-off trip?" Somehow I knew that the Lord's future work for me was somehow connected to these areas, and yet so different from what I had expected it was going to be.

I have found that the people we meet and the things that happen to us in certain periods of our lives can be very significant in helping us discover the destiny that God has for us. Often the most difficult task for us is to die to ourselves and to bury our own motives so that God can develop His plans instead.

> **Our own dreams for our future can be very different from God's plans**

Many of us fail and give up during this training period because our own plans are often based upon our own selfish desires and ambitions. It is "me and my world with others serving my interests", until the big hammer of God comes down and breaks our hard self-centred shell … when the old is broken then the new can grow out.

Our own dreams for our future life and ministry can be very different from God's plans. If God had shown me beforehand what I would do "when I

28

grew up" I would have chosen a completely opposite direction, because I didn't then have the maturity to step into such things. God had to squeeze me through many narrow tunnels, from one situation to another, before I learned to trust His arms to carry me and before I dared to step out in faith.

Our evening meetings lasted really late, and the one on Monday evening didn't finish until 1 am. We didn't sleep that night at all, as we had to be at the airport for the flight to San Jose city on Mindoro Island at 3 am on Tuesday morning.

WESTERN MINDORO

Mindoro is a big island of 10,245 square kilometres, divided by a line of mountains into two parts: Occidental (Western) Mindoro and Oriental (Eastern) Mindoro. It is the fifth biggest island in the Philippines and in prehistoric times it was the connecting bridge between Luzon and Palawan islands, before the sea disconnected them. Mount Matalingahan, the highest peak on Palawan Island looks towards Borneo, just 100 km away from Palawan.

14. Mindoro in the Philippines

In 1987 at a conference in Baguio, a town in the north of Luzon, the missionary Bill Perry spoke about his vision of the Philippines: he saw the map of the Philippines as a soldier. Similar visions came from other sources two years before that. Bill saw Palawan as a sword swung in a strong hand. The hand was Mindoro Island. I strongly believe that in God's plans Mindoro has a special part in revival. These visions have started to come true in my own life regarding Mindoro, from where I believe the fire of revival will travel to many other islands in the Philippines. And you will be hearing a lot more about Palawan later in this book.

The name Mindoro comes from the Spanish words "mina de oro" meaning gold mine, and the original inhabitants of the island are the Mangyan tribes who now live in the mountains.

29

THE MOUNTAINS & THE MANGYANS

There are several big mountains on Mindoro Island, of which Mount Halcon is the fifth highest at 2,587m, located in Oriental Mindoro. Even though it has very inhospitable terrain, there are quite a few people living in this mountainous region. The Mangyans are nomads who roam around the area with their cattle. This nomadic life has caused them to lag behind developing society around them and has left them in a miserable position socially. Because they don't have any permanent homes, they gather around their camp fires at night, and so it can be seen from some distance away where their camps are on the mountains.

15. *Mindoro*

To those readers who might think it is somehow romantic to live like Mangyans in the wilderness, I want to tell you that their life is far from paradise. Their life expectancy is low, their children's death rate is high and tuberculosis, malaria and other diseases can devastate the population. Body malformations and mental illnesses are common. Marriages often take place between close relatives and even siblings, there being few moral rules in these matters.

Mangyan people are often seen early in the morning close to market places in towns and villages, selling beets and handicrafts. They stand out from other members of the population by their appearance and their clothing, which for the men is often minimal.

Because of their nomadic lifestyle the tribes do not have land for cultivating, so hunger and deficiency illnesses are very common. Some Mangyan tribes have settled down close to towns and villages, building primitive huts that stand on bamboo poles. Downstairs is reserved for the animals if they happen to have them, with the people living upstairs. The garbage system operates quite efficiently with food leftovers falling downstairs through the bamboo floor where they are consumed by the pig "waste disposal unit" or taken care of by loose dogs that hang around the villages.

In the Philippines, about 100,000 people belong to the Mangyan tribe, and in Mindoro Island they are about 10% of the entire population, but just 0.1%

of the overall population of the Philippines. The Mangyans can be divided into eight tribes but normally they are all just called Mangyans. Before the time when Spaniards conquered the Philippines, they used to trade with the Chinese using their primitive national boats. They sold cotton, beets, various medical herbs, beeswax, dishes and so on.

Even though most of the different Mangyan tribes look alike, they still have different cultures within their tribes. The Alangan tribe lives in Mindoro. Women of this tribe still dress according to the old tradition: they cover their upper body with the "ulango", made from Buri palm leaves. Sometimes ladies use a red scarf on top called a "limbutong". The lower part of the body is covered by a woven skirt. I have also met many tribes women who live close to the towns, who seem to wrap themselves in whatever old fabric or cloth they happen to find, layer after layer. Men's clothing is much more simple: they wear a tiny g-string with a small decorative tassel in front, somewhat strategically positioned.

16. Mangyan hut

The Iraya tribe lives near the town of Mamburao which was to be our mission field. Irayas look a bit different than other Mangyans with their curly hair and dark skin. Often they don't wear their national dress, and instead put on whatever old used clothes they can find. Women from the Ratagnon tribe wear a cotton skirt reaching from the waist to the knees, with the upper body having a covering made from woven vines.

Even though most of these people are in contact with modern Filipino society while living in or visiting towns or villages, the men have generally not given up their g-strings. Sometimes during celebrations the men might add an embroidered coat on top. In other words, the males don't tend to be particularly sensitive to the whims or trends of current fashion.

The tribe members often chew palm seeds, called betel or "nga-nga" which produce similar effects to narcotics. This traditional habit takes hunger away and involves meaningful ceremonies when taking it with others. Betel can be chewed the whole day or can be smoked in a tau-buid (pipe), the latter being the preference of young people.

THE NPA ARMY

The Mangyan tribes are not the only inhabitants of the mountains. The Mindoro Islands have problems with the New People's Army whose troops tend to hide in the mountains; so I don't recommend "nature trails" or mountain hikes in these areas. I have preached and evangelised in NPA areas, including to members and soldiers of the NPA. Some of their troops have become believers, but have remained as members of the NPA. How much one can trust the depth of their Christian commitment only time can tell.

The NPA group is considered to be a terrorist organisation by both the USA and the European Union. It operates mainly in the countryside and it targets politicians, business people, army, police and anyone who in any way represents the government. It has murdered foreigners and burned schools that have rejected their demands to teach their communist ideology. It is not rare to see NPA "shadow governments" in the provinces, which collect "taxes" and blackmail small companies and politicians demanding protection money. Their reign of terror is not just limited to wealthy people but extends to the poor as well.

In the year 1995, the NPA shadow government declared that marriages between same sex couples were allowed and in 2005 two commanders of the NPA army married the first homosexual couple. The Maoist NPA has connections with the Communist Party of the Philippine (CPP).

In September 2007, President Gloria Macapagal-Arroyo signed Amnesty Proclamation 1377 pardoning members of the Communist Party and its military offshoot the NPA. The declaration also covered another communist rebel group and their protection organisation the National Democratic Front. The amnesty covered all political crimes and acts of rebellion but not rape, drug trafficking and similar criminal activities, even if it was claimed they were motivated by political beliefs. It is very difficult to say how well the NPA army has complied with Filipino law after this declaration – certainly during 2008 the NPA army has continued to shoot people.

> **they have little compassion towards the poor**

Because my mission field is to slum communities, I meet there people whose relatives the NPA has murdered. It seems they have little compassion towards the poor - the very people whose good they are supposed to be working for. In this context I sometimes find it difficult to understand why the NPA finds it so easy to recruit new members from amidst the young people living in such misery. But if you are already outside society's norms, there are no other choices than to live on the streets, to belong to one of the countless youth gangs, or to grasp the ideology that the NPA offers you.

In January 2008, Avelino Razon, the Philippine national police chief, announced that after the military had attacked thirteen NPA targets in the previous year, there were only 5,700 NPA terrorists left. At its height the NPA army had 20,000 members. During the years about 40,000 people have died in NPA attacks[1].

17. Mangyans on the way to market

---

1   source: Wikipedia

18. San Jose seashore

19. San Jose town

CHAPTER 5
SAN JOSE

SAN JOSE

San Jose is the main town of Occidental Mindoro. It started to grow when the official capital Mamburao was affected by terrorist activities and Mamburao's airport and harbour facilities were closed down.

20. San Jose on Mindoro

When we arrived at San Jose airport we found it full of Filipino army soldiers. They questioned us over and over again about the purpose of our trip. They couldn't understand why any sane person would come to the island as a tourist at a time when people were being evacuated because of the danger there. This was a time when NPA terrorists were kidnapping foreigners and it was pretty clear that we weren't locals, with our flour-coloured skins in the middle of a bronzed population. Well, at least we Finnish people weren't going to miss each other in a crowd in this country!

It was at this point that Chris started having some serious doubts over the wisdom of his decision to come with me. The soldiers were looking sternly at his camouflage trousers, similar to the ones that the partisans used, asking why a young, fit-looking man in military clothing was coming to the island. Try and explain to the suspicious soldiers how terribly expensive these fashionable trousers were in Brisbane and how all the young men at home were wearing them …

LUXURY

Mr Tala knew a good cheap hotel in the city but didn't remember its name. He promised to pay for us as well, so we walked in the direction where it was supposed to be. We eventually found it and as we stood at the front entrance, he mumbled, "It's strange, they seem to have renovated the place and changed everything both inside and outside." He paid in advance for our stay at the reception desk and commented, "Inflation has doubled the prices – such a pity that they have done this renovation!"

Chris liked the look of the hotel. After staying in Manila in quite primitive accommodation and now with a hammering headache because of the heat, he found this to be a refreshing change. We were happy, the room was luxurious, with air conditioning, TV, and best of all we had a big bathroom – really great. Because it was still morning, we went out to the balcony for breakfast and marvelled at the scenery: down below there was a garden straight from wonderland and next to that, a sparkling sea. Mr Tala looked at the views and mumbled some more. Suddenly he jumped up and shouted: "Now I know why everything is so different; we are in the wrong hotel. Look there, behind the corner, that hotel is the one that we were trying to find." Behind the palm trees there was a very simple building. I was very happy about Mr Tala's mistake as we could now sleep at least one night in relative luxury. But that night was our last one in such comfortable surroundings.

In the morning we woke up to the sound of knocking: it was Pastor Sonio's daughter Nheng (who was also called Methusela) and their friend Brother Boy who had come to pick us up for the bus trip to Sablayan town, in the interior of Mindoro Island. Brother Boy used to be the head of a well known Bible school in the Philippines. He and Nheng said it would take between three and four hours to get there on the bus, depending on how many tyres we would have to change during the trip.

The bus was a typical local one with double seats, on each of which five Filipinos managed to sit. There were also about twenty people hanging on the roof, because these buses were always very crowded and not everyone could fit inside. We managed to get seats at the back of the bus. It didn't have any windows, only openings, and after a few kilometres I understood why local people now and then bent down and pulled the hood of their coats or terry cloth towels in front of their faces. The ones at the front of the bus saw when there was traffic coming towards us; that meant that a cloud of sand would soon be blown in. I quickly learned that everything had a reason, and that it was worth watching what others were doing and then quickly following suit.

21. Nheng

The woman sitting behind us had a cockerel in her lap, that crowed straight into our ears for the whole journey. At one point I wondered what another weird noise was close to my ear. Chris told me later that it was a lobster moving its "scissors" close to my hair, threatening to trim a bit from one side. My hair was mainly sticking upwards because the wind was so strong, and after one hour's journey it was a real mess, resembling a 1960s beehive style: the dust had been a very effective hairspray.

Suddenly the bus stopped and we were left wondering why. We found out that the next bridge ahead leading over the river had been blown up. The bus driver told us that it had still been there when he drove towards San Jose town from Sablayan a few hours earlier, so that meant that the NPA army was somewhere close by. We started to drive through the river at a worryingly slow pace from its most shallow point. In the rainy season this would have been impossible but soon the old bus was complaining with squeaks and shudders as it climbed over the stones on the other side of the river. With great difficulty it managed to reach the road again and we set off again with a great sense of relief.

But our relief was short-lived. Suddenly everyone around us dived to the floor and the bus careered to a sudden stop. There was total silence on the bus, very unusual in that society as Filipino men and women tend to talk constantly. I leaned over and peered through the window to see what could be the reason for the deathly hush. I saw a huge lorry which had turned over beside the road, with its contents strewn all around it. Soldiers in camouflage clothing were poking through the lorry's cargo with their machine guns and one of them was just walking towards us. Chris pulled me down on our seat. "Mum, try to be invisible, keep down, they are NPA men!" Invisible? How could we possibly blend in to look like local people? I quickly understood what kind of mess we were in, and tried my best to look as small as possible in a country where people normally reach only as far as my shoulders.

> **'Mum, try to be invisible, keep down, they are NPA men!'**

Luckily we were right at the back of the bus. Mr Tala was sitting away from us, nearer towards the front, and the soldiers hopefully would not be interested in a seventy year old white-haired man. They glanced around at the travellers and then let us continue on our way. Apparently they didn't want anything from this old bus and its poor country passengers, having prospects of better plunder elsewhere. Chris murmured: "You and your trips; I should have known that coming with you was going to be far from a normal holiday!"

Our companion Nheng tried to reassure us by saying how safe Sablayan town would be, as it was full of army soldiers because of a political murder that had just happened. They would be guarding the town for at least the next two weeks.

CHAPTER 6
SABLAYAN & THE SONIO FAMILY

SABLAYAN TOWN

We finally arrived at the town of Sablayan to find it stiflingly hot: it was the hottest and driest season of the year when the temperature is normally around 40°C.

The plan was to stay for a few days in the town and then move to live in a house outside Sablayan belonging to a young lady who at the time was an acquaintance of mine from Brisbane. Let's call her Lea Wando. I had known her family when she was a teenager, and the wide difference in our ages and lifestyles had prevented us from getting to know each other, but this was going to change on this trip.

Lea knew the Sonio family well, having lived in the town for some time. She

22. Sablayan

had not yet started her university studies and so she had time to work with us for a while..

Mr Tala, Chris and I found the only motel in town and Chris asked at the reception desk for a room to meet his criteria: "We want a room with an air conditioning unit, a shower, a toilet, and two beds." All his questions got positive answers, so we booked in.

ROOM WITH AIR CONDITIONING

Since I was older, I chose the bed besides the air conditioning (AC) unit. So Chris got first turn in the bathroom. "While I am in the shower," he said, "would you switch on the air conditioning to cool down this horribly hot room?" I agreed to wait and followed his instructions, but when I pressed the switch on the AC, nothing happened. Hmmm … we obviously hadn't asked the right questions at reception. We didn't ask if the AC unit was working, only if there was one in the room.

It was rather quiet in the shower room so I asked Chris to hurry up, but there was no answer. I called, "Are you in the shower?" The answer came: "Yes I am, but there is no water." "OK," I called back, "then please come out of there so I can go to the toilet." The answer was even more frustrated: "All right, I'll come out – but the toilet isn't working either."

> ... **something big and grey just ran under your bed**

There was a small electric fan in the room and I put it on, now understanding why it was there. It made all sorts of strange noises like a death rattle. Chris came out of the bathroom and fell exhausted onto his bed. "How long do we have to stay here?" he sighed. Well, we had only just arrived. Suddenly Chris sat bolt upright staring at the floor under my bed: "Mum, you won't like the sound of this but … something big and grey just ran under your bed."

It turned out that the big grey one, or rather ones, lived inside the foam mattress where they had dug tunnels. That whole night I listened to their noisy family comings and goings. And in spite of the horrible heat of the room, I wrapped myself in my sleeping bag, preferring to melt there like butter on a hot pan, rather than let these creatures run over my body. Right now they were just running on the floor and making rattling noises in the waste bin.

Chris went to investigate the shower room that was at the end of the corridor and soon came back to inform me: "Yep, there is a shower but no spray

40

head." It was interesting to see how the water came out, when it now and then decided to do so. It came only at certain times of the day, five water jets as thin as a hair's breadth and all of them going in different directions. You could choose which of them you wanted to use. And just when you thought you'd mastered the schedule of when the water might be coming, the authorities decided to change the time. Once I had made a good lather of shampoo in my hair and then suddenly there was no more water. I had to rinse my hair in the toilet as no other water was available. Some days the supply was cut off for hours, if it ever came at all. Electricity power cuts too were frequent, typically happening every day and often in the middle of our meetings. Filipino people call these periods "brown time".

Chris' natural inventiveness really came to the fore on this trip. As a young boy he had delighted his younger sister by inventing a system of lights for her dolls house and even a working lift for taking the little dolls from downstairs to upstairs, all working by batteries. As he got older he used to build tree houses, again with a working lift to take his friends up and down. And now his imagination and creativity were invaluable to us since many things seemed to be "nasira" (a Tagalog word for broken).

> **The blown air from the fan turned the jeans into a wind sock**

In our Sablayan motel room he rigged up an automatic laundry drier that also acted as an air conditioning substitute. On this trip he had learned to wash his jeans in a bucket, and he then hung them on the electric fan, which was fixed to the wall. The blown air from the fan turned the jeans into a wind sock. Water was sprayed across the room as the fan blew and turned back and forth, freshening and cooling down the room at the same time as the trousers dried.

PRISON COLONY

The first place we visited was a prison colony in the mountains. It held about a thousand prisoners in a sort of colony community in a very remote area. Mindoro has always been a prison island. At the other end of the island were all the political prisoners and terrorists, but at this end where we now visited were located other criminals, murderers, thieves, and drug offenders.

The prison colony was carefully guarded. We travelled there in the back of an open lorry, with big planks fixed for seating on both sides and in front, and people sat on them in lines, virtually in each others' laps. Pastor Sonio's congregation did a lot of prison ministry and as many of them as possible wanted to come along with us, since we had come from as far away as Australia to preach to the prisoners. I felt like a live sardine packed into a tin.

They had set up a plastic chair for me standing at the end of one plank. Not such a good idea, as it fell over on every bend of the road, either backwards or forwards and I always found myself on someone's lap or on the floor. My bottom got a lot of bruises but I thought that others had it worse – yet no one complained, so I didn't either. Travelling through the mountains, we passed by several prison checkpoints. If someone ever managed to escape from this place, there would still be a week's swimming trip to the mainland.

23. Outside the prison

Finally we came to the prison area. The prisoners had built a shed for the meetings, giving shelter for 200 prisoners. Around this shed there were old buildings; further away were buildings for the more dangerous prisoners who were not allowed to come to the meeting at all. The ones that were permitted to come were life sentence prisoners or double life sentence prisoners. I asked how dangerous those other ones then might be, but no one answered me. I was only told that they were serving three life sentences. In the Philippines a life sentence is shorter than in western countries, and a "double life sentence" means about 22 years in prison.

If you saw what the jail was like, you would know why the guards did not allow cameras to be taken in. A two person cell held as many prisoners as they could make stand in the room. This was a colony jail, in which several worked on the fields and so were at least allowed to move around in a fixed area. Happy were the 200 or so prisoners who were permitted to come out of their cells to attend our meeting, while others could only listen from afar via the loudspeakers. I was told that in some jails the prisoners can do whatever they want in their cells; if the guards would dare to try and stop them, there would be riots, the jail would be destroyed and many people would die.

The prisoners had been brought to this jail from other islands. When they are freed, many of them have to still stay in the prison area living in small bamboo huts: where else can they go? They do not have money to travel even to Sablayan, let alone any of the countless other islands of the Philippines. Most of them cannot read or write and they do not have any occupation. Many of them speak only their tribal language, of which there are a hundred different varieties in the Philippines. Life can be agonisingly lonely.

I watched the prisoners as the meeting went on. I saw how each of them wanted to say something, to tell about their own island or their home region. Some were singing in their own tribal language and were weeping as they sang. I didn't understand their words but I could feel the hopelessness in their voices. The meeting went on like this for two hours … two sultry hot hours, with the thermometer showing more than 40°C and no breeze at all. The

> **I could feel the hopelessness in their voices**

person who had arranged the meeting came over to me and said that it was my turn to preach, and then Mr Tala would close the meeting.

I was embarrassed as this was a men's jail and I had not intended to preach. What could I say? My head was totally empty as I climbed the platform. I had never before felt so short of words. Normally words just run out of me, whatever the topic might be. I started to speak something or other, but then I felt a change happen inside me, and a deep compassion and love towards these people came over me. I found myself speaking words that I had not articulated. It was as if I was a stranger even to myself, like listening to someone else talking.

I heard myself telling my listeners the story of how God had healed me from cancer, even when the doctors had given me only a 0.01% chance of survival. It had been more than a life sentence for me – a literal death sentence. This had happened in August 2005 after coming home from Europe, where I had spent three months preaching in different countries. My doctor said I had a cancer which was growing very aggressively. It had already spread so widely in my body that there was very little – if anything at all – to be done for me surgically. Nevertheless the specialist still scheduled an operation. In the meantime very many people prayed for me, but nothing seemed to happen.

So I went for the operation, but determined that I would come home the next day after surgery, in spite of the fact they had planned to keep me in hospital for at least a fortnight. When I came round from the anaesthetic and told the nurses that I would now leave for home, they persuaded me to stay overnight so the specialist could see me next morning. He told me that the operation had been one of the biggest ones ever done in that hospital, and that I had to be very careful indeed to let my body to recover. I listened, nodded and said, "Thank you for your marvellous job, doctor – but I am still going home." To cut a long story short, God gave me a supernaturally quick recovery so that the day after the operation I did go home and later the specialist said, "You are a walking miracle, this is totally impossible!"

On getting home, I jumped into the swimming pool outside our house, and swam 100 metres. And that was my daily exercise from then on, as I felt like a generator was charging me from the inside. As for the stitches, they just seemed to disappear the moment I touched the water in the pool. In the same week I held a meeting in my home and there I suddenly felt the desire to do somersaults, as I had so much energy inside of me! I loved my new energy levels, I loved my life and did not care what people might say. God healed me totally. So never give up but choose life!

After telling my story to the prisoners, I suddenly realised that nobody was interpreting my words into the Tagalog language any more. I turned to see where the interpreter had gone, and saw that he was standing at the corner of the platform weeping. I asked, "What's wrong? Please come and interpret." He replied that he couldn't because he was crying too much. I turned towards the audience and wondered what to do now – all the prisoners were crying too. Then I recognised that my cheeks too had tears rolling down them. It was really odd as I never cry – the tears were coming from somewhere deeper. This was a supernatural stirring from deep inside, caused by the Holy Spirit.

I stopped my sermon but one of the staff came crying and pleading with me to continue. I tried to speak in English and didn't know if anyone was listening or understanding or even whether that mattered at all. After a while I jumped down from the platform and walked away down the central aisle.

As I walked by, the prisoners stretched out their arms towards me crying. I passed by a man, who stood there covering his face and crying. The guard told me later that he had been unable to move for one hour after we had left – paralysed there, a double life sentence murderer who wanted to be saved.

I remembered a vision that someone had for me at a prophetic seminar a year before: they saw me walking in the narrow corridor of a prison and on both sides of the corridor were numerous prison cells. From these cells stretched many hands trying to reach me. In the vision the hands belonged to people from many nationalities in the Asia-Pacific region, and even Muslims were included. The words came: "Through the gaps between the jail bars they try to reach to you, lots of hands, lots of hands stretched towards you, so many are those in need."

At that time I believed the vision was symbolic, with me as some kind of bondage breaker, rather than it being real prison ministry. I hadn't understood God's ways with my natural mind. As the Lord says in Isaiah: "For my thoughts are not your thoughts …" (Isaiah 55:8-9). He knows our destiny much better than we do.

When we left, the prisoners held out their hands offering their handicrafts to us. They had crafted statues out of plastic bottles. These little gifts had other meanings as well – inside the ornaments were hidden tiny messages in blurred handwriting: "Please call this number and tell my wife that I am alive."

All the messages gave similar information to relatives from men who had spent years away from their families. The relatives had no money to visit their husbands or fathers in prison. Someone whispered as we passed by, "Winter is coming and we do not have shoes, blankets, or clothes, can you give us any?"

Countless hands were held out to offer different handicrafts for us to buy, to get money for food and medicines. Apart from rice, the jail supplied nothing else – no clothes, no flip-flops to replace ones that had worn out ages ago, no blankets. They used banana leaves as plates for their rice because there were no dishes, and they pulled out grass from the little lake to use as a salad. There were also some fish in the lake that could be caught by those who were allowed to work in the fields.

I had much to ponder as we made our bumpy journey from the mountain prison back to Sablayan.

THE SONIOS

Edwin Sonio and his wife Nena were the pastors of the Foursquare Church in the town of Sablayan. Nena originally came from Romblon, an island to the east of Mindoro. She told us that she had financed her high school studies and Bible school by washing people's laundry in cold water, and as a result she developed rheumatism in her hands.

After Bible school she travelled to Mindoro Island to work as a missionary and she founded the first Foursquare Church in Sablay-

24. Nena Sonio

an. It grew rapidly; Nena had a beautiful singing voice, and she used it to good effect as she travelled from village to village communicating the good news through both preaching and song.

No one in her new church could play the guitar and there was no guitar to play either. Then Nena heard that the local young baker was a talented guitar player. So one day she walked into the bakery and asked the young man to come and take care of the music in her church. That man was Edwin Sonio. At first Edwin wasn't interested – why on earth should he go to her church when he had no interest in faith or God or anything like that? There was only the rather nice looking Miss Nena …. And she was so persistent in her pleas that Edwin soon became the musician of the Foursquare Church, but he made up his mind that he wasn't going to fall for the silly games of these believers. He was just going to play his guitar and get this Miss Nena as his wife.

Some time later a preacher visited the church and held a meeting where there was prayer for the sick. Edwin looked on with suspicion as the man walked around and prayed for individuals in the meeting. As he approached a blind lady, Edwin said a silent prayer: "God, if you are real then give sight to that blind woman. If you do, then I will believe in You and give my life to You."

The evangelist prayed for the blind to be healed and at that very moment the lady received her sight. Edwin told us that this really scared him, knowing what he had promised God in his silent prayer. But he was a man who kept his promises so, putting his guitar on one side, he marched to the front of the church and gave his life to the Lord. And the baker soon became an ex-baker and one of the most hard-working members of the church.

THE FOURSQUARE CHURCH

I held two meetings in Edwin and Nena's church. They told me how the church had suffered a major setback just a few months before – a visiting evangelist with a deliverance ministry had split the entire congregation. He sought to "free" that healthy congregation from something that they didn't need to be freed from, and as a result things got very bad. Many started to suffer from anxiety and depression, one half of the congregation got into a fight with the other half, many left the church, and the handful that didn't leave ended up spiritually wounded.

> a visiting evangelist had split the congregation

46

The Apostle Paul says in his letter to the Galatians (Gal.6:8)

If they plant to satisfy their sinful selves, their sinful selves will bring them ruin. But if they plant to please the Spirit, they will receive eternal life from the Spirit.

The teaching of this visitor was obviously not in balance with the Word of God. It perhaps had started as biblically true teaching, but it had become twisted, and then it was inflicted upon the weak and immature hearers. Instead of gaining freedom, they became bound in the chains of fear.

The pastor couple sadly recounted to me that as a result of this disaster they expected very few people to come to my meetings. But to their surprise on the first day of meetings the church building filled up, even including people who had previously left the congregation – perhaps there just out of curiosity.

GLORY CLOUD

Before I had left home for the Philippines a prophet had come to bring me a word for the coming trip: "You will see the 'cloud of glory' come to your meeting and people will be healed just like when Peter's shadow touched the sick." I had thought over these words and interpreted them as a symbolic picture of God's power coming to the meetings. The shadow of Peter means the presence of the Holy Spirit around us.

> **You will see the 'cloud of glory' come to your meeting**

So what is this 'cloud of glory'? God is so huge and His glory so glaring that He clothed Himself with a cloud when He appeared to Moses. That was because no one can gaze upon God's full glory without a sheltering shadow:

Then the cloud covered the Meeting Tent, and the glory of the Lord filled the Holy Tent. (Exodus 40:34)

The glory that radiates from God sheds light on everything that is in our heart, revealing its darkest corners and its sins. The Israelites in the wilderness looked at this glory from a safe distance, saying to Moses, "You talk to Him instead of us." When Moses went up onto Mount Sinai, the Bible says, "… the cloud covered it." (Exodus 24:15)

Paul saw a small measure of the glory of God on the road to Damascus and that transformed him.

> On the way there, at noon, I saw a light from heaven. It was bright-er than the sun and flashed all around me and those who were travelling with me (Acts 26:13)

A man is changed when he sees the glory of God. And the part of this glory that we are allowed to see is only a small glimpse of what God actually is. The glory cloud is not even a microscopic drop of the infinity of God, because His glory fills the heaven and is like a sun whose rays go everywhere. Habakkuk 3:4 says:

> He is like a bright light. Rays of light shine from his hand, and there he hides his power.

MASS DELIVERANCE MEETING

I finished the sermon at my first meeting at the Foursquare Church and I asked for sick people to come forward for prayer. I was shocked to see everyone run to the front. "How can they all be sick?" I wondered. The church staff helped people to line up and I came down from the right hand side of the platform. I decided to first walk to the left hand end of the line, as I saw some elderly people and children there, who I presumed would not be able to wait for very long. Since then, I have learned that we should not underestimate children's ability to receive; they are the best listeners and absorb your every word like blotting paper.

25. Sablayan Foursquare Church

Something really amazing happened as I was trying to push through the crowds to the other end of the prayer line: as I was passing by people, they started to cough, one was vomiting, and other weird things started to happen – I was totally confused. I had not even started to pray for people! What on earth was going on here? Line after line of people were falling down under the power of the Holy Spirit, crying and behaving like bad stuff had just left them.

I had never thought that deliverance was my ministry, and I have always left it to people with that special gift from the Lord. Yet here I was in a mass deliverance session that the Lord himself had set up. I was helpless and didn't know what to do. It can't be this easy, Lord – how can it be that I am just walking by people and they are being set free?! So I just walked up and down the lines as I didn't know what else to do.

Much greater powers were now at work than I could even imagine, and without knowing it, I had ended up in the "Peter's shadow" ministry! God was also showing me that when He does the deliverance, man's memorised lists, theories and methodologies are not needed. It is the power of God that makes a person free. If that power is lacking, then no jumping, shouting or waving our arms about in our own strength is going to make any difference at all. The most difficult thing for an evangelist is to do nothing and just be. Many evangelists are used to waving and shouting like auctioneers in order to get people into the Kingdom of God. But God was showing me that when He is at work, such techniques are totally redundant.

Next day the astounded Pastor Nena told me of many people who had come to ask forgiveness from her. They had really been set free from something that had covered them as a congregation in a black gloomy shroud for many months. Those that had left the congregation came back.

A CHANGED CHURCH

This was the first time that I have seen a whole congregation set free in one go; and we learned later that the deliverance was permanent. At the end of that month when our small team was about to leave Mindoro Island, the Sonios came by motorbike to meet us in San Jose town: they told us that a permanent supernatural healing and deliverance from the powers of darkness had taken place. Depression, quarrels, disagreements and many other things that had been burdening the congregation had disappeared. God not only heals our physical illnesses but our souls and spirits too.

26. *The man whose back was healed*

After the amazing deliverances in that first meeting at Edwin and Nena's church, many new people started coming along. During one sermon, God started to give words of knowledge to a man sitting in the front row. Afterwards he came to me literally dancing and said: "Fire was coming out of your eyes and hit my heart." He

49

started to feel the fire in his back and was wriggling in his seat, not knowing what was going on but by the end of the meeting he realised that his back had been healed. Previously he had been unable to bend down because of a back injury, and now he was bobbing up and down, dancing and rolling around. In his excitement, he told everyone how God had healed his back without him even leaving his seat.

Later he admitted that his relationship with God had not been right and that he had been backslidden. He had come to the church meeting just out of curiosity to see what is happening there. Through this healing miracle his faith was renewed and during our whole crusade he followed us and witnessed to everybody who would listen, how God is the healer. He would jump up and down as eagerly as in the first meeting and bend himself double, to show that he was telling the truth.

What a witness to a permanent miracle – not just a momentary healing testimony in a meeting, that wouldn't last until the next day. Where Jesus walks among His people something always happens. In Christ there is resurrection power that changes the world, bringing revival and freedom, breaking the spirit of apathy and sickness. Every believer carries the same power of the Holy Spirit of Christ in himself or herself that sent the disciples out from the Upper Room into the streets to work miracles.

LEA'S HOUSE

Lea Wando had been living for a while in Sablayan town. She had been married to a man from Vanuatu, off the eastern coast of Australia, but when he died,

27. Lea's house

she decided to move away. While visiting the Philippines, she was captivated by its beauty and she settled in Sablayan, close to Pastor Sonio's church. That is where she had a house built for herself and her little daughter, Princess. It was her home while she was in the Philippines, but she also had a place in Australia. Lea offered to put us up while we were in Sablayan, so we happily moved in to her house.

It was built like all the other houses in the area, with bamboo walls and a roof of local material resembling dried grass. Because the windows were only holes in the walls without any glass, wind blew in and we found it much cooler to sleep in than the motel room. Local people know what kind of house construction fits their climate. The house was in the middle of a field and after the meetings we would stumble our way there in the dark, as even a torch didn't help much – the light seemed to sink somewhere into the vegetation.

One night as I was making my way back to the house with my son Chris, my speedy pace was brought to an abrupt halt by some sort of wall in the dark path. The light of the torch revealed a big eye and I was horrified to see that I had stumbled into a water buffalo.

I shouted to Chris behind me: "Chris, help! Look out! There's a water buffalo!" I turned round to check where he was, only to see a blurred shape whiz past me in the darkness. Then his voice called from many metres ahead of me: "Run Mum, run, or else you're dead meat!" So I ran for my life and the buffalo came after me like a tank … until it was suddenly yanked to a stop, at the end of the long rope to which its owner had fastened it for the night. It didn't help much when the locals told me afterwards that water buffalos are "friendly". This one certainly got pretty irritated when I disturbed its beauty sleep!

28. *The unwelcome turkey*

There was no running water at Lea's house so water for washing and drinking had to be carried in by bucket from a pump 100 metres away. The toilet too worked in the same way, by water that was carried in. There was only one room in the house, with a small part separated by a bamboo wall to be a sleeping area. An everyday occurrence was "Operation Ants". They came in from every split in the walls or floor and had to be destroyed by a burning petrol cloth. The place regularly became a crematorium for hundreds of them, but soon there were plenty more again.

One day as I was resting on the bumpy bamboo bed in between meetings, I felt something upon my stomach. I opened my eyes and there was a big turkey breathing in my nose and its five wives were standing on the floor in a line staring curiously at this weird creature lying on the bed. I was not raised on a farm so my first reaction was to scream and jump up wildly. The turkeys probably got more scared than I did and out they rushed through the open door, gobbling away in their own language. But soon they became my everyday companions, and in fact they developed a particular interest in my hair drier. The turkey ladies would stand in a line like soldiers stretching their necks and wondering at the strange noise coming from the machine. Perhaps they were pondering how quickly their feathers would become curly in that sort of wind.

29. The Sonios' congregation

CHAPTER 7
MEETINGS AT THE ASTRODOME

SABLAYAN ASTRODOME

On the main street of Sablayan there is a large meeting place known as the Astrodome that for some time had hosted only cock fights. The town council had promised it to us for our meetings. So the church ladies spent a whole week cleaning it up and making it fit for human habitation, as the whole venue, and especially the platform, was full of soil, feathers and other leftovers from these crowing gladiators. The locals didn't have many other forms of entertainment so they enjoyed betting on cock fighting. Wealthier people kept several cockerels but poor people had to make do with only one bird, which they then pampered as if it were a baby. The cockerels had bets placed on them in a similar way to horse racing in other countries. Good fighting cocks were expensive to buy and the owner would receive quite a few pesos reward if his bird managed to win its battles. But the cocks now had to step aside to make room for our meetings.

The soldiers, who had been promised to us as security at the venue, never materialised but they were not needed after all. Military helicopters buzzed over and around the area trying to locate guerrilla hiding places, making a lot of noise and generally disturbing the meetings. I also heard that there were 500 Philippines army soldiers sited in strategic places around the island.

Before we arrived, five NPA commanders had been put in jail and the remaining NPA military had disappeared to hide in the mountains. The capital of Mindoro Island, Mamburao, was the most dangerous area and one of the strongest bases of the NPA. Another hazardous place was Abra De Ilog, the port area to the north east of Mamburao, through which all lorries and heavy transport passed en route to the rest of the island. Mamburao became a strategic area for the NPA army, because it took only three hours to travel to Abra from the mainland, compared to the sixteen hours it took to get to San Jose town at the southern end of the island. It was also the subject of NPA activity because it was the capital, not only of Occidental Mindoro, but also the whole island. As such, it housed government offices and the officials who were a favourite target of the NPA.

VEHICLE VARIETY

People arrived at the meeting from the surrounding area in all sorts of transport, their only common denominator being wheels. Typically they originated from

30. A jeepney

Second World War days, being vehicles that the Americans had left behind. At that time hundreds of surplus WW2 jeeps had been given to the Filipino people. The locals had converted them to carry several passengers by adding side benches, and so was born the jeepney, the vehicle for which the Philippines is famous. Their sizes vary but they are designed to carry about sixteen people, and frequently many more Filipinos tend to cram inside them. Because the Filipino people are very religious, they christen their jeepneys with wonderful names like "Heavenly Transport" or "God is Great" and often decorate them with colourful pictures. I saw one jeep in Manila with a big picture of Jesus painted on its side; at least it was a bit different than the pictures of the Virgin Mary that were everywhere.

Sablayan had been one of the American bases in World War Two. When the troops left the town, businesses ground to a halt and prosperity changed to poverty. But because many of the local people are very skilled mechanics, they can make almost anything move that was originally made for moving, however long ago. They are very ingenious and seem to be able to create something out of nothing. Once I happened to ask Pastor Sonio why he didn't have a motorbike helmet. Next day he had one … and there was something rather familiar about its shape. Somewhere he had found an old German soldier's helmet and had painted it black. Recycling certainly works!

It was quite a sight to see the different vehicles bringing people to the meeting. Flat-bed trucks had been instantly converted into buses by arranging plastic chairs in closely fitting rows in the back, one after another. Those who couldn't fit inside the jeepneys travelled on their roofs. Motorbikes with sidecars were often seen, and even tractors straight out of the rice fields were used for passenger transport. They usually had just a long metal bar on which the driver's seat had been fitted, and several people would squeeze onto the bar, one after another, sitting in each other's lap.

31. Edwin's helmet

The venue started to fill up until there were about 800 people in the meeting. Pastor Sonio got a call from a group whose old lorry had died in the middle of the dark jungle leaving them stranded half way to the meeting. But later on this same group of people managed to join us, having combined their mechanical talents and fixed the engine.

EVENING MEETING

Filipino people tend to be very musical. They really come alive with their Tagalog songs and the youngsters love to dance. I am especially fond of the Filipino national dances. There was beautiful dancing during the worship time at our evening meeting.

Pastor Sonio had asked Pastor Eduardo Aeupido from Cornerstone church in Manila to interpret for me, because the poor country people do not speak English. The language is taught at school but few poor people have any chance of attending school. Eduardo has been the interpreter at many big meetings, for example for Benny Hinn, and he really put his heart into it. He made the effort to travel to meet us in Sablayan the day before the meeting, so that he could chat with us and get familiar with the Australian accent and the personality of the preacher. Interpreting is an essential part of the sermon, it either flows or it doesn't.

At the beginning of the meeting something funny happened. Pastor Sonio stood up and invited "the 80 year old evangelist from Australia" to come to the platform, and then pointed at me. I looked around me to see if any elderly Aussies had crept in behind me, but sadly not, so he was apparently referring

32. Brother Boy, Edwin & Eduardo

to me. My age had instantly increased by a couple of decades. The audience took Sonio's description of me as a fact. Well, there was at least something positive here, as Filipinos do tend to honour older people. On the other hand, in Asia even sixty year olds are considered to be on their last legs.

Lea and I had a good laugh about this afterwards, but next day we met two girls at the local supermarket. The little ladies stared open-mouthed at the first pale-faced foreigner they ever had seen. The younger one asked me straight out, "How old are you?" I answered politely: "Please, have a guess!" Both of them scrutinized me closely before one of them supplied her estimate with considerable conviction: "81 years old". Dear me, I definitely must change my brand of wrinkle-preventing cream, as overnight I had aged by yet another year!

HEALING MINISTRY

The meeting was nearing an end and all the sick and those wanting to be saved were asked to come to the front. Everyone came forward. In the Philippines, a blessing means a lot and no one wanted to miss out. I turned to Nheng and asked, "Surely they can't all be sick or wanting to get saved, can they?" She answered innocently: "At least they're sick, because they can't afford to buy medicines or see the doctor, so they've come here." It was pretty clear to me at that point that I couldn't produce faith through my own efforts and if there was any religious cloak on the shoulders, it fell off then and there. The real power of God was needed, the power that can move anything and everything.

As I started to pray for people in the prayer lines, the locals, who are naturally chatty waited quietly and patiently for their turn. I knew that Jesus does what He has promised in His Word and that He was now working in the midst of these people. He doesn't care about anyone's religious rules or belief systems but He heals the sick by the power of His word. He gave this same authority to His disciples as His messengers, and it has continued from generation to generation because of Jesus' name. (Mark 16:17,18)

I came to a woman who was carrying a boy of about seven years old in her arms, and she showed me his paralysed legs. I prayed for him but didn't notice any visible changes. His mother just cried and after a few moments walked towards the doorway, while I continued to bless the people. Suddenly a commotion started close to the door and many people started to run to that direction. A young lady who was helping me went over to have a look and soon came back to tell me, "God has done a miracle, the paralysed boy is walking!" It was so interesting to see how the healing power of God often worked after the meeting. This showed

the paralysed boy is walking!

that Jesus is the healer and so the honour could not possibly go to any human being. Their level of faith grew as people saw how the impossible was made possible, and as a result many sicknesses were healed.

Mr Tala was praying for people at the other end of the venue; there one boy, the son of a pastor, was instantly healed from a horrible skin rash. I came to a lady with a paralysed hand. I was just about to lay my hand on her hand when she put it over her heart … I didn't understand why, but it didn't matter whether or not I knew what her illnesses were.

Later someone told me that this woman had a serious heart condition and had travelled to the meeting from Manila, after visiting several doctors. In this meeting her heart was healed and her hand started working again. I am not a doctor and I do not know what physical link there is, if any, between the heart and hand. The main thing was that she was healed. Another lady had a tumour in her neck; in Jesus' name it just disappeared and I was amazed, looking and trying to find it on the floor – I had never seen anything like that before.

Believers in the western world are often troubled by cynicism and doubt. They find it difficult to believe that the resurrection power of Jesus is working today. And yet that same power has been given to us all. The disciples didn't stay inside the upper room and be a "Galilean Cult", but they went out and brought the upper room reality to the people. Wherever they went, signs and wonders followed them. Jesus commanded his disciples in Matthew 10:8 "Heal the sick, raise the dead to life again … I give you these powers freely, so help other people freely."

History tells us about many "men and women of faith" who in spite of humiliations and tragedies fought through to victory. What they all had in common was that they walked through the door of possibilities as it opened in front of them. When one preacher encountered family sorrows, sicknesses and accidents, he just said: "A rose must be crushed before the right aroma is produced."

As I looked at the digital pictures at the end of our series of meetings in Sablayan, I was astonished to see a clear golden, veil-like cloud hovering above us wherever we prayed. The Lord had promised to appear as a cloud of glory in the meetings and that is what He did.

MEETINGS AROUND SABLAYAN

After these meetings in the Astrodome, we travelled outside the town to visit churches in the surrounding area. One Sunday I decided to wear my best black trouser suit to the meeting, as the local people were also wearing their Sunday best. That was a mistake; we had to travel for an hour to the meeting on the back of a motorbike and the sandy road often disappeared into bushes. When we arrived, my black suit was grey and my hair was like a large corkscrew. In fact I bore a remarkable resemblance to the Australian palm cockatoo, a big grey bird with high tufts on its head.

At least the local people had fun. Most of the people at this meeting were children, almost filling the entire hall. It was Mr Tala's turn to preach but he quickly asked us to swop: "I can't preach to these children, that's your job." I answered: "You'll get the chance to preach anyway as the adults will come later." The grown-ups weren't much bothered by timetables.

I decided to gather the children in the front of the room and started to tell them about heaven. Edwin Sonio interpreted and made the story into an even more colourful Mindoro version, fitting the part of the island where we were. The kids again got very excited about the wonders of heaven and all wanted to be saved. Adults had been wandering in while the story was continuing. At the end we prayed again for sick people, and one lady came forward with a big goitre in her neck. While we were praying, the lady started vomiting and whoosh – a big green mucus lump flew out of her mouth and onto the floor. At the same time the goitre disappeared. Please don't ask me how this is possible – I can't explain. But the woman was a pastor's wife and her friends told me later that she was totally healed that evening.

It is totally biblical that signs and wonders follow when the Word is preached. When Philip preached, signs and wonders followed him and the town of Samaria believed (Acts 8). Paul preached the Gospel in Lystra with signs and wonders (Acts 14:10). And Jesus commanded us all, "As the Father sent me, I now send you ..." (John 20:21). It is time for believers to become real believers, rather than "a little bit of this and a little bit of that". The early church had no choice in the matter, they had to have real faith. If we believe only 40% of the Word, it is no wonder that there is no revival.

33. The glory cloud at the Astrodome

34. The mayor's house in Santa Cruz

35. At the Santa Cruz stadium

CHAPTER 8
SANTA CRUZ

TO SANTA CRUZ

The next big meetings were to be held in the biggest hall in the town of Santa Cruz, halfway between Sablayan and Mamburao, which was a strategic place at that time because of attacks by NPA troops. Pastor Sonio contacted the mayoress of Santa Cruz and asked if there was any accommodation available in the town for our big group, as there were also dancers and musicians travelling with us, and the local believers' small "nipa hut" houses were not big enough for all of us. Only the youngsters could stay in these grass-roofed cottages; but they were used to sleeping anywhere, even under the stars.

36. Nipa hut

The mayoress replied that it was too dangerous to come to the town at this time. But Rev. Sonio wasn't going to give up, as the hall had been paid for and the meetings had been advertised. People were coming so what else could we do but go on with the meetings as planned?

The mayoress gave some further thought to the situation: there was no place safe in the town right now and the only guarded house was her own home which was still under construction, with scaffolding around it. She decided to tell the carpenters to stop working for as long as we were staying there, and she herself would move to the town hall overnight. We happily accepted this incredible offer - how many other mayors would put up an unknown evangelist and her group in their own home?!

> **how many other mayors would put up an unknown evangelist?**

Our journey to Santa Cruz started in Pastor Sonio's old jeep, with lots of people packed in. I was partly hanging out and Chris' feet were pressed against the windscreen as he sat on the back seat. The local people were sure that Chris was a basketball player, because he was head and shoulders taller than them. Mr Tala was the oldest member of our party, so he got the front seat, but he shared it with two other people! Altogether there were about a dozen of us in that five-seater jeep. Travel sickness didn't affect me on the bumpy road because I was partly in 'outer space' outside the vehicle, so I certainly got enough fresh air during the drive. Each time the car hit holes in the road, I collided with a metal bar, and so each time my rear end got a few more bruises.

37. *Santa Cruz*

Edwin decided to shorten the trip by 10 km by driving along a dry river bed. At one point we had to drive across a stream but before doing that we stopped and let the tyres cool down to prevent them from exploding in the cold water. In the rainy season this route would not have worked. The bed of the dry river was like the base of an old crater but it was safer than the steep mountain road.

Buenavista, El Dorado … the names of small villages ran past our eyes as we travelled. These names are remnants from Spanish rule, before the Philippines became an American colony. The Philippines gained independence in 1946 after the Pacific War. Their culture is a mixture of Spanish-Latin, American and also Roman Catholic. If this were not enough for a real cocktail, let me tell you that before the Spanish came, the name of the Philippines was Maharlika, which in the ancient Malay language means "Noble Creation". Few other countries or peoples have this kind of royal heritage.

YOUR STEPS TODAY BECOME YOUR FUTURE

Almost everyone I met during this journey to the Philippines connected with my coming ministry in some way. We are called to fulfil certain God-given tasks here on earth, and we do not carry them out alone but we need each other. Some people are called to bigger tasks, some to smaller ones. Humanly we often gauge the size of a ministry according to how visible it is, but God evaluates our ministry according to our hearts – our attitudes and our motives.

There are many different tasks and roles in a battle – from the general to the private soldier – but all are vital. The general formulating his strategy needs up-to-date information – both from the front lines and, if possible, from behind enemy lines. Reconnaissance troops working in secret will not be prominent figures, but the knowledge they bring can change the war. Aaron and Hur were vital to Moses in the war against the Amalekites. They held up his arms when he got tired as the battle was raging. Without Aaron and Hur Israel would have been defeated. It was their collaboration with Moses that brought victory to the Israelites, as we read in Exodus 17:11-13.

Today we cannot find many Aarons and Hurs because the enemy knows that moving strategic people away from their posts is his key to gaining victory. That is why the enemy attacks the Aarons and the Hurs – without them there will never be breakthroughs in the ministries they support.

> **These prayer soldiers fought things through in secret**

My intercessors Hilja and Paula back in Finland were my Aaron and Hur, even though my own task was very much at the grassroots level too. God had placed them as my reconnaissance troops, or perhaps even better described as spy satellites over the land of the enemy. These prayer soldiers fought things through in secret and their seamless cooperation brought victory in all situations.

Yes there were crisis situations too. On one occasion I was in a very difficult situation for a couple of days and I called for help from the Lord as my own strength was running out. "Lord, please would you wake up Hilja to pray for me?" Shortly afterwards I received the following by e-mail:

"For the past three nights Hilja has been woken up by the Lord at between 2:00 and 2:30am. She has seen your face in a round picture frame. Each time she prayed for you and then went back to sleep again. What is going on there?"

God never gives up and we shouldn't either.

Hilja, Paula and Anja, a third woman of prayer, were again interceding during my journey. When I got to Manila I found this message in my email inbox:

"We were praying and Hilja saw a stormy cloud over the sea. Out of the cloud came letters and words as you talked. When people saw the words they calmed down, and started to read and listen. They were astonished, saying, 'What on earth is happening?' As you spoke, the storm calmed and the wind died. You are in the Lord's purse. It is a big elastic purse stretching with you as you move, and it is travelling smoothly like a boat on the waves."

That is exactly what happened. There was a furious storm around us but wherever we travelled it became calm. For the first time in their lives people saw God's miracles and they understood that the word of God really is true.

AT OUR DESTINATION

The mayoress of the town of Santa Cruz was waiting for us in front of her unfinished house. Wow! We had a real house to stay in, after living in tiny huts and cottages. And a shower that worked and lots of big rooms. My son Chris and I got the mayoress' own bedroom. What luxury to sleep in a real bed with a real mattress!

Our celebratory mood lasted as long as the lights were off but then reality 'crowed' in. Next to the bedroom window was a yard containing the mayoress' 100 fighting cocks and beside it was a betting arena. Small shelters had been built for the cocks to protect them from the rain, while at other times they crowed loudly from on top of their shelters. Because they were so aggressive, their legs were tethered so that they could not reach each other. But they still tried to attack each other, fluttering their wings and showing off their tails. I had always thought that cocks slept in the night and then acted as alarm clocks in the morning. But these cocks didn't go to sleep at night and so we didn't sleep either.

On our second evening in Santa Cruz the electricity went off – brown time again. We sat there in the darkness expecting the lights to come on at any moment, when suddenly Chris started jumping around and yelling, "Mum! Get the torch, get the torch! Something is walking up my leg and it's biting! Owww it's burning, it's burning!" I scrambled around for the torch, found it, dropped it, and in all the hassle it rolled right under the bed.

In the meantime Chris was hopping around on one leg and bumping into the furniture in the darkness, trying to pull his jeans off.

In the dark it was impossible to see what strange creature had attacked his leg. But whatever it was had eased its grip and fallen off and my son calmed down. I gave him antihistamine and mosquito cream as I couldn't find anything else. In the morning the top of Chris' leg was full of strange pink blisters and even the local people didn't know what had caused it.

I saw the funny side of this nocturnal drama but my son was not amused, "It's easy for you to laugh, Mum because it wasn't your leg. I could have died!" Think-

38. The mayoress and Anne

ing back, I felt that the two of us were now even. I well remembered that night-time sprint in the rice fields in Sablayan when a 800 kg water buffalo had wanted to make minced meat out of me.

SUPERNATURAL POWER

Santa Cruz stadium was filled with hundreds of people, many of whom had travelled long distances to get there. They had heard about the Sablayan meetings and healings, and in fact knew more about them than we did.

Before the meeting started, I was taken to a very thin man who was holding his paralysed wife in his arms. His friends told me that he had come from 100 km away to the meeting as he believed that God would heal his wife there. The woman seemed to be in such a bad condition that I could not be sure that she was completely aware of what was going on around her.

I asked the man to bring his wife to the front of the meeting and to sit down on the plastic chairs arranged for them there. Pastor Sonio promised to pray for this lady together with the other pastors. When the meeting ended, as usual everyone rushed to the front into the prayer lines, as nobody wanted to leave without a blessing. Everyone wanted our heavenly Father's grace to be saved and to be healed.

John 20:21,23 says:

> **"Then Jesus said again, "Peace be with you. As the Father sent me, I now send you ... If you forgive anyone his sins, they are forgiven. If you don't forgive them, they are not forgiven."**

The power of God is mightier than any political or military or economic influence: only His power can change human beings and hence cause a real change in society. Nothing is impossible for God, and the Holy Spirit is not self-centred like we are. Out of his love he gives to everyone who believes.

MANGYAN LADIES

I prayed for two very fearful sick women, so timid that they sought safety even from each other, hanging their heads down and wrapping themselves under the cover of the dirty rags of clothes that hung upon them. They were Mangyan women and it had taken a lot of courage for them to come to the meeting, because their tribe has nothing to do with outsiders and especially with Christians. But sickness is no respecter of persons. When a person is desperate enough, they will push through whatever barriers surround them.

> **A deep love towards these women filled my heart**

A deep love towards these women filled my heart. They probably came from the Iraya tribe who live close to Santa Cruz. The Irayas have darker skins than the other Mangyan tribes and they dress in a similar way to other people. Because they were so poor, the women had old worn out clothes, other people's cast-offs, in which they wrapped themselves layer by layer to try and keep out the cold from their long nights on the mountains.

They had long lank hair and were so small and thin that I could hold both of them in my arms at the same time. Even though we didn't share a common language, we were all women together – "sisters". The local people wanted to avoid them but of course Jesus does not pass anyone by. Mangyan people often carry infectious diseases, even tuberculosis, and their hygiene standards can be lower than civilisation demands. But that didn't matter to me. What did matter was their courage in daring to come to the meeting. I firmly believe that when they went back to their own people, they told their tribe everything that had happened.

LIKE THE BOOK OF ACTS

There were large numbers of sick people and many others full of distress and anguish. The queue of people wanting prayer seemed endless. Then one blind woman started screaming in fear: she was seeing light for the first time in her life! No doubt it would make anyone scared who previously hadn't even been able to imagine what light was like. Excitement filled the hall. The paralysed woman brought by her husband and sitting in the plastic chair at the front stretched her arms and legs out as she felt them straighten. Pastors took her by the hands, helped her to her feet, and started to walk her around. With each step her legs grew stronger and joy filled her eyes. God's creative power was restoring her limbs and she walked faster and faster all the way round the big hall.

It was like the third chapter of Acts:

> **Then Peter took the man's right hand and lifted him up. Immediately the man's feet and ankles became strong. He jumped up, stood on his feet, and began to walk. He went into the Temple with them, walking and jumping and praising God. All the people recognised him as the crippled man who always sat by the Beautiful Gate begging for money. Now they saw this same man walking and praising God, and they were amazed. They wondered how this could happen. (Acts 3:7-10)**

We had two evening meetings in Santa Cruz, on Thursday and Friday, and Lea Wando was there for the first time helping me. During this month together in Santa Cruz we got to know each other quite well, through long and deep discussions. Lea was wondering about moving back to Australia from the Philippines, as the situation on the island had become too dangerous for foreigners.

FAREWELL TO THE MAYORESS

It was Saturday morning and time to start our journey back from Santa Cruz, so we drove with Pastor Sonio to the City Hall to return the key to the Mayoress' house. We arrived at the City Hall early, at the start of our long and strenuous cross country trip, as Pastor Sonio didn't want to drive at night because of the war. The City Hall was made of simple bamboo walls and had just one room with a few pieces of bamboo furniture. It was there that the Mayoress received people and that town council meetings were held. When we arrived at the door and said who we were, a helper went off to find the Mayoress. She wasn't far away,

39. The mayoress

just sleeping in a small corner behind the curtain. I was astonished! She had handed over the keys to her wonderful house to us, a group of total strangers, and moved to this room the size of a wardrobe for the duration of our entire stay in the town.

Pastor Sonio boldly asked the Mayoress if she had had the time to come to our meetings. She replied that her work commitments had prevented her but that she had sent her adult son there. He had brought her news of how sick people had been healed and how the meetings had been a blessing to many people's lives. I was even more amazed to see what a humble person she was. We prayed for her and we blessed both her and the town of Santa Cruz. She told us that we would be welcome to come back in the future and that her house would always be open to us: she was preparing a nice house so that she could accommodate all those important visitors that might come to the town.

Santa Cruz, like many other small towns in the area, lived under pressure and fear because of the NPA Army. To prevent continuing attacks from the NPA, the town had to pay this communist army what it called "support money". The payments were in no way voluntary – if you didn't pay then punishment was

> **Poverty was excellent fertile soil**

the result. Fear made people do whatever the NPA wanted. They also recruited youngsters from the slums to join their army. Poverty was excellent fertile soil on which to seed their Marxist propaganda into people's minds. Scarcity, corruption and misery breed anger and resentment towards the administration of the country and towards everything that represents power and wealth.

I was told that Santa Cruz as a town paid their support money in food, and that sacks of rice changed hands. Maybe that was some sort of solution, I don't know. But from my heart I blessed the Mayoress of the town who had opened her home and her town to the Word of God.

CHAPTER 9
FINAL WEEK

RETURN TO SABLAYAN

After another long and bumpy journey back to Sablayan which took most of Saturday, we settled back in at Lea's house. We talked together and recognised that the security situation in the island had deteriorated even further. So Lea decided to give up what had been her home in Sablayan over the past couple of years, and to start packing up her belongings ready to move back to her original home country of Australia. She contacted Qantas to try and get a ticket on the same plane as us on Monday 1 May, just over a week away.

40. *On the way back to Sablayan*

We decided to move away from Sablayan to Pandan Island and spend a few days there before travelling to San Jose. At least it would be safer there. So we loaded Lea's belongings into a local boat and said goodbye to Nena and Edwin Sonio. Their children Nheng and Loloi came with us to Pandan Island as we needed all the help we could get to carry Lea's belongings – the boxes almost completely filled the motorboat.

Before we left, Pastor Sonio asked me for prophetic advice about where he and his family should move to work as pioneers. He felt that the work in Sablayan town was done. I suggested Mamburao to him: this town had been on my mind for a long time and I knew that God has a plan for that place, even though I didn't know quite how the pieces of the jigsaw puzzle were going to come together. My suggestion left him thinking. At that time Mamburao was the most dangerous place on Mindoro Island. Edwin also asked advice from Mr Tala, who came up with the same proposal. Time was up for the Sonio family in Sablayan. Edwin and Nena had founded the Foursquare Church there and had ministered in much of the surrounding area – now it was time to break new ground and to hand over the Sablayan congregation to a new pastor.

There was also a Foursquare Church in Mamburao but its best days were long gone. Many people had left the church and the church building was rundown. The only church members left were the pastor and his family and the owner of the nearby building, who had rented his poor quality nipa hut to the pastor as his home. In Foursquare churches pastors can only move if someone else agrees to take their place. No doubt the current pastor would jump through his grass roof for joy at the prospect of leaving that besieged town.

I said to Pastor Sonio that there must be something wrong if all the people had fled and nobody was attending this church. Edwin wondered how active the pastor had been in his role. He and Nena were certainly very active, as they were both always evangelising, preaching the word, and inviting people to come to meetings. Sonio also had an official license to marry couples and through that he easily got to know a lot of people in the area as many couples got married in his church.

I couldn't get Mamburao out of my mind: I had to get there by some means even though it was impossible at this time. There would always be another time. I have a habit of pushing myself in where other people don't want to go and now I was pushing Rev. Sonio and his family into Mamburao.

PANDAN ISLAND

Pandan Island is not far away from Sablayan, only about half an hour's boat ride from the mainland. It is a small island of about 30 hectares. There were a few grass-roofed nipa huts for divers as the famous coral reefs are nearby. This beautiful island was owned by a Frenchman who had married a Filipina lady. A foreigner is not allowed to own land unless by marriage: in developing countries like the Philippines only the local people can legally own land, otherwise rich westerners would move in and buy up the best parts of these poor countries. With its clean beach, this peaceful island was an idyllic spot for us to relax after all the hassles that we had been through.

We moved our things into a rented house and started to make it home for the next few days. In the meantime, Chris decided to have a look around the island saying, "At least I can walk around here in peace. No need to worry about some NPA soldier jumping out at me from behind the nearest bush. This is such a deserted place that only people like us are here."

41. By boat to Pandan with Loloi

All tourists and travellers had been evacuated from the island and no newcomers were arriving while the political situation on Mindoro Island remained hot. Our only fellow inhabitants were a few workers in the accommodation area and some divers who disappeared out to sea during the day and only came back in the evening. It felt like the war that was going on in the main island would never reach this deserted place.

So Chris packed his camera and went off for a walking trip and I promised to join him with Nheng as soon as I had finished my jobs. But Chris' expedition didn't last long … Less than half an hour after he left, he returned at top speed. Rather than giving a calm account of this idyllic holiday island, he was hardly able to breathe.

"Well that was quite a short island!" I said to him as I waited for him to stop panting. "Oh no, don't go in that direction!" Chris gasped. "In fact don't go in any direction at all! As I was walking over there, a man with a machine gun leapt out from behind a bush just in front of me. I have never run so fast in my life, not even that time with the water buffalo!"

We guessed that he must have bumped into one of the government soldiers who were guarding the island. Well, at least we were well guarded, whoever the soldiers were. Throughout each night a patrol boat would circle the island, now and then lighting up our hut and the surrounding area by searchlight. Looking on the positive side, it meant that we weren't going to get lost here, or if we did, we would soon be brought back to our nipa hut, by the scruff of our necks!

After staying on Pandan Island for a couple of nights, we travelled back to the mainland, for the long bus journey to San Jose. However the journey

turned out to be even longer than expected, as the old bus got a flat tyre on the way. All the passengers had to get out, then all the luggage had to be unloaded, and then a trap door was opened under which the ancient spare tyre was found. It took a long time with all the necessary discussions about all the possible alternative methods of changing a tyre, and nobody seemed to be in any hurry at all. We sat for about an hour by the side of the road in 45°C heat. Somebody had the

42. Bus with flat tyre

audacity to complain to the driver, who replied angrily, "You should be happy that the bus is going at all! The previous bus crashed when the driver fell asleep."

That put an end to all complaints, so we went back to counting the stones by the side of the road and counting our blessings, "At least we are still alive!" It took four weary hours to get to San Jose.

MEETINGS IN SAN JOSE

A typhoon had hit San Jose on 20 September 2004, pulling up trees with their roots, taking the roofs off of houses, and knocking down the walls of many houses. Nothing seemed to be spared in its path, as it destroyed schools, churches and even the health centre of one village, sucked up into the air. Hundreds of children suffered in the chaos, especially those who lived in the slum villages along the seashore. Typhoons and other natural disasters are part of life in these areas of the Archipelago.

Yet here we were in San Jose, a town full of life and energy. We planned to hold just a few meetings in the town and then to travel back to Manila. We let Chris choose the motel to stay in as no other accommodation had been reserved for us. He wanted somewhere very close to the airport. "At least we can run to the airport if everything else collapses on the island," he thoughtfully decided. My son was a good source of practical advice! In fact our motel was right next to the military base.

The meetings at the Foursquare Church in San Jose were a success, with a church full of people and the power of the Holy Spirit coming down mightily. The pastor commented afterwards that they had once before had a visiting team who had brought with them a drop of Holy Spirit rain, but this time there was a complete waterfall. God touched the sick and needy; the wind of God literally blew through the venue, and as that wind swirled around invisibly, people fell under the power of God. There was no need for human touch as God's Holy Spirit again did His powerful work.

The audience was mostly women and I wondered where the men were. The pastor explained that they were out at sea. San Jose is a fishing port and they have to stay at sea for months at a time until they find fish. It was a difficult time for their families as they had neither money nor food and not even a guarantee of their men finding fish on this trip.

On our last night in San Jose we were woken up by the sound of machine gun fire, as the army started to take measures to protect our surroundings. Our plane to Manila was due to leave early in the morning, so why did they have to start shooting now? Chris stayed awake the entire night with his suitcase to hand. I didn't get a lot of rest that night either but my sleeplessness was caused by internal rumblings rather than external ones: we had all suffered various forms of sickness during this trip, and now it was my turn.

43. San Jose through the bus window

At 6 am the SE Asian Airlines plane from San Jose landed at Manila airport. We loaded our own suitcase and what felt like a hundred pieces of Lea's luggage into the minibus and set off to the international airport. Lea and I were dreaming about letting loose the "spirit of shopping" and taking a trip by taxi to the Makati Manila shopping centre, as our flight to Australia

73

wasn't until late that evening. It would be pointless to spend the whole day at the airport. So we asked the minibus driver if he would take us to the city after first dropping off our luggage in a safe place. His eyes widened in horror at the suggestion and he kept shaking his head, "No that is not a good idea! I certainly won't go there and I'm sure no one else will take you." We were astonished – what was wrong with us?

For the past month we had had no access to news, whether TV, newspapers or radio and it was as if Manila had dropped off the map. The driver told us that army soldiers had laid siege to central Manila so no one could go there. Coup, coup! Makati was the centre of the crisis at the moment. We were amazed – what a strange country, just when the previous crisis was over! Chris was very amused about this and our foiled shopping expedition. In some ways he said that "the end" was really the high point of our trip.

As we sat on the plane, Lea leaned over and asked me cautiously, "Anne will we ever travel to the Philippines again?" "Of course we will," I replied. "Actually I'm missing it already."

Even though we had to leave Manila without our shopping souvenirs, we did manage to bring back something with us to Australia. When I got home, the first thing I did was to rush into the shower. But at that very moment there was a power cut and the electricity stayed off for 2½ hours. Good old brown time again … maybe some sort of electricity demon had decided to follow us home.

PART THREE. MAMBURAO

44. Pastor Sonio & beach kids

45. Feeding the beach children

46. By motorbike near Mamburao

Chapter 10
Called Back to Mindoro

The Inner Call

Believers have inside them an invisible compass pointing to their future – the God-ordained call over their lives. You cannot see the end of the road yet, but if you keep your eyes open for the right signs you will find your way to the destination. It is God's wisdom not to show us everything beforehand, not until the time is right and we are ready. In the waiting time He allows storms to come and blow off dead branches from us, as His way of preparing us. The strongest quality of a believer is the ability to look ahead towards what's coming rather than staring back at what has passed.

In my view, getting stuck in the past is one of man's biggest weaknesses. We should never be afraid of stumbling or falling down: those who are afraid of taking risks will never win a big victory. In spite of past defeats let's press forward, as many good things are still ahead of us. Real Christianity is radical and it will take us through fire, storm and wilderness. Radical Christians are not afraid of challenges.

Our next trip to the Philippines came quite soon. The Sonios had moved to Mamburao town after the prophetic words from both myself and Mr Tala at the end of April. They sent me a message: "Come over quickly, we need your help."

It was September 2006 and I had just come home from a European evangelism trip. I felt nice and comfortable at home – why should I leave my home comforts to rough it again out in the bush? But my conscience nagged me: "It was you who wanted to go to Mamburao and you even persuaded others to go and live there." While I was in the Philippines, Mamburao had been at the forefront of my mind but now it had faded away like a wisp of cloud.

> **The Lord had put hooks in my jaw**

I found an old letter from Paula that had arrived before my first trip, in between all the changes and flight cancellations. I read it and understood that I didn't have any choice but to respond to the Sonios' pleas. The Lord had put hooks in my jaw and was pulling me. So I assumed it would all become clear in Mamburao why we were supposed to be there. At the same time Lea had also made up her mind to travel to Mamburao and had found a cheap flight on the internet.

The Letter from Paula

Paula had written:

> When you wrote that you weren't going to travel to the Philippines, we felt disappointed. Hilja told me on the phone that we cannot know the timing of the events that we saw in visions before your trip – maybe it will all happen later. But anyway we agreed that we are not going to give up now. However, of course it's not us who has to travel to that place full of guerrillas.
>
> But I have just found a piece of paper where I wrote down more details about the vision in connection with the Philippines. I'm embarrassed to say that I didn't dare tell you then, as you had just cancelled the trip.
>
> Anyway, I saw how a strong white tornado left Australia from Brisbane and moved towards the Philippines and I got the word: power evangelism. That is what is needed there, nothing less will do. Hilja and I then prayed together that there would be a spiritual landslide and coup. Be brave, my sister. *Sisu* and blessings! Paula

So I emailed Paula: "I am going on another trip to Mindoro Island, destination Mamburao town, and will probably need some prayers." My worries were pointless because the Lord had already spoken about the things to come. Paula wrote back:

Hello Anne, I had a picture of you earlier, leaping on the water with **long** jumps. It looked like you were somewhere in the islands of the Philippines and on the surface of the sea, but then I realised that there were rocks under the surface, just in the right places. So go forward in faith, there is the Rock underneath you.

> **go forward in faith, there is the Rock underneath you**

You also seemed to be in the valley of Jehoshaphat. The sun came up and you started moving; the words came: 'Look, how the Lord fights for you!' You will go in peace and thank Him for what He is doing. Also a group of angels suddenly appeared out of nowhere and started to fly towards the Philippines. It seemed to me that a whole squadron of angels had been commissioned to do the job. In all of this it looks like there is a real rush on and a lot of things are going to happen quickly. Hilja prayed that the money would multiply and that feeding miracles would happen there.

What an encouragement from God!

In 2 Chronicles 20:15 we read what a prophet said:

> **"Listen to me, King Jehoshaphat and all you people living in Judah and Jerusalem. The Lord says this to you: 'Don't be afraid or discouraged because of this large army. The battle is not your battle, it is God's."**

79

47. Mindoro agriculture

48. Water buffalo transport

CHAPTER *11*
TAGUIG AND THE SLUMS

ON THE WAY TO MANILA

Sometimes it's best to only get to know the full picture afterwards: when you are not aware of all that there is to know, you get less stressed and you can stay blissfully ignorant, with your feet planted firmly in the clouds …. At least, that is until you get hit by reality.

49. Israel Forbes

That's what happened to us in October 2006, on my second visit to the Philippines. I went for a fortnight, together with Lea Wando and her five year old daughter. At that time in the Philippines, monsoon rains together with heat and a typhoon had hit Metro Manila, and this combination made the air steam like in a sauna.

Israel Forbes from Mount Moriah Church came to pick us up from the airport, but he was an hour late. Driving in Manila traffic is like being inside thick porridge; when you sink there, you can't see the bottom. Traffic pushes forward without any traffic lights, roundabouts or lanes, and with just one rule: "Don't give way, that is cowardice; it's the driver whose nerves fail first who is the one who gives way so that others can drive on." I asked my Manila friend: "How did you pass your driving test in this chaos?" He looked at me rather embarrassed: "What driving test? You hand over some money, take the driving license and then jump onto the merry-go-round."

50. Traffic policeman

They say that traffic policemen stay in that work for a maximum of five years. I wondered whether the statistics just list those who are still alive after that time. The policemen stand inside the hot bubbling porridge without any safety platform and wearing a gas mask with a woollen sock wrapped around it. The air is so grey and sticky through the exhaust fumes that you feel you could cut it with a knife ... and then make nice wrap-around safety bumpers out of it for your car.

Everyone who cares anything about their lungs and their life covers their faces with terry cloth. But when you get stuck for hours in a traffic jam, you would need more like a plastic bubble over you as pollution protection.

DOWN IN TAGUIG

The smog comes straight down on the Taguig suburb, one of the poorer and lower lying districts of Manila where our accommodation at Mount Moriah Christian Academy was to be found. Taguig is a rambling, mainly industrial area in Laguna Bay, at the lakeside.

There are about half million inhabitants there, although it is doubtful whether anyone knows the exact amount. On its better side it extends to Makati town area in the North, but in the opposite direction is Laguna Bay and a huge slum area with a derelict cemetery where street children and criminals live.

The railway cuts it in two and on both sides of the rails people have rigged up little huts and stands. Dwellings are even set up on the rails themselves, even though a goods train passes by once a day. The huts are dismantled before the train comes and then quickly set up again afterwards, because the people are so short of space and even this little piece of ground is good enough.

82

Some calculations say there are between three and four thousand children living in the streets and about 150 gangs that they have formed. Everyone belongs to some gang or other, as that is their family. Some children have been thrown out of their homes for various reasons while others have gone to live on the street to escape violence at home. For them their substitute family is their fellow street children.

51. Huts on the rails

There is a big jail in Taguig, holding many children of varying ages and sentenced for varying crimes. According to the law, children should not be sent to jail, but in practice they are in jails, crammed into their own wards. In the middle of all this chaos stood the Mount Moriah Church, together with its Christian school. The school offers simple guest rooms for missionaries, and that is where we were heading for.

Israel Forbes told us that we had missed the typhoon by just a few days. The eye of the typhoon had hit Taguig, resulting in about 80 confirmed fatalities and 40 unaccounted for. Some of the schools flooded by the typhoon were still closed and the electricity was only on in some areas. But the Mount Moriah School Centre had got its electricity working just moments before we arrived. This area of town has no street names, but the slum huts have sprung up side by side everywhere. No one asks permission to construct their huts. The lower into this shanty town you go, the bleaker and gloomier it gets and the narrower the

hungry dogs & even people scavenge, trying to find something to eat

streets and lanes become. People throw their garbage onto the streets, and as a result there is an unending stream of plastic bags where hungry dogs and even people scavenge, trying to find something to eat.

Because there are no addresses in this part of the town, you have to find your way by landmarks. Taguig is a place where people never seem to sleep, and its main artery throbs day and night with its small, one-room shops open 24 hours a day. Everyone tries to make their living by selling something to each other. Someone sells rice, another clean water, the next one home-made soup and someone else has put up a barber stand in the street. One euro and your hair is trimmed. One entrepreneurial businessman put his TV onto a one square meter stand and for 50 cents you can watch one program. Poverty makes you come up with new ideas to try and get bread somehow.

A Filipino friend of mine from Australia told me how their businessman father had been kidnapped in Manila as he came out of a bank in the SM City Bi-

52. *Taguig slum hut*

cutan shopping centre near Taguig. He disappeared for three days without trace and then on the third day showed up at home. His neat business suit was dirty and he bore signs of having suffered. The man told of how the NPA army had kidnapped him but that he had managed to negotiate his freedom by promising to pay them ransom money. In fact he lost a great deal of money to the NPA: it wasn't just his own money that he was taking out of the bank but also the wages of his employees. The NPA freed him on the basis of continued "support money" from his company. Of course his family was delighted to have him back alive, but this was yet another example of the terrorist tactics of the NPA. Whether you own a small company or a large company, you always run the risk of being kidnapped and having to pay a price for your life.

SM City Bicutan is a big shopping centre close to the Taguig suburb in Manila. Further down, deep in Taguig, there is a no-go area used as a hiding place by criminals, terrorists, drug dealers and many others who have left society's rat race only to fall into a pit of corruption. And yet this part of the city is also a potential mission field for God's work. It may not look like a place where His glory could appear, but God sees the bigger picture far beyond our limited understanding, and He is prepared to show up in the darkest of places.

MOVING HOUSE

One local inhabitant told me a story about a slum hut, which had collapsed through poor design. Its builder had put the base of the hut on the waste pile of plastic bags. Of course this idea wasn't so good: the foundations failed when floods and rains came and the house slid slowly and with dignity into the canal leading to the sea. It didn't cause a big catastrophe as the canal was already full of plastic bags holding waste, and the hut just floated upon them. Apparently it just became a house boat! May-be the Filipino Bible should say: "Do not build upon plastic bags, but upon the rock."

The slum dwellers can-not be blamed for the waste problem – if there is no garbage collection system, what else can you do but throw your rubbish bags out on the street. But even with all its problems, Taguig is a place which has quite an attrac-tive atmosphere. When you live there, you are counting down the

53. Rubbish stream by the road

days until you can leave, as if you are in military service. But when you are not there, you want to be back. Taguig is ripe for revival and there is plenty of work for the evangelist there. I believe that from the midst of all this misery there will rise up an army for God, as it says in Joel 2:7

They charge like soldiers; they climb over the wall like warriors. They all march straight ahead and do not move off their path.

The Philippines as a whole may look small and insignificant compared to the rest of Asia, but God has chosen it for a special task in the last days. He doesn't look at the size of a country, nor its finances or wealth of natural resourc-es. The real wealth of the Philippines is its multi-million population. And the key that it holds is its location; the whole population of Asia can be reached through the Philippines because of its proximity to the rest of the continent.

MERRY-GO-ROUND

God had been at work again through my two Finnish co-workers, Hilja and Paula who interceded for me. Hilja had seen two visions before this trip. One was a very apt description both of the future and also of the situation at hand. She saw a merry-go-round full of shapes that changed to different parts of the Philippines, all fields of work for me.

The merry-go-round spun clockwise at a constant speed and eventually walls grew up around it to cover it. In this fairground we were on the merry-go-round but we kept on spinning perfectly safely and the Lord's favour was over everything that we did.

That whole first day in October 2006 had been like sitting on a merry-go-round … a seven-hour flight from Australia to Manila, followed by a one hour crawl through the city traffic in an old pickup from the airport to Taguig. We sat in the back of the pickup on side benches, the first of which collapsed when I sat on it. Well, I couldn't care less where I sit, I thought to myself.

One of the guys who came to pick us up kept the door closed by pulling a rope tied to the back door. The door lock was broken and at every bump the door burst open and had then to be pulled shut by tugging on the rope. When I leaned out of the open window to take some photos, Israel shouted at me: "No, Anne, no!" I couldn't understand why not. "Isn't it allowed to take pictures here?" I asked. "Oh yes, you can take pictures," Israel replied, "But if you lean out of the window like that, someone will pinch your camera!"

MOUNT MORIAH

Finally we reached our accommodation at the Mount Moriah school guest house, and I managed to grab our luggage before the horrendous downpour started. Rain poured down like a waterfall all through the night and the downstairs of the house flooded.

In the morning the floors of the classrooms were full of water but the assembly room was dry, so we gathered the primary school pupils there to listen to the message of Jesus and the story from a book called "My Heaven" that I published in 2006. The children were excited about the pictures and the story, and when I asked, "How many of you want to know Jesus?", they all said yes.

This was the first time that I had used the "My Heaven" picture book as a tool for evangelism and it really worked. God had given me the theme and the pictures for the book in visions as long ago as 1993, but at that time I didn't understand the real meaning or why He had done so.

54. The 'My Heaven' book

I also didn't understand why God delayed the publishing for so long. I had previously worked as a book illustrator and when I used to get a new task sent me from a publisher to illustrate something, it usually meant that the book would be published within a few months. I couldn't understand why my Heavenly Employer gave me an illustration job to do, which I then did promptly, but He then withheld His permission to publish it for ages, so it just gathered dust in a drawer.

Humanly we want everything to happen straightaway, but God in His wisdom was causing the material in the book to gradually ripen until the right time came. He knew that I wasn't at that time ready for the job or for some happenings that would relate to the book.

We had promised to help the Joshua Care organisation, in their work of telling the children about Jesus and helping to feed them. This would enable us to get in touch with and understand what working amongst these poor street and slum children was like, before we travelled to Mindoro Island, to do what God

55. Children's meeting at Mt Moriah

had prepared for us there. We certainly couldn't foresee what a huge mission field was waiting for us, nor did we understand that what we now were involved in had a significant connection with the task to come.

In the evening the assembly hall at Mount Moriah school was filled with 300 children of every size and age. Sharon, the leader of the Joshua Care organisation from Australia had given us suitcases full of plastic toys – small plastic animals, cars and dolls. The playthings caused such joy as these were kids who had never owned any toys at all. But sadly the toys quickly ran out and I said to Lea that I'd never again want to do this when I saw the faces of the hundreds of disappointed kids that were left without any.

However thankfully there was enough food for all of them. Slum children are always hungry as they very seldom eat at home, and if they live in the streets they have to beg for their food. When the food was distributed, all the sorrows over the lack of toys were forgotten. I told them about Jesus and I used "My Heaven" picture book again. The children loved it, as Lea read out Bible verses that fitted the story while her daughter sang and walked around showing pictures from the book.

56. *Enjoying 'My Heaven'*

In the book there is a picture of heaven where all sorts of wonderful delicacies and special foods are laid out for the children to eat. But a slum child isn't familiar with any of these special treats, so I just told them that in heaven no one is ever hungry because there is plenty of fish and rice for everyone.

The story of heaven brought such joy and expectancy to these slum children. Hope came into their eyes and a deep longing for a place where this constant hunger does not exist, and where there is no sickness or suffering. Immediately all 300 children wanted to get to heaven. One small child asked me in a disappointed voice, "Can't I go there now?" Another one poked him and said knowingly, "You have to die first."

Next day the work among these children continued, with new ones being brought into the hall. One four year old was delighted as he had just got a sponsor from Australia who would pay for his upcoming schooling, and money had also been collected for him to get an operation. The child had been born with his bowels outside of his body and they were tidily collected in a plastic bag on his side … the other kids didn't pay any attention to it. Many poor children living in the slums or tip areas have such bodily malformations.

57. *Food in 'My Heaven'*

Pastor Sonio's daughter Nheng and her brother Loloi arrived from Mindoro to guide us on the next day of our trip. We also needed some extra pairs of hands to carry the luggage as we had brought lots of clothes and other stuff as gifts for the local people. So they stayed with us in our room at Mount Moriah on the night before our journey.

Vision of a Pillar of Fire

Hilja and Paula had again been praying for us and I heard by e-mail that Hilja had seen a vision of some papers with writing on them. It was my handwriting but quite small, with the words filling the pages, apart from the lower right hand side. Next the page slid away from her sight and was replaced by another picture where a large scroll of off-white paper was gently unrolled open. Inside the scroll was some embossed writing. Hilja saw a group of people looking and reading; the scroll was in front of them like a screen, and they calmly read it as it rolled opened. It was all a single long sheet of paper.

58. Anne preaching with 'My Heaven'

Then Hilja saw a white sandy beach with waves lapping against the shore and slowly covering the sand. The sea was turquoise and light blue. On the beach she saw lots of people, mainly children. In the middle of the people rose a fire – like from a big bonfire – between two and a half and three metres high and maybe 70 cm wide.

Hilja watched as the fire grew higher but narrow like a pillar and it sparked smaller fires along the whole coastline. It would only be a few days before we would see this vision become reality.

59. Girls at Mt Moriah meeting

60. Preparing the food in Mt Moriah

CHAPTER *12*
JOURNEY TO MAMBURAO

TO THE HARBOUR

Next morning, 7th October, we got up early to make a start on our journey, but I noticed that Nheng's brother Loloi was nowhere to be seen. I woke Nheng up and told her that I couldn't find the boy anywhere. We eventually found him fast asleep underneath an iron bed and of course we couldn't understand why. There were two iron beds in the room – Nheng and I, being slim, slept on one of them, which for some reason was on a slant, causing me to roll over on Nheng from time to time. Lea, her little daughter and Loloi slept on the other bed, or at least that had been the plan. When we found

61. Bus station

91

Loloi, Nheng laughed and told us that he wasn't used to sleeping on a mattress so he'd preferred to lie on the concrete floor under the bed. I have often wondered how it is that many Filipinos seem to be able to sleep anywhere and in any position, even upright.

We waited and waited for our promised transport to take us to the bus station, but the driver had overslept. This delay turned into a chain reaction and we ended up missing our planned boat journey as a result.

We also had some drama on our bus ride. Soon after we had got on board the bus and settled down in our seats, Nheng got very anxious and wanted us all to get off again straightaway. I couldn't understand why, as we had just managed to get all eight suitcases in, found seats for us all after trying and pushing hard, and we had even paid for the suitcases as well. Nheng was insistent: "I am scared because you are the only foreigners here and the bus is full of men, so anything could happen." I settled down even deeper into my seat and said firmly: "I am not going anywhere; only a madman would go out there."

The bus station was in the middle of a notorious criminal district. Where would we go with all these suitcases? We couldn't just stay on the street waiting for suitable-looking fellow travellers to appear. En route to the bus station the driver had even told us to lock all the car doors from inside when the vehicle got stuck in a traffic jam. We had watched through the car window as a group of young men had taken just a few seconds to rob an unsuspecting passerby.

62. Batangas

There was no way that I was going to wait on the street in that sort of "porridge". The bus full of people took considerable interest in our conversation, obviously an enjoyable part of the on-board entertainment programme provided for them. The bus started off towards the harbour but Nheng didn't start to relax until we were at least halfway there.

It took us more than two hours to travel to the Batangas harbour. There we heard that the afternoon ship to Mindoro had been cancelled and so we had to wander around in harbour area until evening. We could only hope that the captain of the night ship would have the motivation to actually make the sea crossing; the stifling harbour hall was already crammed with people and I wondered how we would all fit into one ship.

FERRY

The night ferry finally arrived and we sprinted to the entrance along the half kilometre long bridge. Everyone had the same target, to get a seat or a wide bench to lie down on. Nobody wanted to stand up for three hours on the rough seas or to sit on deck in the heavy wind.

Princess ran in front of us with her backpack and a pink Barbie bag hanging from her shoulder. I pulled one large piece of hand baggage and a heavy suitcase. Lea ran behind me with even bigger cases shouting: "Run! Run! Run!" Loloi and Nheng tried their best to manage our other bags. We pushed, shoved and stumbled in the total darkness, knowing that it was the slow ones who would be left on the shore. Soon I felt that my legs couldn't manage another metre at this pace. My mind was filled with lovely thoughts: "This is not a job for a sane person – what on earth made me come here?"

On the ferry we piled up our bags in the hold next to where the cars were. Not a good idea. Afterwards we found they had got really wet as dirty oily water had soaked them all for the duration of the crossing.

In spite of our mad rush to the ferry, the best seats had already gone, let alone any sleeping possibilities. So I tried to learn to sleep upright like the locals. Loloi found

63. Sleeping on board the ferry

a tool box to lie down on and there he slept contentedly – 13 year-olds can certainly sleep! Nheng slept on the life jacket box. At least that was one of the safest places to choose as ferries very often sank on these archipelago routes through storms rising up suddenly.

Lea always takes a very positive approach: once before she had made this journey, in the opposite direction and she was singing the praises of the views and scenery as being really mind-blowing. We had a good laugh, whether out of tiredness or hysteria I don't know, about her travelogue on the views because it was as dark as pitch out there! The seemingly endless journey finally finished as the harbour lights of Abra De Ilog came into view in front of us and we saw the majestic mountains of Occidental Mindoro silhouetted against the sky. We were one step closer to Mamburao town.

MINIBUS TO MAMBURAO

Long before the ferry arrived at Abra port, we pushed our way down to the hold to wait for the doors to be opened. In the very dim light it was impossible to see where we were walking and soon our shoes were as wet as our suitcases.

Nheng said she would run on ahead of us to reserve seats in the minibus. Getting luggage off the ferry was just as manic as our struggle to get on board. All the passengers had the same idea – to get their luggage off and to get themselves and their luggage into the waiting vehicles. So chaos again ensued as people bumped and elbowed each other, trying to fight their way to the front of the queue.

64. Mamburao

The local people thought we "big people" were taking up far too much room when we wanted to sit on the whole bench of the minibus rather than just a quarter of it. Together with Lea we fought tooth and nail to keep our parts of the benches, as Lea already had her daughter on her lap and I had our hand luggage in mine. Nevertheless I lost half of my seat to a chap who had obviously forgotten to use his deodorant that morning.

The driver pushed more people in and I screamed from the back seat: "No room, no room!" But he seemed to have the opposite opinion and yet more crowded in, while a trembling falsetto voice gurgled from the radio: "Love me tenderly". Tenderness wasn't a big feature of this trip.

We travelled the whole day. The many army checkpoints slowed down our journey, as the soldiers wanted to make sure that there were no NPA men or weapons hidden in our minibus. Mamburao was still a hot spot that could boil over at any time.

We finally arrived at midnight. As it was so dark, we couldn't see much of the town of Mamburao but we could just make out the invitingly lovely shape of our small motel standing there on the main street. Nheng had reserved us a room, and her parents, Edwin and Nena Sonio, were waiting there for us, together with some other acquaintances who had moved to Mamburao following the Sonio family.

The only thing I could think about was sleeping; Princess was already fast asleep in Lea's arms. So I threw myself onto a bed which seemed to be quite clean and I fell asleep im-

65. Welcomed by the Sonios

mediately. But not long passed before I woke up with strange tingling sensations on my skin – which I rapidly realized were actually bites … I jumped up and switched the lights on, only to find that my bed was full of ants. Why had they built their nest right there?!

66. Happily inside, minus a couple of buttons from my cardigan and one shoe

95

67. *First meeting at the Sonios' church*

68. *Anne & friend*

CHAPTER 13
FIRST MEETINGS IN MAMBURAO

THE SONIOS' NEW CHURCH

Pastor Sonio was excited when he came to wake us up for the morning meeting: the church was already full of people. They had all come early to make sure they would get a seat. We were the only white foreigners in town, and many people had also heard of our previous trip in April, with the healings and other moves of God in our Sablayan and Santa Cruz meetings.

Edwin had worked hard, travelling around the town and surrounding areas inviting people to come to the meetings. He went from home to home, and also to those who had in the past been members of the congregation.

The Sonios had started the church from rock bottom when they arrived a few months before. The church building was in a decrepit condition with everything in bad shape, like an uninhabited house. Next to the church was a piece of land and a nipa hut, which the owner had promised to the Sonio family for them to live in. I looked closely at that little nipa hut, if it really could be called that; it had bamboo walls and only one room, which had been separated into two little halves by curtains to make sleeping areas. The kitchen was outside, together with a small

> **The Sonios had started the church from rock bottom**

97

covered area for eating, which was right next to the road. Every time a motor bike passed by we were showered with dust, and when we had our meal the local people would gather hungrily to watch us eating.

There were seven people in the Sonio family and everyone had to fit into that one room. I asked where the 20 year old twin boys and Loloi slept, and was told that they slept on the wooden benches in the church. Back in Sablayan they had had quite a comfortable pastor's house provided for them as part of the same building as the church.

69. Frances

With the Sonio family in this same little hut there also lived an 18 year old girl called Frances. The previous pastor couple had given her a place to stay in the hut during the time that she studied in high school. She slept with Edwin and Nena's seven year old adopted daughter Mijan, whose mother had been a member of their church in Sablayan and had gone off with a man, leaving the child behind in the church.

Later the Sonios learnt that the little girl had tuberculosis. I do not know what kind of nursing she received but the girl had her own plates and bowls and she ate apart from the rest of the family. Abandoning children is quite common in poor areas and they tend to be just left in churches. This is a substantial burden for the already poor pastors, who often find it difficult providing for their own families. But Mijan was looked after and she helped with the housework and cleaning in the family.

As well as Mijan, the Sonios had also raised up a couple of boys after their parents, relatives of Nena, had died. As often happens in countries where there are no social services, these orphans were placed with the closest relatives, and that was Edwin and Nena. One of the boys was Jonathan and he went on to be a pastor like his stepfather.

The start of the new congregation was not very promising: just nine people, almost all of them from their own family. Gradually some children from the neighbourhood started to pop in now and again, and with them Nheng started a Sunday School. Little by little through the Sonios' work, people started to come to the church's Sunday meetings.

SUNDAY MEETINGS

On that first morning, I preached a sermon about the lame man who lay beside the Bethesda pool and was healed by Jesus. These people needed both mental and physical healing.

In the meeting it was stiflingly hot and humid; the moisture made the pages of my Bible stick together so reading it was impossible. These people needed a Living Word so that they could see how God works. That evening I carried my torch with me to the meeting. I thought I would be able to read some Bible passages with it in the darkness of the pulpit, hoping it would be cooler and less humid so I could turn over pages. However my idea wasn't that bright after all, because I ended up with a microphone in one hand and then didn't have enough spare hands to hold both the torch and the Bible!

70. The Sonios' church

The venue was so full in the evening meeting that not everybody could fit in and some had to listen to the message from outside. God's Holy Spirit was present, healing people. At the end of the meeting, as I waited for the people to come to the front for a blessing, I climbed back onto the platform with my camera, intending to take some pictures of the congregation. But before I could manage to take any, something really strange appeared on the dark screen of my digital camera.

PILLARS OF FIRE

There were two fire pillars stretching from the floor to the ceiling about 70 cm apart and about a metre wide. Each was made up of many small flames in a variety of shining colours with some delicate lilac ones too. I was stunned! I shouted to Rev. Sonio to come and have a look.

> **There were two fire pillars stretching from the floor to the ceiling**

This was no night-time exposure error on the camera – I felt I was watching a vision on the camera screen. I wanted to know whether Edwin would see the same … and he **did**! He was so excited that he announced the phenomenon to the whole congregation, so they all rushed towards the platform to see the fire pillars for themselves. I tried to figure out at what position in the meeting hall they actually were, and I immediately recognised that people were falling under the power of God right in that place. How amazing!

I had eliminated all natural causes why the camera might be showing such things on its screen. I was very familiar with the camera and I knew how to take photographs. I have a degree in photographic design and have worked as an arts director in an advertising agency, with responsibility for photographic sessions. There was no possibility at all that through ignorance I might have mistaken some lighting effect on the camera. But now I really didn't understand what was going on. Later on after the meeting had finished, I made a point of testing my camera in exactly the same spot with exactly the same lighting: there was nothing to be seen.

What made me believe that this was a miracle of God was the vision that had come from Paula and Hilja before I left for this trip. I had written down their visions when I heard them, as I planned to go over them again during our trip. So after the evening meeting I checked in my notes for these fire pillars. There they were, pictured exactly how we had all seen them in the meeting. I had thought that this vision was just a symbol of the things that would happen during the trip but now God had made it a visible reality too.

In the vision my intercessors had seen two pillars of fire showing up in Mindoro, about 70 cm apart and made up of many small flames – in exactly the same colours that we had seen them on the camera screen. That would be a sign from the Lord that revival will hit that town.

Still later that same night I took my camera out from its case, switched it on and reviewed the photographs that I'd taken in the meeting. The flames could not be seen on the photographs and the lighting was totally right. I believe in miracles but I am also a down to earth person. I am keen to eliminate every natural explanation so that when the supernatural really does show up it will be clear for what it is – a phenomenon for which there is no rational explanation. God does not need any advertising hype: He can manage very well without that.

There had also been another vision from Hilja that I found in my notes: "A flame, orange and gold coloured inside, with greenish edges, followed me and our little party like a pillar of cloud in the daytime and fire in the night. There was also a rock and water was coming out of it."

On that trip I didn't see any water coming out of a rock, but in one meeting I felt water raining down on me, not for the first time in my life. I am quite used to feeling the rains of the Spirit falling upon me before He comes down on a meeting. In one prayer situation in Australia I saw how a giant water drop fell from heaven on my friend's hand. I thought it was just a vision but suddenly the lady screamed: "Water, water!" and showed me her hand upon which a huge drop was floating.

FOLLOW UP AROUND THE TOWN

Next day people everywhere were talking about the fire pillars that had been seen in the meeting. Edwin and Nena's church increased in size in one huge leap following our visit – with 80 new members. I promised to work together with them, both in Mamburao and wherever the Lord might lead us.

Edwin told me that they all were going hungry and that they also needed money to buy petrol for the old motorbike on which they travelled to the surrounding areas. This is the reason why many pastors do not travel around to evangelise such areas and many localities are left without the gospel. But we did have money for motorbike fuel and for other forms of transport so we did travel, from one village to another. We went either by motorbike or by a three-wheeler and sidecar, in which we could fit more people. Lea and I sat in the sidecar, Rev. Sonio drove and two slim locals fitted behind him. Lea's daughter sat upon the petrol tank in front of him (there are no European-style safety rules in Philippines), and then there were two extra people who sat on the floor of the sidecar as I sat on the bench with Lea.

71. Edwin by motorbike

The floor of the sidecar was so close to the ground that the metal and my bones clanked in turns against the bench. I pointed out to Lea that she mustn't put a single centimetre more on her hips or else we wouldn't manage to sit side by side. The bike was slow and a real "dust-eater" but there was no alternative for us to get round the area.

101

72. *Coconuts*

73. *A heavy burden*

Chapter 14
Beach Kids

Nena's Dream

One day, Edwin and Nena took us to the beach area of Mamburao. There we found big crowds of children who swarmed around and followed us, so I asked Edwin, "Whose kids are these?" He told me that they were "beach kids" as there is a big slum area on the beach in Mamburao. The children came from there, some having parents, others a granny or relative, and several having no one at all – "Cinderellas".

Nena Sonio had a dream of starting to minister to the kids on the beach but they didn't have money for that kind of work. Nena had visited the slum village to get to know the people, but visiting was not enough; there was a big need to do something. Lea and I talked this over together. We agreed that this was it, this was our piece of work, our ministry. We would give Nena money for

74. *Preparing the food*

food, she would find ladies to prepare it and then we would all go with the food to the beach to gather the kids together.

Soon our "soup-kitchen" was on the go. We thought that spaghetti would be a nice start as that is something the kids never get, as it is far too expensive. Rice is the common food, although even rice is not always available. Milkfish came from the sea if the fishermen were lucky, but normally fish were always sold to get some money. Lonely mothers would walk from house to house selling just one fish, starting very early in the morning. They usually asked if they could wash someone's laundry too. There was no kind of social help; if you didn't have money, you didn't get anything to eat.

FIRST BEACH MEETING

The women that had come to the church worked through the night preparing food in the outdoor kitchen, while we planned the feeding programme from one beach to another. Pastor Sonio visited the village communities to tell them about the meeting to be held on the beach.

About sixty kids came to our first meeting, rather timid and frightened. There were also some very small ones, about three or four years old who came with their mothers. One little girl of about two years of age had a withered arm. Another mother brought a boy whose legs were paralysed.

75. Beach meeting

Edwin Sonio played his guitar and taught them to sing Tagalog language songs. He also interpreted when I talked to the kids and told them about Jesus and heaven. In the end I asked who would want to give their lives to Jesus … and all the hands went up and then they put their hands over their hearts to pray.

Suddenly the Holy Spirit pointed out a paralysed boy to me and I clearly heard Him say: "Take the boy and walk with him – I will do a miracle." I was astonished, as I don't tend to operate like that. I never pull someone up and command them to walk – in fact I have opposed that type of method, believing that the power of God will push a person up if that is needed. But now

I had to obey. God wasn't bothered about my religious beliefs and preferences, and He often likes to totally undermine my logical reasoning …

So I walked over to the boy's mother, and said: "God is going to heal this boy today. You take one hand and I'll take the other – and now we'll go for a walk." The boy was about five or six years old and he got scared. "Don't you see that I can't walk?" he whined. His legs dragged lifelessly behind him along the sand as his mother and I walked along the beach holding his hands. But his mother was trusting completely in what I had said.

I said to the boy: "Walk! Jesus will do a miracle." The boy started to take steps but kept on whining: "No, I can't walk!" As we walked around the beach the other children were watching us out of curiosity. Suddenly the boy got an invisible jolt in his legs and they started to move slowly without dragging; he was astonished as well. But then he started to take steps and soon it turned into walking. I said to the mother, "Let go of his hand." Mother did so and the scared boy shouted: "No, mum, no …!"

76. *Paralysed boy healed*

Now he just had me holding on to his other hand but we continued walking and his legs got stronger with every step. Suddenly I released my hold on his hand … the boy stopped, looking at me astonished … I told him to walk and that is exactly what he did: he walked and finally he ran a full circle on the sand!

EXCITING NEWS SPREADS

What joy this miracle caused in that group of children! The two year old with the withered arm who was on her mother's lap started to swing her arm in her excitement and the arm was healed as a result of the first miracle!

After all of this excitement we passed out the food to the children. We had so much food that many of them got two helpings, which they greatly enjoyed. Some kids were so enthusiastic that they finished their portions within a second, as if they were scared it would disappear.

The kids carried the news about the healings to the next beach where there was a bigger slum community: God certainly takes care of our advertising.

> **God certainly takes care of our advertising**

Our ministry had started and 60 small souls had come to Jesus. Pastor Sonio promised to take care of them in the future, as we desperately needed a church where they could belong.

In the evening a resident from the slum village came to ask if we had seen two small children, of 3 and 4 years old, who had started to follow us after the meeting. They were found later in a deserted old cemetery, where they probably had stopped, after running a couple of kilometres after us until their legs could run no further. I do not know if they had parents or not; maybe they just had decided to become our children.

Next day, many of the kids who had come to Jesus arrived at the church, and Nheng started to teach them songs and dances. The ex-paralysed boy was there too, now running like all the other kids. Nheng decided that she would let the children show what they had learned in the following Sunday's meeting, so they would naturally join in church activities. So the children's work had a speedy beginning in this congregation, where the Sunday school room would immediately be too small for all these sixty new little believers.

A VISION ABOUT A WIDE SCREEN

Later I found an internet cafe in the town. It looked a bit strange as there were masses of wires running along the walls and the floor. The computers were old, the keys of the keyboard stuck to my fingers one letter at a time and they had to be pushed back onto their holders over and over again. The mouse pointer wandered about with a mind of its own and sometimes your whole text mysteriously disappeared, especially if a power cut happened in the middle of your writing. It was hotter inside the room than outside, but if you survived the heat you could even read some emails. And I had one from Paula and Hilja.

Hilja had seen a vision of me and Lea's daughter walking on the beach. I had somehow crept around on tiptoe and played with the girl. Then Hilja saw a screen open up in front of her, on which pictures from my book "My Heaven" appeared one at a time. There were also a lot of people watching it as if they were in a cinema. Then three clouds of lilac blue appeared on the screen, and eagles came out of each of them, flying towards the earth. The screen was then folded up in the shape of a 'Z'. Next a big globe of planet earth started rolling around on a pedestal in every direction, one after another. Hilja felt wind blowing as the globe rolled, and she also heard the sounds of animals. Then the word came: "The book goes around the world."

Paula told me that she had not mentioned anything to Hilja about my book. I was astonished at this email, as it was exactly what was happening. The book was serving as a marvellous tool for the gospel, not only with children but also adults. These kids don't have any books and they understand heaven better when they see it in pictures rather than just listening to stories. I had brought the book with me on this trip even though we didn't have a clue what we would be doing with it. Before the trip, meetings had only been arranged in churches – we had not planned any work with beach kids.

77. *From 'My Heaven'*

78. *Beach children*

107

80. *Mangyan mother & child*

79. *Mangyan families*

Chapter 15
In & Around Mamburao

Hospital

Our days were spent busily distributing the contents of our luggage: toys and clothes, amongst other things, to the poor kids. I only planned to keep my own personal belongings until we were about to leave the country, then I would give them away too.

The town was smaller than San Jose because terrorism "taxes" had forced a lot of companies and families out of Mamburao. The harbour had been closed and moved to Abra De Ilog, and the airport was no longer used either. Grass grew on the runways and the only thing left standing at the airport was the deserted air traffic control tower. In any case, why should the townspeople bother about the airport? During the rains it flooded anyway.

The central hospital of Mindoro Island was located in Mamburao. Someone told me that it was a place where you would only go to die. Almost the only things available at this hospital were the rusty iron beds. Medicines you had to buy for yourself, and the same applied to food. Some kind relative of the patient had to prepare their food and bring it to them. That is why the rooms were full, not just of patients but also of their close relatives. There was a manual respirator provided and the relatives kept it working by taking it in turns to pump it. If the pumper got tired and stopped, the patient died. The hospital could not be blamed for deficient nursing as this was the system, when there was not enough money for the upkeep of the hospital.

Medicines were available from the pharmacy without a prescription, but poor people didn't have money. When the doctor advised them to get antibiotics, they bought only one tablet and then complained that it didn't do any good at all. The first task was to teach people how to take antibiotics, that the whole course of them had to be taken to have any good effects. But the teaching didn't seem to make any sense to them, as they had always managed with just one tablet. The looks on their faces said it all: "Say what you like, white nose, but I know that my relative died after eating one tablet."

What was desperately needed here was a medical mission. We made contact with a medical organisation in Manila that we had got to know on our previous trip, but their timetable was already full for the year. They promised to come next year, provided we would pay for everything: medicines, accommodation, food and travelling costs. I promised to do all of that. I didn't have the money but I trusted that it would come – miracles have to go hand in hand with the practical gospel.

GETTING TO KNOW THE MANGYANS

We visited the Mangyan tribe for the first time. Pastor Daniel, who spoke their language, was our interpreter. He works with these tribes people, trying to help them and to bring them the gospel. We travelled there on motorbikes, I was riding pillion with Pastor Edwin Sonio driving one bike, and Pastor Daniel rode

the other. The village was not far from the main road but we could not ride the motorbikes right into the village itself as the end of the track was only just walkable

We gathered adults and children in a small bamboo shed, which served as their school, and again I used the "My Heaven" book as a tool when telling them about heaven. Sparks of interest were kindled in the eyes of both kids and grown-ups. These people

81. With the Mangyan children

were the lowest of the low and the most miserable. Pastor Daniel repeated the teaching, to try and make sure that they understood what it all was about.

The Mangyan tribe is very closed and shy. The children were hiding behind the bamboo posts for this was the first time in their lives that they had seen a white person – something really scary for them. But the pictures in the book drew them closer, like a magnet pulling metal out of a hole. They all wanted to know Jesus, and both young and old were born again into the Kingdom. We had kept some clothes to give to this tribe but we wished we had more, so ragged were their own clothes.

We prayed for the sick people. They were easy to divide in groups as everyone seemed to have some sort of malarial disease. So it was malarial ones in a queue to the left, tuberculosis sufferers to the right, and all the other infectious diseases in the middle. Pastor Daniel thought this was the wisest solution as he then would not need to interpret everyone's disease to me. There was a father who had brought his little son to receive a blessing. The boy had a dirty piece of cloth draped over his head. When I asked the father to remove it, he refused, so I lifted it up to see what was under it, and then quickly put it back again when I saw what was underneath. The head was completely open, a bloody purulent mess. But I still prayed for him, asking God for a miracle. I have not had any contact with that village since then, so I don't know what results there were.

When I looked around the village, I came across a big water buffalo happily chewing on some laundry that had been washed in a muddy ditch. On asking why it was doing that, I learned that even water buffalos were so hungry at this village that they would eat anything that had even a hint of soap left. This time someone's shirt was the main course, and a couple of scarves served as a side dish. The lady of the house had left her laundry half done when we turned up at the village. In Mindoro water buffalos are called **tamaraw**; they are the biggest animals in the country and are often used instead of horses to transport goods or to work in the fields.

82. *Water buffalo eating laundry*

111

On subsequent visits to Mamburao, I made further trips to the Mangyan area with Pastor Daniel. He told me beforehand about the tribes people's liking for sardines, so our equipment usually consisted of Bibles and tins of sardines.

> **our equipment usually consisted of Bibles and tins of sardines**

The empty tins were used as dishes after their contents had been shared quietly and enthusiastically by everyone. After all the sardines had been eaten and only the oil was left, even that was used efficiently. The Mangyans dipped their fingers in it and stroked it carefully through their hair like gel; what a delightful aroma exuded from the assembly!

I thought about the fact that one person's delicacy is another person's nightmare, as the only thing that makes me feel sick is the smell of herrings and sardines. Even the smell of Manila or garbage tip areas can't make me feel sick. Maybe my love towards those little children, rejected by their parents and by all of society, helps me forget the smell.

My dream of joining the tribes people as an evangelist quickly evaporated. They do not accept outsiders and you have to live and behave according to their customs. This was how Pastor Daniel did it.

One day he asked me whether I would eat their food. But when he told me what was on the menu I quickly replied: "No way, let's forget the whole thing." The Mangyans meet their need for protein by eating rats and they may get offended if you say no to this special delicacy.

83. Mangyan mother & baby

Apart from in the area of my dietary foibles, I was an object of delight to the Mangyans. They marvelled at my long straight nose, which I had previously regarded as just a normal part of my face. These people became really infatuated with it: the bigger and more handsome nose you have, the more beautiful they think you are. A wide flattened nose turning slightly upwards tends to be distinctive of the Mangyans themselves.

Fireplace Food

After our trip to the Mangyan village, we returned to Mamburao for the evening meeting, and the Sonios' church was full. Some of the women went off to pre-pare food for our kids feeding programme planned for the next day. The ladies were excited as one of the sisters had offered a big outdoors kitchen for our use and it was there that they pre-pared the food. An outdoor kitch-en meant literally outside fire-places. We had given the church ladies enough money to buy the ingredients; so the women bus-ied themselves cleaning chick-ens, and cutting up vegetables and herbs. It was a real hive of activity, small fires were burning

84. Outside fireplaces

and you could hardly see because of the smoke. "Why not have electric hobs?" you may ask. Well, how would those be any good with the continual power cuts?

Stories about Healings

At the beginning of the meeting many people came forward to testify of heal-ings they had received at Sunday night's meeting. One lady told of how she had been healed of pain in her hip and thigh that had gone on for years. She jumped up and down on the platform, so excited by the fact that she now had no pain and was able to walk normally. She pointed at me and said: "That white lady prayed."

A deep hush suddenly descended on the hall, and everyone looked at me as if they were waiting to see how I would react. "React to what?" I won-dered. What on earth was going on now? Pastor Sonio whispered something to the lady, who then said something in Tagalog and finally he spoke to me, "We ask your forgiveness, Anne!"

The lady looked so miserable when she looked at me … I didn't under-stand anything, could someone please explain? The pastor politely clarified the situation: "This lady didn't mean to hurt you Anne, she just got so very excited and accidentally called you "white lady", which means "ghost" here.

113

Of course I immediately burst out laughing and I laughed so much that I could hardly stop. So that was the name of the game here! My laughter seemed to break the tension amongst the congregation and soon everybody was laughing with me. I thought to myself that perhaps it was time to buy some special cream to make my skin brown. But the trouble was that in this country the shops only had long shelves full of creams to bleach brown skins white.

One man came forward to witness how he had come to the prayer queue to ask for help in selling his house. The Lord had answered immediately and after getting prayer he was able to sell the house next day. In this poor town it was difficult to sell houses, and they often stayed on the market for years as no one had money to buy anything, and as a result the sellers could fall into serious financial difficulties.

Another lady had travelled from Sablayan to Mamburao to tell us how she had had a tumour in her stomach, causing her intense pain, but at our meeting in April the tumour had disappeared and she was totally healed.

Again another person came to tell everybody how her paralysed hand had started functioning again in the meeting. She waved her hand around and around, to show what she had been unable to do before. She told us that her knee had also been hurting and that it was healed at the same moment.

Later on in the prayer queue, an Assemblies of God (AOG) church pastor was brought to me. Pastor Rodelio Hernandez had been in a car accident where four people had been killed. His own life had been spared but he had suffered serious injuries, resulting in two months in hospital just before this meeting. He told me about these injuries. It was a long story but he ended up saying how he couldn't ride his motorbike any more, because his leg could not cope with the pedalling motion and his back injury was painful too. At that point I didn't remember any more what his other ailments were.

> 'I came because the sick are being healed here'

Then he showed me two bones clearly visible in his chest that had been broken in the car accident. The accident had left him with a gap between them, another source of pain for him. Rodelio said, "I came to this meeting because Pastor Sonio told me that the sick are being healed here."

Edwin took me aside from the prayer line for a moment, telling me what he had agreed with Pastor Hernandez: "When the pastor gets healed now, he will arrange to take you to preach in his church."

"Oh, how very simple ..." I thought to myself. At this point I almost lost my faith, but the Lord whispered a reminder to me: "Use My faith." I really cannot be proud of my own faith – I am not the one doing the miracles. The roles were about to be swopped.

So I went back to the AOG pastor, who seemed to be looking rather sceptical as he waited for me. In Jesus' name I told his body to obey the command of the Lord, and the bones to be healed just like they were created to be. I looked on astonished as the two bones that had had a gap between them suddenly clicked together! I don't know which of the two of us was more shocked, the pastor or me. I must admit I never get used to miracles – they are always so amazing.

85. *Pastor Hernandez testifies*

THE FLAMING SEA

At the end of the meeting the Lord again showed me the pillar of fire, made up of many small flames. This time it came as a wide sea of flames upon the people, right across the hall. The Lord is the fire of life to those who honour Him but the fire of judgment to those who keep sinning. Under which fire do you want to be? In the book of Zechariah it is said:

> '**I will be a wall of fire around it,' says the Lord. 'And I will be the glory within it.' (Zech. 2:5).**

After a couple of days, Pastor Hernandez rode his motorbike into the church yard to show us that his leg was healed. He pedalled the fuel excitedly shouting: "My leg is working!" He told us that the Lord had been working on his body one problem at a time. "My back is still hurting, but when you come to my church on Sunday, we'll pray that this pain will go away too!" So, was this an invitation, I wondered? The pastor said that he had witnessed to everyone in his own home area about the wonderful power of the Lord, so the church would be full. The Lord is powerful and mighty indeed. Every day we heard about new healings, as the Lord showed that His Word is living and active.

86. *Feeding the beach children*

87. *Praying for a lady on the beach*

CHAPTER *16*
MIRACLES ON THE BEACH

A LETTER FROM PAULA

Once again I hurried to the internet café to pass the latest news to the intercessors and to send emails to the Pacific Islands. This time it took longer than usual as the electricity was cut right in the middle of emailing, and it stayed off for more than an hour. Happily I managed to read the message from Paula:

> I saw you floating in the air. You were holding an opened umbrella over your head and you looked as colourful as Mary Poppins. Stones rained onto the umbrella, and they were the size of a fist or a bit smaller. The umbrella was red. Earlier Hilja had also seen you floating in the air and then you had moved somewhere. She saw you, Lea and Princess yesterday riding around in a circle on a scooter. You were entertaining the children who were in the middle of the circle; and everyone seemed to be having fun.

> Hilja's vision: She saw a cactus in the Philippines, shaped like a menorah (the Jewish candle stand) at the top. It was knocked down and juice came out of it. People crowded round to drink from it. For some reason the Lord gave us the verse Jeremiah 31:10 - Hear the word of the LORD, O nations; proclaim it in distant coastlands: 'He who

117

scattered Israel will gather them and will watch over his flock like a shepherd.'

Hilja also saw a spotlight especially pointing out certain children in the group. We do not know why the Lord highlighted some of the kids, and we even wondered whether some of them could be of a Jewish origin?

With blessings, Paula

MARY POPPINS JUMPING

The group of us left for the beach to meet the children, with the food packed into boxes – the same sort that are used in Australia to pack hot takeaway food – altogether enough for 250 kids. There were lots of children on this beach area, because the biggest slum was close by. Edwin carried his guitar and the ladies found a bamboo shed near the shore where they stored the food and everything else that we needed. Kids started to gather around, full of curiosity, and all the while more came running from further away. Edwin started playing his guitar and encouraging the kids to sing with him.

Nheng arranged the kids in a circle, and it grew bigger all the time as children came from everywhere. We organised funny games and competitions for them. The kids were jumping with joy, literally jumping, as I arranged a Finnish "letka-jenkka" dance line behind me. This is a dance rather like the conga where each person holds the waist of the one in front. Around we went, kicking our legs and jumping along, while Sonio sang and played a children's song in the Tagalog language.

Yet more kids joined on the end and hundreds of little feet were kicking up the sand around us. We jumped, we weaved in and out, we circled and sometimes I would stop suddenly, causing the whole line to concertina into itself and kids to collide like dominoes. What laughter and screams of joy that caused! Even some of the adults started joining our line. I literally felt like I was Mary Poppins, and would soon be starting to fly! And my umbrella was not far away – at this time of year heavy rains were common and people also used umbrellas as sunshades. Laughing and giggling kids covered a wide area of the beach.

After we had played enough such games, we gathered the children in a circle again to hear what I had to say. I told them about Jesus and heaven, with some short stories about the miracles Jesus is doing. Children were listening, in a total silence like adults. They really lived along with the stories, sometimes saying "oooo-oh ... aaaaah". When I finally asked which of them wanted to know Jesus as their Saviour, all said they wanted to. So they put their hands on their hearts and together we said aloud the sinner's prayer. Many of the children wept. The Holy Spirit really touched them visibly. I even saw some adults break down in tears too, wanting to receive Jesus into their hearts.

Most of the children and adults that had come didn't know about the food distribution. We had given out information about it, but many new kids had come along, just to see what was happening. Finally everyone wanted the blessing and they pulled my hand onto their foreheads. I should have had many more hands up my sleeve for this. Someone tugged my shirt wanting my attention: "Mum, mum!" (a common title for an older woman). So I turned around to look. A small boy pointed out two lads a bit further behind the crowd of children: "They want to be prayed for too."

NICO

The children moved to one side so I could get through the crowd. I didn't quite understand, but I saw two boys one of whom was pulling the other smaller one along the sand, as his legs were paralysed. I walked over to them and bent down. The other kids made a circle around us staring with curiosity and wanting to see what would happen. The boy who had towed the paralysed one, said: "This one wants to start walking too." Well, that was a very simple request! He had heard how God had healed another boy of the same age, on the other beach. The paralysed boy told us that his name was Nico.

The crowd of children was pushing too close and Nico was already getting plenty of sand in his face so I told them to move back a bit. Nico's legs were like pathetic thin sticks through lack of use.

88. Praying for Nico

I tried to find out how it had all happened and someone said: "He just got paralysed when someone hit him and he fell down. The doctor said he'd never walk again and he just stayed like that." It was a simple story of disability, but it

119

was clear that his big brother had to have faith and plenty of *sisu*, to start towing Nico to the beach. Nico's brother himself was so frail and thin that it wouldn't have been possible for him to carry his little brother. Wheelchairs were unknown here, and even if they were available no one could have afforded one when it was a struggle to buy even food each day.

I asked the bigger boy how he knew we were on the beach. He innocently replied: "I heard someone shouting: "Let's hurry to the beach, two *kanas* are there." Lea and I looked at each other dumbfounded: "*kana*" is a Finnish word meaning 'hen'. Do we look that much like hens? How have they learned Finnish words here in the Philippines? Later Pastor Sonio told us that 'kana' is a Tagalog language word for all foreigners. It was not until my next visit that I learned where the word actually came from in the first place.

I put my hand on Nico's heart and felt it beating much too fast. He was probably scared but clearly he had something wrong with his heart too. He was

> **You will walk, that is the Lord's promise to you**

finding it difficult to breathe, as the dust was hanging heavily in the air around us. It was burning my eyes as well. Suddenly I felt words of knowledge just come bursting out of my own mouth: "You will walk, that is the Lord's promise to you." Something like that had only ever happened to me a couple of times before, but now the Lord was taking over my own reasoning, in order to achieve His purposes.

The crowd of kids around us was abuzz with the words: "Nico is going to start walking." Nico himself was tense; I picked him up in my arms and said: "It is too dusty here. Do you have a mother?" He nodded. "Would you ask your mum to bring you to the church tomorrow?" I asked. "Then I will pray for you there later. Now I will pray that Jesus would touch your heart."

I said a very short prayer and asked Nico if he had understood, what kind of promise Jesus had given to him. He nodded, saying, "Jesus will heal me and I will walk." I felt it was important for Nico to feel free and relaxed with me without tension, fear, and panic and without hundreds of other kids standing round staring at him.

NOW THE FOOD RAN OUT

The ladies called for the children to come forward, as it was time to distribute the food. Kids were arranged in queues and we were surprised to see that nobody tried to push in or jump the queue. We tried to position the smallest ones, three to four year olds, at the front of the queues, but it was difficult to tell their ages when even the older kids looked so frail. Lack of vitamins and nutritious food had affected their growth. The children were always hungry – the fish they caught often carried worms which were then passed to them. White rice, which contained very little nutrients, was the only other food available to them and that only during rice harvesting time.

Adults could work in the rice fields for two months per year, those that managed to get the job. At other times there was nothing to eat. Rainy seasons were the worst times, for then no one could go out on the stormy sea to fish. The rice that was still available was mixed with water and day by day this 'liquid rice' got thinner and thinner. Lack of vitamins weakened the immune system and children easily fell sick. Malaria was the worst disease during the rainy seasons

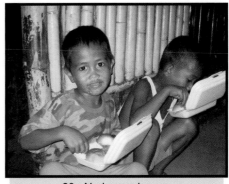

89. No longer hungry

but there were others as well, like Ross River Fever, Dengue Fever and many other tropical illnesses.

But now we had food to offer these hungry children, and it was distributed box by box. Lea's daughter ran with boxes from queue to queue, diligently working to give out food.

One of the church ladies came over to me: "Anne, we have a problem. There is food for only 250 kids but there are hundreds more of them here today. What are we going to do?" Finally we realized that we could reduce the portions and so we got 50 more, but even that was not enough. There were around 700 kids altogether. So many new souls brought into the Kingdom of Heaven … where on earth could I make enough food for them all, as we hadn't expected such a huge crowd of them to show up.

Nothing is more miserable than to see the disappointment in the eyes of the children when food runs out. Those at the tail end of the queue had watched closely as the pile of boxes got lower. One of the little ones came over and asked me: "Will those kids who were left without food today get some tomorrow?"

121

I nodded, feeling I had to say something. These were kids who didn't have food every day, but tried their best to manage through the day until evening. Many of them came to thank us for the food that we had given to them.

Later on, a boy of about 12 years old was keen to show us where he lived. He guided me to an old, half rotten nipa hut and pointed towards it. I replied: "Mmm … 'nice' home". He looked at me aghast and said: "Oh no, I don't mean the hut – my home is that couch!"

Beside the wall, there was an ancient settee that had seen its best days long ago, and on that he had collected some old pieces of worn-out fabric. He was clearly very proud of his settee and that is why he wanted to show it to me. It was a step in the right direction as the children do not normally want to show their homes or the places where they live. I felt that we were on our way to winning the trust of these children.

THE CHAIR LADY

Someone came and took me over to where an old lady was sitting on a plastic chair. I didn't understand what she told me in Tagalog, but I just nodded compassionately. She laid my hand upon her forehead. So, whatever it was that she wanted, I just prayed: "Thank you Jesus that you bless this old lady." I turned around and went over to another old person, who was complaining of neck and shoulder pains and aches in her bones … at least that is what I understood was her ailment from her fussing and gestures … I blessed her as well.

When I walked away from the first old lady, I couldn't know what sort of commotion I had started. I only got to hear about it on my next visit, when an old woman ran up to Nheng and told her the story. Her legs had been paralysed and some friends had carried her to the beach on a plastic chair, where she sat, waiting for the white *kana* to come and bless her. As I left her, Jesus had touched her feet, and she had bounced up off her plastic chair and started running, something that she'd been able to do ever since. Wow! The Lord had again showed His glory; Anne Miettinen's own faith hadn't counted a bit towards the healing. I didn't even pray for her legs to be healed as I hadn't the foggiest idea what the stream of words coming out of her mouth actually meant. Yet again the Lord had showed how to do the business – just like He did it 2000 years before.

The faith of these people was whole-hearted. They didn't understand all the theological intricacies or even that they were supposed to believe all the right stuff before they could be healed. No, they just honoured God and didn't despise the ones that God had sent to tell them about Him. Matthew 10:40 says:

Whoever accepts you also accepts me, and whoever accepts me also accepts the One who sent me.

Faith Anchored in the Word of God

We were the target of open-mouthed stares from the townspeople: as the only foreigners in the area, we were seen as strange albino people who had lost all the colour from their faces. Where could we hide? Wherever we went, kids followed us giggling. They also marvelled at Princess's dark skin which was similar to theirs … but why on earth had her hair gone so brown and frizzy rather than being nice and black and straight like theirs. In the meetings children used to stroke my hair or let it run through their fingers, as it was so very weird and mysterious to their minds.

Nheng told us that not only was the whole town of Mamburao talking about us, but also the surrounding localities. If that wasn't enough, I heard that even the next island knew about us. They were all talking about the miracles that had happened through these two *kana* hens. I thought if there had been more of us, we would have been a real *kanala* or hen house!

90. Strange albino lady

So God was taking good care of our advertising and the gospel was advancing at a rapid pace. If miracles were good enough for Jesus, they must be for us as well. There are immeasurable amounts of unused miracles in the store-rooms of heaven. A doubting heart sets itself higher than God and makes Him out to be just a cardboard figurine who doesn't act today.

Matthew 28:18-20 promises us:

> **Then Jesus came to them and said, "All power in heaven and on earth is given to me. So go and make followers of all people in the world. Baptize them in the name of the Father and the Son and the Holy Spirit. Teach them to obey everything that I have taught you, and I will be with you always, even until the end of this age."**

His miracle-working power and presence is in us. God has given us heavenly gifts to use as His colleagues, and He will not leave us without tools. Many ask in meetings, "Give me more, more!" What exactly do you mean when you ask for more? Do you only want the pleasure – a moment of basking in His presence? Or do you want to receive power to surrender to His will, to go into the refining fire where real changes happen in you; where the impurities will be burned away, where you will die to yourself? Then you will be an instrument of God's power.

91. A boy from the slums & his home

CHAPTER *17*
BREAKING THE VICIOUS CIRCLE

DOING THE IMPOSSIBLE

We talked to the kids that had come to Christ, and asked about their wishes for the future. We wanted to find out how best to take care of them from here on. How could we get their relatives to church so that the children would keep believing in God? Now that the whole thing was fresh and new to them, they ran to church, but what would happen when we left – would their enthusiasm go too? We also wondered why the kids were not at school. They told us that they had no money to go to school, but that they wanted to. This sounded strange to us who had always thought of school as being free for everyone.

We were told about compulsory creche and pre-school where children learn English, which is one of the two official languages in the Philippines. A child does not learn English if everyone else around them is speaking the Tagalog language – normally their parents do not speak English.

The people of the Philippines seem to have a natural ability to learn foreign languages. Many of them speak three or more languages in addition to their own tribal language and the two official languages. There are more than 7100 islands in the Philippines, which causes enough dialect and language confusion to rival the Tower of Babel itself. When a family moves to a new area, they also have to adopt the dialect or language of that area. And I am not talking about mild type of dialects like Geordie in England or "*savo*" in Finland – no, they are different languages on the archipelago.

93. Huge potential

Entry to creche and pre-school was too high a hurdle for these children to get over: poor people could not afford the charges for these facilities. Gradually we began to understand how the system worked. In theory, educational institutions are open to all, but in practice they are not, because the poorest social class is excluded. Then if one cannot read or write, life's possibilities are very limited in a country where there is not enough work available for everybody.

That is why 11 million Filipinos have to work overseas. And even this door is closed to people living in the slums. If you do not have work, there is no money to buy food … if you don't get proper food, your immune system gets weak. In every rainy season kids fall ill. During the last typhoid epidemic in the archipelago about 150 people contracted the disease. Typhoid occurs where sewage is not properly dealt with, and the heavy rains cause the residues to flow into the drinking water. At the beginning of March 2008, typhoid hit in Calamba town, on the outer edge of Manila, and 1200 people got seriously ill. Typhoid is a killing disease.

Life will never improve if you don't have the opportunity to go to school. You live in the tip, you were born there and you will die there – one million poor people live in the huge tip area of Manila. The place is called "smoky mountain" because of the fires burning constantly. The

"smoky mountain",
fires burning
constantly

garbage is burned as there is no other way to get rid of it. Year after year the pile grows and the area gets bigger, and finally it has become a smoking mountain.

Mamburao town was remarkably clean compared to Manila but it was much smaller. Yet even in Mamburao we found rubbish fires burning along the roads in the evenings and the acrid smoke stung the eyes.

126

The poor people of Mamburao had the sea shores to themselves, with million dollar scenery but without the expensive villas. The area was full of grey shacks, between which narrow clay paths wove in and out as makeshift streets. Building materials varied – cardboard, plastic, pieces of metal, bamboo and brushwood. Because there were no foundations to these ramshackle constructions, the annual typhoon blew them to smithereens or the floods washed them into the sea. Nevertheless, they always sprang up again soon afterwards like mushrooms after the rain.

Once I was given the chance to buy a plot of land for a school in the middle of this shack village. An interesting idea, but the potential building site was already occupied by little squatter cottages that belonged to the children that we knew – precious homes to them. It would not have been right to build a school and at the same time rob them of the only homes they had, even though by law they had no right to be there. Especially so since we had no alternative accommodation to offer them.

MISERY A BREEDING GROUND FOR VIOLENCE

Mamburao lived for years under the influence of the NPA terrorists. That influence slowly turned a once lively and thriving city, the island's capital, into a frightened and poor community. As businesses and companies fled to the mainland and people no longer dared to come to the city, the airport closed, ships used other harbours … and the city died.

The bank filed for bankruptcy following a terrorist kidnapping that effectively put a stop to tourism: the owner of the French hotel was seized and murdered and his body was never found.

People lived under constant fear. The NPA terrorised even the slum community keeping it under constant terror by killing people without reason. Goods trucks and other vehicles were robbed as they travelled along the only main road to the other side of the island that went through Mamburao. All goods brought to the island were originally carried through its harbour, but the NPA bombed a ferry there and shipping companies swiftly moved elsewhere.

94. From poverty to education

In spite of this reign of terror, NPA terrorist ideology still sank its teeth very firmly into the young people living in these miserable conditions. Bitterness towards the local administration and officialdom kept growing. The people's lack of knowledge and education made them fertile ground for NPA propaganda lies. But a drowning person will clutch at just a straw, even though he knows it will not hold. Chewing nga-nga induced drunkenness; soon violence and its partners-in-crime came to fruition in the fertile ground of hopelessness and misery.

In April 2006, there had been heavy fighting in the area and it had left behind many personal tragedies. One such tragedy was a boy of about twelve. He was also notable to look at because he suffered from a large malformation in the middle of his face, from nose to forehead. He wasn't the only one disfigured by this sort of disease, but especially at his age it was a horrible affliction. He wept quiet tears in the prayer queue. Perhaps the meaning of the spotlights that the intercessors had seen was that the Holy Spirit was pointing out certain children to us, such as this boy and also Nico.

I asked the boy if he had a mother, and he started trembling hysterically. Someone came over to tell me that NPA terrorists had attacked his village and had machine-gunned his mother before his eyes. A week after that his oldest brother had contracted polio. His father was an alcoholic and had not seen a sober day since the time of the NPA attack. The boy was living in the trauma of all that had happened and I was speechless; how much anguish can a child cope with? I hugged him and somehow he calmed down.

> **how could this vicious circle of poverty be broken?**

Back at our accommodation Lea and I talked over many big questions … how could this vicious circle of poverty be broken? We offer Christ to the kids and that solves the spiritual dimension, but what about the practical side? How would it lift them up from that deep hole of inferiority into which they had sunk? What would Jesus do in the similar situation? Would He just say: "The poor you will always have with you – now that you have dealt with them, move on"?

I really don't believe He would have treated these little ones so offhandedly. Jesus loves children and wants them to be blessed, so we decided to find out how best to help them. It only takes one person who is willing to step inside a dark room and find the switch; then the light comes on and the darkness disappears.

A SCHOOL FOR THE POOR CHILDREN

Now some kids were saved they had a connection to the church, but their lives weren't going to improve without a radical practical change. As we talked, the same idea came to our minds : "A school, let's set up a school!" The same thought popped up in both our minds at the same time but then of course the practical questions followed: how we could possibly start a school here without any money and even more importantly how on earth we could make it keep going after we'd left. So we prayed together and asked the Lord to help us find out how all of this should be done: "Lord give us the answer in some way. Help us (in Finnish "auta"). Is this really your will?"

Suddenly Lea shouted out "autan"! I didn't have a clue what she was talking about "Errr, I beg your pardon but what did you say?" She ran to the table and picked up the bottle of mosquito repellent that was lying there. She held it up to me, laughing: "Autan! Autan! Do you not see that the answer is Autan?!"

Okay … so what has Autan mosquito repellent got to do with anything? We were on completely different wavelengths and I hadn't the faintest idea what this woman was so excited about. Lea threw the bottle over to me and then pointed out the text on the label. The brand name of the repellent was there …. a big word in clear Finnish: "AUTAN", meaning in English, "I will help." Suddenly understanding dawned and we both burst out laughing! The rest of the label was in the Tagalog language and we didn't understand it at all, but there in big letters was God's answer – *Autan*, I will help!

95. Help

The Lord has many ways of speaking to us, but at that moment the text on that insecticide bottle was fine for us as His answer. The Designer of the Universe had just said: "Autan", I will help, so why should we try and solve the problems with our pea-sized intellects? Let's just jump by faith into the unseen, with the Lord as our Helper doing His stuff. Our real help comes from heaven; if we try and live according to earthly realities we will never achieve very much.

96. *Making plans for the school*

97. *Some of our potential pupils*

CHAPTER *18*
A SCHOOL IS STARTED

FINDING A BUILDING

We got in touch with Nheng and told her about our idea. She got really excited as she is a teacher by profession but was unemployed after moving to Mamburao. Back in Sablayan she had held occasional jobs in a creche. Also her mother Nena Sonio had a degree and was a qualified teacher too.

Well, we now had a teacher. So what we needed next was a rented room for the school: we started looking in the town for a place suitable to be a kindergarten and pre-school. Pastor Sonio knew a man who worked as a school supervisor in the area and was a believer, so we called him for an appointment.

We also found another believer who owned a big building with a couple of empty rooms. He had complained about having part of the place empty, as a result of the previous tenants not paying their rent for half a year and having to be evicted. If we wanted more room later, he told us that would also be possible soon, because the last tenants were moving away. There was also a tiny little corner shop in the same building. Behind the shop there was a kitchen, where we could make food for our school children if we had enough money. We agreed on the rent price and I paid the owner for several months in advance. This meant that our travel money was going down and we still urgently needed more for registration costs, to renovate the rooms and to buy tables, chairs, and school equipment.

Finances

Lea and I talked over the financial situation and came to the conclusion that we would have to set up a charitable organisation in Australia with its own bank account. Then I could get a bank card with which to withdraw money from

the account whenever needed. Many Australians had already expressed interest in donating for such a purpose as this but we just lacked the account.

I promised to send more money after they had given us an estimate of how much the renovation would cost. I sent express telegrams to my "Manager on the top floor" saying, "Lord, please arrange some buyers for my paintings when I return to Australia," as I had quite a few paint-

98. Corner shop beside the building

ings piled up in a cupboard at home. The Lord soon answered when I was back home … a businessman who had bought some of my paintings a few years before called me asking if I still had some available. His son was about to move to England and wanted to buy some to remind him of the collection on the wall in his Australian home.

What about the pupils? There are some Christian schools in the Philippines but all of them are private and require fees for the pupils. I got a bright idea about our fees: the school would not be free,

> a weekly charge - a compulsory Bible study lesson

but there would be a weekly "charge" by which everyone who wanted to send their child to the school would have to participate in a compulsory Bible lesson. These lessons would be once a week and attendance would work as our payment. This way we could reach the whole slum village and get everyone who had some connection to the kids saved on the seashore involved in Bible study.

Ground Work

The Sonios eagerly went to work. We formulated a budget, designed the teaching programme, agreed the logistics and chose the administrative officers. We went to meet the believer friend of Edwin's who was a school inspector and he got excited about the idea, promising to help arrange the necessary permissions and registration. He gave us lots of useful and practical advice, both at that time and in the future. Nheng went over to the slum area to tell the villagers about the school and to figure out how many kids might possibly come.

We also visited the prospective school building and the owner promised to build up a fence after I complained that the kids might stray onto the busy road. These were young children and they couldn't be allowed to roam free in the street like sheep on a hillside. The fence had to be built by the owner as we were regularly paying tenants, from whom he was going to get a lot more benefit than the previous ones that he had had to evict.

99. *Looking round the building*

Active Faith Works

The building was in poor condition, but at least it was a start and with some small renovation it could be made serviceable. The best thing about it was that it was only a short distance away from the places where the kids lived: we had heard that it was obligatory to arrange transportation for children who could not walk to school. The idea of running a free school felt humanly impossible but nothing is impossible to the Lord.

Mark 11:23 says:

> **I tell you the truth, you can say to this mountain, 'Go, fall into the sea.' And if you have no doubts in your mind and believe that what you say will happen, God will do it for you.**

In the evening there was another meeting and the locals eagerly joined in. A lot of children came along too after being in our beach meetings earlier, so we decided to arrange a programme for them. Filipinos love music, dancing and singing, so we sang some songs together and I showed them how to make a tunnel of arms through which both kids and adults happily ran. Loloi played drums, Sonio was on guitar and Nheng sang. The tunnel curved all around the church and everyone could go through it. After some energetic running and jumping it was easy to settle down and preach.

I preached about miracles and Jesus' healing power. These people needed living examples from everyday life – dry theological texts weren't suitable for them. To my hearers, miracles had to be for now. I also mentioned the idea of starting a school and that caused an enthusiastic buzz to go round the hall.

In the end many came forward to receive healing or to be saved, and the atmosphere of faith grew as people gave testimony. One lady received healing in her back and shoulder; earlier she could not lift her arm higher than shoulder level, but now the pain was gone and she could stretch her arm up normally.

The boy whose paralysed legs had started working in that first beach meeting ran and jumped with all the other kids. He witnessed by his very behaviour of the work of Jesus in our midst. A mother from the slum village testified about her healing from breathing and heart problems. Her heart was now working normally and she could breathe freely without pain.

NICO'S PROGRESS

Earlier that day Nico's mother had told Pastor Sonio about the change that had already happened in her son. He was breathing normally and his heart

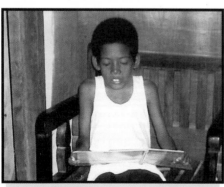

100. Nico enjoying a book

was healed. She could now take him out to see the other children playing, something she had never been able to do before. She was embarrassed as she explained how she had put Nico sitting beside a wall, but when she returned to check if everything was alright, he had mysteriously moved to another place. No one had moved him, so how had that happened? Perhaps Nico had been able to take his first steps in faith or perhaps he had done an experiment to see if his legs would work already, as I had told him that Jesus would heal him.

Nico's mum came to the meeting carrying her son with his younger brothers and sisters running around her. I went over to them and carried Nico to the front. I held him until it was time for me to preach, talking with him and quietly praying for him. Nico even shyly smiled to me. I told him that I was so happy that he had kept his word and came to the church. Nico replied: "I really wanted to come."

At the end people just didn't want to leave the church building. The pastor asked several times for them to go, so the doors of the church could be locked, but the people just sat on their seats and someone shouted: "We don't want to go, it's so nice here."

I asked Nico about his birthday and he answered that it had already gone. "What would you like as a birthday present? What could I get for you?" He glanced shyly around him: "Nothing."

I encouraged him further, "Please tell me something you'd like?" The boy replied: "That I could walk and get to school." I reassured him that Jesus would indeed heal him and that we would take him into our school. I had a big torch in my hand so I decided to give it to Nico. He looked at it curiously. He and his family needed it more than me, I felt.

I also asked Nico's mother what he would like, but the answer was the same … "We do not need anything. My son is now able to breathe and his heart has been healed – that is such a big gift." I asked her to think more and if something came to mind, she could pass me a message in Australia through Nheng. I honoured this woman – she lacked everything, even money to buy food but she did not want anything.

> **My son is now able to breathe and his heart has been healed**

I had secretly put a small amount of money into Nico's hand and whispered: "Keep this for yourself, don't tell the others, so you can buy something later …" He kept the money hidden, grasping it tightly in his fist. It was so amazing to see such strength in his hands. The day before his hands hadn't worked properly and the money would have just fallen through his fingers. I remembered seeing his arms just hanging limply by his sides and just stiffening sometimes out of excitement. I said to Nico: "Remember what I said, you will walk one day soon. Don't look at what you are now, God will do this for you at the right moment." As Mark 11:22 says, "Have faith in God." I watched them leave towards the slum area, feeling their way in the darkness of the night, with mother holding Nico in her arms and the smallest ones clinging tightly to the edge of her dress hem.

God's Big Plans

When rumours about the new school reached the people, Nheng's registration list filled up quickly. There were 300 kids wanting to come to school but we could only take 63 at the most and even that was too many for just one teacher.

Nena Sonio promised to help. She is an absolute model of efficiency and a bundle of energy who manages to do numerous different things, all at the same time. Frances, who lived in the Sonios home, became an assistant to the teacher. She had started studying at vocational school but had had to stop when her money ran out. Now she had a job too.

The pieces of the puzzle started to come together in a seamless pattern. All the members of the church came to help – some people volunteering to do the painting and renovating jobs, others promising to build school tables if I only would send money for the tools and materials. The school was starting to take shape.

Some months later while I was on my preaching trip in Europe, Lea made another visit to the Philippines. She had collected used picture and school books and brought big suitcases of them to Mamburao. That is how we created a simple library for the school. We could not give abacuses to the children but we collected white stones and they were used instead for their arithmetic.

Chapter 19
Church in Pasua

Everyone is the Target of God's Love

Saturday was the only day that week without a meeting at Edwin Sonio's church, so we planned to travel to the locality called Igsoso Pasua where we would speak at an Assemblies of God church in the evening. This was the church of Rodelio Hernandez, the pastor who had been healed in our meeting earlier.

That morning some sick people had come to the Sonios' church to try and find me and they were disappointed to hear that there was not going to be a meeting there in the evening. Edwin suggested they should come to the Sunday meeting or to the AOG church in Igsoso Pasua, but this caused a few of them to burst into tears: the place was so far away and they didn't have any transport.

I was totally unaware of this drama as I was enjoying my first free morning of the trip without either children's meetings or Mangyan tribe's visits. Next to our accommodation was a small street that I walked down ever day and on one side was a large tree. I often stopped at the tree to say hello to the little monkey that lived there. Its owner had tethered its leg to the tree, so it could not go anywhere. So there it sat every day, staring through the branches and throwing seeds and leaves at the passersby. Life in that tree must have been very boring without company.

Whenever I had chance I went into town to an internet café where I could read my e-mails. As the electricity seemed to be on today, it was nice to see that the computers were working. Life had to be arranged around the availability of basic utilities like water and electricity in Mamburao. The town allowed its inhabitants one day for doing their laundry, and on that day poor people wandered around asking if they could do others' washing, as this was often the only job that was available in the town. The laundry came back clean, after it had been hand-washed in cold water, but the heavy handling often caused these 'Made in China' T-shirts to lose their colours and shapes in a short time.

101. Laundry time

The washing machine called 'Lea' was much better. Lea used to put water into a bucket and then tread our laundry clean with her feet. This amazing washing machine had different programmes too: the first phase involved jumping into the bucket quickly as the water was ice cold. In the second phase it didn't feel quite so icy anymore, so the washing programme slowed down. It was good exercise for the feet too.

At the internet café, I found that Paula and Hilja had sent me an e-mail. It was always so amazing how these intercessors knew what was happening here in Mamburao, even down to the smallest detail that I thought had absolutely no spiritual significance at all. Maybe the Lord used these details to demonstrate to us that everything was in His hands.

Paula wrote: "I got a picture of a monkey while I was praying with Hilja, and it was such a happy looking little creature. What could that mean?" So even that little monkey was caught in the heavenly album!

She continued, "Hilja was woken up on the night before last to pray for you. She saw a huge crowd of people gathered together with you standing at the front, and white hoods descended from heaven onto the heads of those people." I took this picture to mean that the Lord was working with us. White is the colour of righteousness and so the picture was talking of salvations and healings, as people experienced the power that changes lives. The Lord was saying that minds were being renewed as His transforming grace was released.

IGSOSO PASUA

Pastor Sonio had an old jeep which on our previous trip had been in a pretty reasonable sort of condition but now was on its last legs. For our trip to Igsoso Pasua, one of Edwin's twin sons drove and the road was what you can expect in these circumstances. It went through the rain forest, sometimes up into the mountains, down again, and tree branches poked inside the open cab as the jeep leapt from one side of the forest road to the other like some sort of mad young calf. Its road-holding even on reasonably level surfaces was shocking. I asked our driver whether he was aware that something seemed to be wrong with the steering. "Oh yes," the young man calmly informed me, "The axle has almost split in two – that's why the jeep is jumping from one side of the road to the other." A stupid question on my part obviously.

Edwin rode his motorbike behind the jeep with his wife Nena sitting behind him and a couple of three-wheelers were putt-putting along after them. All the vehicles were full of passengers.

Night was starting to draw in by the time we drew up in Igsoso. It was a small village with a partly collapsed Catholic church building and the AOG church next to it. We first of all exchanged the normal Filipino pleasantries and the pastor cut a coconut in half to offer us something to drink. He had knocked it down from the palm tree which stood nearby.

The seats for the meeting were under a bamboo roof and they were so high that everyone's feet dangled in the air. I knew from asking earlier that this was so that in times of flooding people could sit down without getting their feet wet in the water that was running over the ground beneath them.

102. The AOG church

The church filled up with people – so much so that not everyone could fit inside the building. Happily the congregation had its own electricity generator, so we were at least able to see each other. The meeting started with the pastor, Rodelio Hernandez, telling everyone about his own amazing healing. He said that on the very next day after being prayed for he had been able to ride his motorbike, and he made a point of showing how the bones in his chest had moved back together – a real creative miracle from God.

After the sermon Rev. Sonio asked the music group of the church to come forward to be prayed for. Pastor Hernandez himself also belonged to that group and so he came to the front too. When I came to pray for him I happened to touch his head and his hip without thinking. At the end of the meeting he came to tell me how at the precise moment when I touched his head and his hip, the pains from both of them had disappeared. Now his whole body was healthy again. Even his back which had still been giving him problems before had been healed during the previous week. His full healing had been a process because there were so many injuries in his body as a result of his accident.

He asked me how I had known about the problems with his hip and head as he hadn't mentioned them to me before. But I told him that I didn't have a clue – it was just an impulsive action on my part. Sometimes the Lord works this way. We don't need to know the whole story or the full medical diagnosis. The Heavenly Doctor knows every last detail.

Many testified of their healings

There were more miracles: the Lord healed one man of an injured arm and he waved it strongly in the air like a victory salute. Many others testified of their own healings but as it was all in the Tagalog language, I couldn't understand what they were saying, just their excitement. Everyone was so thrilled that they forgot to interpret to me.

The area was full of mosquitoes as the church was on the edge of rain forest at the foot of a mountain which rose steeply beside the building. Lea had wrapped herself in a big scarf to try and avoid getting bitten, as she always attracted mosquitoes like a strip of fly-paper attracts flies. So at least I had double mosquito protection: I had sprayed "Autan" repellent on my skin and I also had Lea next to me.

Our return trip back to Mamburao from the church was even more problematic as we had to drive in the dark. We couldn't see the pot-holes in the road so we had no chance to brace ourselves before impact and likewise the tree branches leapt out of the darkness at us – whoosh-whoomphh-whooaahh!! The lights of the jeep weren't working so we just had a torch tied to the front of the car. I wondered if there would be any unbruised places left on my body by the end of the journey. Well, at least we didn't get bored by the routine of the trip.

IT DOESN'T MATTER WHO YOU ARE, GOD IS WITH YOU

I believe in miracles because I know who **He is**, and I don't focus on what I am. God has promised to be with us until the end comes and we are called to bring truth and light to dark places. If we want to know who He really is, we need to accept His power. Never compromise with this truth. You are the ambassador of God's Kingdom and you represent it with His power, as the Apostle Paul says in 1 Cor.4:20, "because the Kingdom of God is present not in talk but in power."

Our Sunday morning meeting was at 8:30 am and the church was again totally full. The children had been practicing to perform a dance and some songs and it was so wonderful to see the saved kids eagerly and actively worshiping God. At the beginning of the meeting a lady who had been sick for months came forward to tell of her healing from back, hip and leg pains. Then her husband came to the platform and told everyone, with tears of joy running down his face, how no doctors and medicines had been able to help, but now his wife was totally healed. As he was telling the story, his wife was moving her hips back and forth, bending up and down and jumping like a rubber ball.

The boy who had been healed in our beach meeting also wanted to tell again of how Jesus touched his legs. He was in the kids dance group, so it was very obvious for all to see how well he now was. It was so moving to see the enthusiasm of this boy to witness about the Lord's goodness.

In the meeting that evening the healings continued, including a lady with a deaf ear who received her hearing amongst many others. The power of the Holy Spirit swept across the people and they ended up lying everywhere, sideways, crossways, and even topsy-turvy on the dusty floor. Happily most Filipinos are fairly small and light so no one got injured. Many of them wept as God seemed to

> **they ended up lying everywhere**

do a mass deliverance from their inner burdens. People who had only heard of God's miracle-making power now saw and felt for themselves what God was doing in them and for them.

141

103. *Followed by kids from the graveyard*

104. *Our new friends*

CHAPTER 20
MANILA & THE GRAVEYARD

BACK TO MANILA

Next morning we had an early wake up call – at 5:30 am the Sonios came to take us back to Manila. The trip took seven hours by various means of transport, the rain poured down, and we were tired of travelling. But at the same time we were so thankful for an amazing trip – how the Lord had so quickly opened doors for our ministry.

We realized that within a few months 2000 kids had got saved, a church had been founded and the Sonios' Foursquare Church in Mamburao had grown from an initial congregation of nine to 100 members and was still growing. That was not including the people who night after night filled the church in my meetings. Pastor Sonio had received a new enthusiasm for the work and now knew for sure that it was the Lord who had sent him to this town. We had started a school for poor children and Nheng and Frances now both had employment.

Yes, we had suffered problems like heat, stomach illnesses, headaches, pollution, heavy rains, constant travelling, getting lost and exhaustion. But all of them shrank into insignificance when compared to the results.

We had learned so much from our experiences and we had been able to encourage our Filipino brothers and sisters. Everything is possible to those that believe. We believed that revival was going to come to Mamburao and that our experiences so far were just a start.

> **The kingdom of David is like a fallen tent, but in that day I will set it up again and mend its broken places. I will rebuild its ruins as it was before. (Amos 9:11)**

PEOPLE IN THE PLACE OF DEATH

On arriving back in Manila we went to lodge again at the Mount Moriah School Centre in Taguig. We had to stay one whole day inside the building as there was such heavy rain pouring down. We had planned to go and feed the children living in the cemetery area but we had to postpone this plan by a day, as the cemetery would be too muddy and the kids would be hiding in the tombs because of the rain.

The cemetery was quite close to our accommodation, and I heard from our friend Israel Forbes that the people living in that area were mourning as they had held a funeral the day before. The four year old boy who we knew

105. *The cemetery*

and who was born with his bowels outside his body had died. I complained to the Lord about this tragedy and the timing: we had just managed to collect enough money for the boy to be taken to Australia for surgery and also to make it possible for him to go to school. In my view the death happened totally at the wrong time. However, God knows the times and boundaries of human beings and He had decided to take this little one to heaven.

We had a rather restless night in our accommodation. This time the iron bed frame seemed to slope inwards from both sides towards the middle, and as well as that the bed head end sloped downwards. We solved the latter problem as soon as we noticed the feet of the bed were in holes in the floor. So after we'd found something to wedge under the feet the bed was at least level in that direction. Lea, Princess and I all slept in the same bed and we two adults kept rolling into the middle of the bed and bumping each other. Princess too slept very restlessly, tossing and turning in every direction and ending up sleeping on top of us and even sometimes hanging halfway over the side of the bed.

In the early hours I finally got fed up with being a holy roller and said to Lea, "Now the mattress goes on the floor." When we pulled the mattress onto the concrete floor, Princess got moved with it. We looked at the old iron bed frame – no wonder the mattress sloped inwards from the sides – the frame was split in the middle. The rest of the night passed in peaceful and undisturbed sleep as at least the concrete was level.

The next day in Manila was typically hot and humid and we made our way to the old Catholic cemetery. It wasn't safe to walk there so Israel Forbes, who looked after the operational side of the Joshua Care organisation in Manila, took us there in the van of the Mount Moriah centre.

There were gates at the entrance to the cemetery and in front of them was a small tip area, where some of the kids had built shelters on the ground into which they could crawl. Their building materials were cardboard, pieces of metal, scrap iron and the like – whatever other people had thrown away. The ownership of the mausoleums and tombs inside the cemetery were determined according to arrogance and muscle power, so adults had claimed the best ones with ceilings and sometimes a couple of walls.

106. Tomb home

People made their homes in these morbid surroundings and there were even families living in some of them. Grave slabs acted as sleeping places or tables. The area was like a city suburb or even a slightly odd looking stony desert. In some ways the dwellings looked much better than the cardboard huts that have been built beside the streets in many areas. One such place had been burning to ashes as we passed by in the van earlier. The inhabitants tended to do their own wiring to get power from the city's electricity poles and one not-so-skillful DIY electrician had succeeded in burning down the entire village.

These shack villages have no utilities or sewage connections as they have been built illegally on whatever empty piece of land could be found. The villagers have no option but to defecate into plastic bags and then throw the bags out onto the street.

Lea told me of an occasion when she herself had to sleep in this kind of shack . She had just arrived in the Philippines and had nowhere to stay, but a friend of a friend told her where she could get a place for the night. Lea ac-

107. *At the cemetery*

cepted it and her hosts happened to have one of these shacks next to a very busy road. They were very friendly to her and, as this kind of living was all they knew, they couldn't understand why their guest would only spend one night in their home.

Lea vividly described to me how the walls were a living and moving mass of cock-roaches. She could have endured that, if only the rats would have stayed in their holes. We are both used to living and travelling in the tropics and with practice you get acclimatized to everything that crawls or flies or whines. Many such creatures of all shapes and sizes have their home in the tropics but at that time it just was too much for Lea.

One good thing about the tombs was that they were solid enough to withstand the typhoons. They had a soil floor and some of them a stone bench and a tall tiled grave slab on which people could sleep and keep their meagre belongings in plastic bags. The slabs were decorated with name plates of the dead as these were family graves. Some of them were real mausoleums with their own iron gates outside, but there were not enough of these 'houses' for everyone.

I do not know how their current occupants had got them but I expect that each tomb had been fought over somehow. Maybe guarding your own tomb house took a lot of energy every day as there were many aspiring rival owners for the best tombs. The weakest ones had to make do with just a tombstone and perhaps then be imaginative enough to build a roof structure over it to make a shelter.

CEMETERY CHILDREN

Strangely enough there was a homely sort of atmosphere in the cemetery. Laundry was hanging out to dry beside the tombs; old sooty pans bubbled away on open fires and mothers took care of their babies. Many of the mums had no teeth and looked wizened and older than they actually were. Kids were small through lack of food and some of them had deformities and development disorders, hardly surprising in those circumstances. But the mothers were still friendly and willingly came over to make our acquaintance and to tell us about their worries. They knew Israel Forbes so they accepted us too.

Lea's daughter sat on one of the grave-stones and handed out sweets to the kids around her – we had bought a lot of sweets to give to the children. The Joshua Care people had fed the children just one week earlier and Israel thought that it would not be wise to arrange another feeding programme for the kids right after the funeral, but instead to give them something that they wouldn't normally get. That way it was easier to get to know them.

Even though the people living in the cemetery had fallen off the end of the social ladder, it was still possible to drop even deeper down. That meant the "Smoky Mountain" tip area which I described earlier. The cemetery had muddy paths leading in between the tombs, creating the streets of this strange community. As we walked along these paths, some people pulled my hand to come and visit their own tomb houses as they wanted desperately to show me their homes.

108. Cemetery children

As we wandered around the cemetery and talked to the kids, we noticed a group of men who were carefully watching where we went and what we did. They were sitting together in a shed discussing some sort of business deals. Maybe they were part of the "Cosa Nostra" that prevailed in the area – I won't interfere with your business if you don't touch mine.

The children ran in a horde behind us, not understanding that in the eyes of most city people they were the dregs of society. They knew no other

147

way of living at the moment, but it would dawn upon them as they got older. As I said, at least these cemetery people were one step higher than those living on the streets or in the garbage tip – they at least had "a stone house" and one person's death had meant another one's good fortune.

The previous week there had been a cruel attack in the cemetery, in which a man had been tied to a pole and stabbed to death. Probably something to do with drug dealing conflicts. Violence was normal in this community; as was stealing, narcotics, prostitution and everything in between. The children were being brought up to fend for themselves in the dark ways of the criminal underworld … but Jesus is the Saviour and He has never given up on anyone.

TIME TO THINK

On the plane on the way back home, I thought back over the situation. There in the slums of Manila and other places in the Philippines, the doctrinal and con-gregational squabbles of the western church had just felt laughable. Problems related to the right positioning of a comma in a proof text seemed to be wholly irrelevant here. The spiritual crop in the Philippines is mature for harvesting and that crop was right in front of our eyes. Our task had become clearer than ever: we had been called to these children by the Lord Himself and I knew where we had to start the job. All that was needed was funds.

> **we had been called to these children by the Lord Himself**

> **But Jesus called for the children, saying, "Let the little children come to me. Don't stop them, because the kingdom of God belongs to people who are like these children." (Luke 18:16)**

When the plane landed at Brisbane airport, I found my husband Erno waiting for this exhausted traveller, ready to bring me home. It felt like I had been on a half year journey around the islands, endlessly on the go with little time to rest. But my heart was still filled with joy, as I remembered all that God had done in people's lives during this trip.

A few days later we were entertaining some visitors at home, and one of them was discussing my recent trip with Erno. I happened to hear him ask Erno, "Why on earth are you allowing your wife to leave you and go on such trips? Surely the place of a wife is at home?" I listened to Erno's answer with a great interest. He calmly replied, "If I would try and stop my wife from working for God, our family would lose the many blessings that God has for us."

148

CHAPTER *21*
BACK HOME FOR A WHILE

SCHOOL STARTS AT MAMBURAO

I soon got news by email that our first pupils had registered for the new school. Members of the Sonios' congregation had together renovated everything ready for the school, and had built tables for the classroom although there wasn't enough money for chairs. As I had very little money myself, I suggested to Nheng that the kids would sit on the floor. She replied: "They already sit on the floor but then all I can see of them from behind the edge of the tables are a few hairs sticking up. Anne, we need chairs."

Then Lea got a brilliant idea: "Let's make a rule that everyone who comes to school, has to bring a chair from home with them." Wow, how smart Lea was, I thought, nodding my head in agreement and very pleased with this idea. But when I voiced this to Nheng at the other end of the telephone line there was first a pause and then laughter: "Mum, these kids don't have chairs, they don't have any sort of furniture at home – they have nothing, they are beach kids."

Oh dear, how could I forget, and so quickly! Most of the children lived on the beach, and their homes were what they were, if there were any at all. Nheng told me that there are 6 or 7 year old kids who didn't even know what school meant, as they had no money to go to school before. And now here they were at our school because it was free.

109. *Classroom at Mamburao*

"We borrowed 10 plastic chairs from the church that you founded," Nheng told me, "but we need to give them back ready for the Sunday meeting. Frances has her own classroom too, as the mothers have brought their 3-4 year olds to school. We've had to start a creche for these little ones. They couldn't be left in with the older children. Their mothers just leave these tots here, to make sure they will get to real school next year. The rumour quickly spread that this is a free school."

The money problem was solved without any effort on my part at all: I received a letter from the Queensland state saying that it had started to grant a special artists' percentage to book illustrators, in addition to library percentages, for every book that is on the market. As I am an illustrator, that included me. The Lord has great timing in everything. A cheque was included with the letter and was big enough for the needs of the moment.

This bonus was quickly changed into pesos and sent to the Philippines, and so the school got its chairs and that was all that was needed for now.

A LETTER FROM NHENG

Nheng wrote:

> In the middle of a lesson one of the little girls started to cry. I asked what was wrong and she told me that a worm was coming out of her bottom. I ran with the girl to the toilet and she was right – there was a white worm coming out, and not just one but two. I pulled the worm and the girl cried. I have never had to do anything like this before so I probably made just as much noise as the girl, but there was no one else to do the job. Later on I thought that it was quite an experience. Then next day the very same thing happened again but with another pupil. Anne, we need money for worm medication for all of our children. They eat local fish that have worms in them.

SECOND LETTER

She wrote again:

> We read your picture-book "Emily's Day" in the lesson. We have all your books but we need more books, pens, exercise books, drinking glasses, and a fan. The parents cannot buy anything as they have no money. Some of the close relatives are very disappointed because we can't accept any more pupils and the mothers come and cry as they beg for just one more child to fit in. We have only one classroom and the room where Frances and I live, but the creche is already meeting there.

THIRD LETTER

In her third letter, Nheng wrote:

> We have one adult pupil of 22 years old, a married woman. She cannot read or write. I felt such pity for her when she asked if she could come to school with the children. Within a few weeks she has already learnt to read a bit and to do arithmetic. She goes around selling fish and she needs these basic skills.

> We pray that the extra room that the landlord promised us will soon become available, so that we can get our youngest pupils in there. That would become the nursery and then we could divide the older children into two different age groups, kindergarten 1 and kindergarten 2, which are pre-school here. So the children could be three years at our school. After that the Catholic school would surely accept them into their prep school.

> The children now have their new uniforms – white T-shirts with the school logo and the girls have blue skirts and the boys blue shorts. They are clearly proud of their uniforms, as they now look the same as the other kids in town.

> It has really lifted up their self image. They want to wear school uniform even after school so that people can see that they are going to a real school. Anne, some of the kids even come on Sundays to school wearing school uniform! They find it difficult to believe that there is no school then. Others just drop into school whenever, as there is no one to wake them up at the right time.

151

Pastor Sonio has started to teach the Bible to our pupils' close relatives and mothers, as it was agreed, and everyone has come. The result has been that some of them have already found Jesus. Bible classes take place in the evenings at school and now some of the attendees have joined our congregation. The church has grown again because of this.

Blessings, Nheng

The school had started well, even though I had never led a school before and I didn't have a clue on how to handle many of the matters. Lea had had experience of teaching English in an Asian college in Brisbane, but that was all.

Every day we had to solve new problems but the Lord was with us in it all. In the areas where we felt out of our depth we just did our best, with a smile on our faces or our tongues in our cheeks.

The first two months were quite an ordeal both for the pupils and for the teachers, while the kids adjusted to the school rhythm. We needed to remember that these kids had been used to flutter around as free as birds. What helped a lot was the fact that they really wanted to go to school. It had been their dream and within two months we could see a miracle in all of them as caterpillars changed into beautiful butterflies.

110. A wonderful pencil box

Soon the new apartment in the building became available to us. At that time financial support had come through for the kids including some donations from Finland and I could rent more room, pay the teachers' salaries and even employ one more teacher. Our new recruit was called Sharon, whom I had got to know during my trip to Sablayan. She was the top student when she graduated to be a teacher, but after that she hadn't been able to find a job. There were just no jobs for new teachers in Mindoro Island. So Sharon together with her mother moved to Mamburao and the school started to grow.

We decided to travel to Mamburao in December. The kids had been practicing keenly for the school's Christmas celebration programme and were really looking forward to our arrival in Mindoro Island.

PART FOUR.
CHRISTMAS 2006

111. At the Mangyan village

112. *Pastor Sonio at the Mangyan church*

113. *Results from the typhoon*

CHAPTER 22
TYPHOONS

BAD NEWS

One day in November 2006 back in Brisbane, I received a distressed phone call on my mobile from Nheng: "Help us! There is a typhoon, the house is blowing down …" Then the call was cut off. Both Lea and I tried to call her back but there was no answer. I sent an email to her and tried several other possible phone numbers, but nothing worked. For a couple of days we got no further information on the situa-

> **'Help us! There is a typhoon, the house is blowing down**

tion at all, then finally we heard on the Australian news that a typhoon had hit the Philippines. It had affected Mindoro Island as well as several other islands.

The Philippines is in a typhoon-prone area, but for some reason Lea and I had always managed to leave there before a typhoon hit, or to arrive just after one had finished battering the archipelago. I was very concerned about the children – what had happened to them? What about their little huts? How was it with the school building? There had been four typhoons one after another hitting the Philippines, and the weather forecast announced that the fifth would arrive around Christmas, just when we planned to be travelling there.

A week passed and then we finally got through by phone to Mamburao - that meant that the electricity was back on in the area. We were very relieved to hear that the kids were all safe. The flooding had of course washed away huts and the wind had done a lot of damage, but the school was still standing. The house of our landlord was on the sea shore and it had been blown down, and the same had happened to the Sonio family's bamboo hut. All their earthly belongings were soaked and useless or had been taken by the wind. They had escaped to the church building when the typhoon hit, together with all the other local inhabitants: the stone structure of the church had managed to stand up to the typhoon's rage.

The Sonios had no alternative but to live in the church, as at least it had four walls and a roof. Nheng, Sharon and Frances lived in the school. Their small room had also suffered from the floods that came with the typhoon, and it was

116. Devastation from the typhoon

the same room that was used for the kindergarten. We had noticed evidence of flood damage previously when we were there, because it had smelled mouldy and we could see where water had penetrated the ceiling and run down the walls.

The typhoon had pulled huge trees out of the ground with their roots, and one had come down quite close to the church. For the Sonios it was a real gift from God; Edwin and the boys sawed the tree in pieces and used the timber for building material. Edwin also used some to build a bunk bed at the church for believers that might come from other villages or towns to take care of their relatives in Mamburao Central Hospital.

Filipinos are very hospitable and such generous acts were always expected from a pastor, which of course could often be quite a burden. In the Sonios' old one-roomed hut there hadn't been enough room even for their own family. Now there was a bunk bed and it was placed outside, next to the church wall. Edwin also used some boards to build a sort of shed around it. The building did not actually belong to him, but it was owned by Brother Binny, who was also the owner of our school building.

After the typhoon the area became a hive of activity with everyone searching for pieces of boards or sheet metal – just anything that they could use to build a hut for their families. I often marvel at the endurance of the Filipinos to reconstruct their dwellings – and for that matter their lives – from broken fragments over and over again. Floods, heavy rains, mud slides, hunger, earthquakes, mafia, NPA army, corruption, violence, unemployment, no social services, Al-Qaida with its links to the Abu Sayyaf Islamic militants, coups, illnesses … to mention only some of the problems the resilient Filipinos have to face. We would easily lose our nerve completely with a lot less challenges than that. But the poor cannot give up: they have no Plan B if their original plan is thwarted.

Courage, Risks and Revival

I had an interesting discussion with some of the local pastors about the western epidemic called 'burn out'. They asked me how it is that a person can burn out, and when I tried to explain the various possible psychological causes, they just shook their heads in disbelief, saying, "Surely someone who believes in Jesus just can't burn out." I must admit that I found it quite a challenge to explain to such people who have managed through all these catastrophes, whether from nature, sickness, poverty or terrorism, why it was that western people just don't cope with stress.

> **Even to this very hour we do not have enough to eat or drink or to wear. We are often beaten, and we have no homes in which to live. We work hard with our own hands for our food. When people curse us, we bless them. When they hurt us, we put up with it. When they tell evil lies about us, we speak nice words about them. Even today, we are treated as though we were the garbage of the world—the filth of the earth. (1 Cor. 4:11-13)**

To these poor Filipino pastors, Paul and the apostles were examples of how believers could face difficulties without complaining, even through persecution, stoning, jail or martyrdom. They travelled around on foot preaching the gospel; their daily bread was mental and physical fatigue; their five star hotel was under the stars of heaven. It is exactly like that in the Philippines too. They may not know all the right theology and in many areas their teaching may be deficient, but they live the pages of the Bible.

> **My teaching and preaching were not with words of human wisdom that persuade people but with proof of the power that the Spirit gives. (1 Cor. 2:4-5)**

I believe that the western church is about to undergo the biggest change in its entire history: a return to its beginnings. We are going to return to an apostolic faith that takes risks, out of a passion for Christ and an understanding of what the Cross really means to a believer. When the Holy Spirit comes down to a meeting, He has a purpose and reason for doing so. He has been sent from the Father to set people's hearts on fire for Jesus. The Holy Spirit is not like Superman, flying in to a meeting to do something special on the platform, showing off His strength by making some people fall down, and then flying out again. There are many different visible manifestations of God's power, but the biggest change must still happen in our hearts.

> **The western church is about to undergo the biggest change in its history**

When the Holy Spirit knocks on the doors of churches, many do not recognise Him. And even if they do, they still want to manage His programme and schedule, telling the Holy Spirit: "come at the end of the meeting but make sure You go before it's time to close the doors." People need to meet with the Real God, not the stained glass window version.

DESTRUCTION

117. Damaged homes & boats

In some places on the archipelago, absolutely everything had been destroyed by the typhoon. People told me that they had never seen such huge floods and such damage ever before in their lives.

This was especially true in the mountains, where the storms had caused mud slides and hundreds of people had died. The black mud was like a bleak and sinister stream from Hades that swallowed everything in its path. Whole villages disappeared with all their people under it and large areas were turned overnight into desolate black clay cemeteries.

The typhoon also blew huge waves from the sea over the slum huts on the shore, washing them away. The stormy seas did not calm down for a long time afterwards and those families whose livelihood was fishing just starved. It was too dangerous to go out on such seas in small boats, and the storm had driven the shoals of fish far away from land into the open sea. There was no income and the rice harvesting season was over. The rice fields provided work for only two months in the year; those who managed to get such work got money then … but at other times there was nothing so the rice portions had to be rationed and thinned out by adding water.

118. *Rice for the school families*

Mamburao was now a disaster area and our school kids did not have anything to eat. I got the idea of buying a big sack of rice and apportioning out a certain amount each day to all the families of our school children. We also made a plan to do this every year during the monsoon season which lasted for about three months. I did not have much to give, but this was something I could do. Our mission field was just beginning and we didn't have enough supporters for the work yet.

I believe that one day I will be able to give the school children a portion of rice every day. Many of our pupils have problems in concentrating in the classroom because they are so hungry. Their lack of vitamins means they often fall sick and are more prone to catch malaria. Whenever we saw the absolute destitution of the local people and their courage in facing up to such a life day after day, our own complaints faded away.

It is a fact that the ministry would not have gone forward if I hadn't put all my personal funds into it at that time. I had to start from somewhere – I did not have a big missionary organisation backing me up and sending me a cheque for my living expenses each month, and neither did Lea. The connection between us was our joint vision for the salvation of the Asia-Pacific nations, a task given by the Lord.

This connection was to continue until Lea decided to concentrate full-time on her university studies to become a teacher. While travelling with me in the Asia Pacific islands she received a good grounding in working with children at the primary level and I of course benefited greatly from her input.

BIBLE SCHOOL

The Sonios decided to arrange a Bible school for the children of the area during the school holiday, partly because we had been unable to accept as pupils all the children that had been saved through our outreach work. The idea really hit home and 90 kids ended up registering. It also meant we could feed the children during that week. The course was given the name "Jesus loves small children" and every child received a printed certificate of attendance with the heading:

Daily Vacation Bible School

Jesus Loves Little Children

Christian Mission School
Occidental Mindoro

The Bible school was divided into three classes according to the ages of the attendees. It was clear that our school building had started to grow too small, as such events stretched us to full capacity.

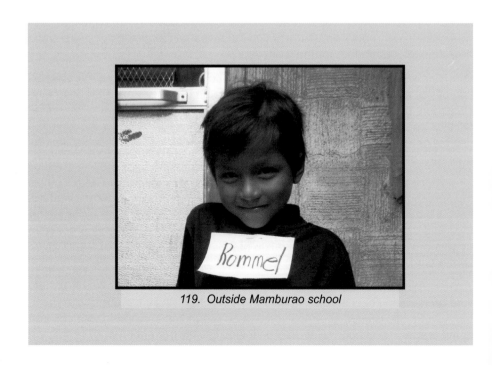

119. Outside Mamburao school

CHAPTER 23
CHRISTMAS CELEBRATIONS

CHRISTMAS 2006 IN MAMBURAO

Once again, towards the end of December 2006, Lea and I packed our suitcases for another fortnight or so in the Philippines. When we arrived in Manila, it felt like we had never been away and that our past couple of months back home in Australia had been just a dream. From Manila we carried on immediately next morning to Mindoro Island. When we eventually came to Mamburao, the typhoon damage was clearly visible, with trees and huts either bent by the wind or collapsed totally. Rubbish and junk scattered around by the storm were everywhere. Electric power cables were partly hanging onto the ground but the electricity distribution had started again quite soon after the typhoon, as the power station was situated in Oriental Mindoro, on the opposite side of the mountains where the typhoon had not had such a strong effect.

The children were waiting for us at the school, together with a group of women from the slum area. We were travelling with heavy suitcases full of books for the school library and school equipment, and our voyage over the sea from Batangas to Abra De Ilog had been exhausting, as the ship had rolled more than usual because of the heavy winds. At this time of the year the winds would come up suddenly and then just as quickly they died down again. The local people didn't know about the new typhoon warning, as they didn't have TV, radio or newspapers. We were in quite a hurry to get a roof over our heads as now and again there were heavy downpours of rain.

AT THE SCHOOL

Before going to the school we dropped off our suitcases at our accommodation, the Travellers Hostel. This is the place where we normally stay in the town, as it is close to the Sonio's home and church, as well as the school and the squatters

village. Although far from being a tourist hotel for westerners, it is reasonably clean and quite safe too. This two storey building with out-of-date rooms may have had its best days before the war, but it is popular with Filipinos who are waiting to go into Mamburao hospital or visiting relatives there.

From there we ran to the school, where we found the yard full of people. The children were waiting in their classrooms and finding it difficult to conceal their ex-

120. *Our accommodation in Mamburao*

citement. They all held out their little hands to us, wanting a blessing. Nheng told us that many of the children who lived further away could not be there today, as they did not have money for the fare by three-wheeler taxi. I didn't know that we had such pupils coming from longer distances to school and not just from the slum area. In fact the whole island was full of shack villages, along the seashore as far as the island went.

I heard of a five year old girl, who lived 15 km away from the school with her grandmother, as her drug user parents had disappeared somewhere. Her grandmother didn't have money, but mysteriously the girl would appear in front of the school every morning as the cock crowed. And after school she would start her long walk back home to her grandmother. My heart broke over such courage and keenness to get to school, knowing that many western children have no enthusiasm whatsoever to attend and some even play truant.

On the following day I heard that one of the mothers of our pupils was wandering around in the market trying to sell a single milkfish; where she had got it from, I do not know. But her selling didn't go very well. I heard that she had used the last of her money to pay the fare for a three-wheeler trip for her daughter to get to the previous day's event at school. She next appeared with her fish at the door of the church and shyly asked if we needed a fish. Mrs Muleta, who cooked for us, bought the fish even though there were already flies buzzing around it in the heat of the day. On impulse I also pushed a small amount of money into the mother's hand – I thought she would have needed the fish herself, so starved did she look.

Pastor Daniel, who worked among the Mangyans and with whom I had visited the tribes people earlier in the year, had a four year old son who was one of our pupils. The fingers and toes of the boy had grown together so that his hands had only two fingers. Mrs Muleta told us how the boy had had trouble at school when the children were learning arithmetic. They used to learn by singing a counting song, where one finger was added at a time until they made ten altogether. The boy wondered how he could do this as he had only two fingers on both hands. Nheng suggested that he could also use his toes to count, forgetting that his feet similarly had only two digits each.

The boy was brighter than many others of the same age and as he was the son of a pastor, he was very keen on praying for everyone. Possibly the anti-malaria medication that his mother had taken during her pregnancy might have caused the malformation. It was impossible to work among Mangyans without taking anti-malaria medication. The Mamburao town council used to spray insecticide along the beach areas to keep down the mosquitoes but the Mangyans lived in the mountains and often along small streams which were breeding areas for these pests.

121. Mangyan mum & child

THE MOTHER FROM THE MANGYAN TRIBE

What surprised me the most on that first school Christmas celebration was to see a Mangyan mother who had come with her children. Pastor Sonio said that it was a miracle, as the tribe shuns contact with other Filipinos and there was no way that her tribe would accept what this mother had done. She really needed a lot of courage to break free of the tribal traditions for the sake of her children's education. What had caused her to leave her tribe and to make this decision, I do not know, but I went over to her, hugged her and whispered, "Never give up."

From the bottom of my heart I wanted to honour this woman. I felt that what she had done resembled the actions of Rahab in the Bible, as she too was an outsider despised by others. But what Rahab did brought victory to Israel and blessing to her and her family, because she saw something that others didn't see. Many women are tied to the prison of their traditions: this Mangyan lady with the courage of Rahab saw an open door to escape and walked straight through it, and in doing so she created a future for her children.

SCHOOL STORIES

I paid for the meal that was a key part of the school celebration. A bring-and-share system does not really work here, as people don't have anything to eat at home. I was surprised when I saw that a couple of mothers had in fact brought something to eat with them and they also seemed to stand out from the rest, appearing to be wealthier and better dressed.

122. Enjoying learning

Nheng was a bit embarrassed about these two, and said to me quietly, "Anne, please don't be angry but there are two children from rich families here." Before I had chance to say anything, she continued, "These two are the mothers, and their children had severe behaviour problems at school. One of them had even been expelled from all of her previous schools. She was a very spoiled girl who was brought to school every morning by servants and she swore, kicked, clawed and spat at them and fought with the other kids. Her mother asked if we could help as she wanted to try a Christian school and upbringing. Within two months this child changed, became a believer and is now a model pupil. Her mother saw what Jesus can do."

Nheng went on to tell me that the second girl was very timid, with a completely different problem. At her previous school she was kicked, beaten and bullied. The teachers didn't understand the girl, and would shout at her, and get angry and aggressive. Of course as a result she didn't want to go to school at all. When she came to our school, the girl was very fearful and timid at first, but a total change took place in her and now she was full of joy instead of fear.

The change in these two pupils had been a witness to the whole community. Their parents were quite influential citizens, the father of one of them being a rich businessman and the other a senator.

> **all were doing amazingly well academically**

I looked at the school reports of our pupils and all of them were doing amazingly well academically, having learned both to write and to do arithmetic. The school inspector was also happy with the results and all the parents were amazed at their children's progress. This school was under the magnifying glass from the town authorities because it was the first free private Christian school in the area. The thought of a free school for slum kids and orphans was a revolutionary one: other private schools charged 3,000 pesos (about €45) each month for every child.

Nheng planned to start a regular Bible school for the children every Thursday in addition to the one on Sundays. And her parents, Edwin and Nena Sonio, travelled around every week from home to home teaching the Bible to smaller groups, to extend our outreach to those adults who had no contact with our school. Weekly Bible study classes were of course compulsory for the parents of our pupils (as our "fees"), but everyone was happy with the system.

We gave out clothes to the children at school as most of them couldn't afford good clothing. We also gave them new pencils and notebooks. Real books weren't available at this time for the children but their notebooks served as books too and were real treasures to them, and most of them stared in awe at their colourful new pencils.

123. School portrait

Every child also received a toy as a Christmas gift from us –something that they had never had before. In later years I was able to give money for buying school books from Manila.

Some of our pupils had to stay at home because they had worms. One child had had five worms coming out of her and more were still coming, or so I heard. Again new worm medication was needed.

I used my digital camera to take photos of all the children for our school records, but the youngest ones had never seen a camera before and some started to cry. Next day I hardly could walk as a result of my rather unexpected exercise – without thinking I had been bobbing up and down more than fifty times as I was taking the photos. More children were brought to be photographed on the following day, and every child later received a laminated name tag with their photo on it, that could be pinned to their T-shirt.

> **These kids had almost nothing of their own**

As I was taking pictures of the children, I happened to sit down on one of the little plastic chairs belonging to one of them. This resulted in a terrible commotion: the owner burst out in desperate tears and ran over to rescue her treasure. She pressed the chair against her chest and showed me her name that was written on the back of it. These kids had almost nothing of their own. This chair was one of the little girl's only possessions and so she jealously guarded it, knowing that it could have got broken when that big white auntie sat down on it.

We heard that in March of the following year another room would become available in our rental building so that we could get our second classroom. Next door to the new room and connected to it was a small bedroom, which would become our library and a place to rest if someone got sick. The town mayor promised to donate books to the school – he had seen how this school for slum children had changed the community. We had started to win the favour of the town officials and politicians.

At the small shopping kiosk next to these new rooms I bought some snacks for the children there. The shop was frequented by passersby as one side faced the busy street. The town is full of this sort of little kiosk, as everybody is trying to sell something to each other to get some form of income. The three-wheeled motorbikes used as basic taxis were not a very lucrative source of income for the owners as they were so common.

Other people tried to earn money through catching and selling fish, but again almost everyone did the same. Doing other people's laundry was yet another way through which people tried to get by.

SPONTANEOUS SCHOOL YARD MEETING

On the day that we arrived, about sixty adults had crammed into the school yard and I took the opportunity to preach a short sermon to them. Rev. Sonio interpreted my sermon to this audience, only one of whom was a believer. I explained about healing miracles, a concept that was totally new to these people.

124. Meeting in the school yard

Pastor Sonio interpreted it all very thoroughly so that everyone would really understand what it all was about. He made a point of explaining very clearly what would happen when they would be prayed over later, and even gave a practical demonstration. He went over to a lady sitting at the front and said to everybody that "when Anne comes and touches you like this," and he touched the woman lightly on her head, "then at the same time the touch of Jesus will heal you." He then continued his explanation.

Suddenly the woman whom he had touched jumped up and started shouting and waving excitedly. I had no idea why - perhaps a wasp had bitten her! Edwin stopped speaking and, with an embarrassed look on his face, he turned to look at the lady who had interrupted him. But as soon as he grasped what she was shouting about, he got just as excited she was. Apparently when he had touched her as part of his demonstration, she had been totally healed of her sickness and all her pain had left her at that very moment!

Now everyone else wanted a similar blessing and to find Jesus as their Saviour. No more explanation was needed, as this very practical example said it all. The healed lady jumped up and down out of joy and told again and again what had happened. No better commercial break could have been hoped for! The woman declared that she would come to church and would bring all her family because Jesus is real. Many others kept nodding in agreement with her. It was amazing how yet again the meeting had turned out very differently than how I had expected as the Lord had showed His power.

When Jesus puts the spotlight on something – just like He did here – it really communicates, and people of course understand and accept it. Pastor Sonio was absolutely thrilled and told us over and over again how he only touched the woman and then a miracle happened. I was delighted to see that my earlier encouragement to Edwin had paid off; when I first met him I had urged him to: "Pray in faith for sick people! Then God will take care of His honour and will prove His word to be true."

> **'Pray in faith for sick people!'**

In the months since then, Edwin had prayed for people and blessed them but had seen few results – perhaps some element of faith had been lacking. He had seen people being healed through the prayers of others, and in fact it had been a key to him first coming to Christ. Now here it came through him, somewhat accidentally, but a genuine experience of God's healing power. God sometimes tests our endurance in these things, but now the waiting was over and the miracle had happened!

125. Blessing the children

Chapter 24
Supernatural Power

Fifth Typhoon

The wind had grown stronger by the time we returned to our accommodation, and it was already blowing sand and small objects up into the air. Later that evening our windows started rattling and all sorts of banging and clattering noises could be heard outside. I said to Lea, "I feel so sorry for these people! It looks like they'll now have to suffer from the fifth typhoon in a row this year – just when they have managed to build up their homes again. Let's pray that the wind turns away and a miracle happens."

So we started battling in prayer against the storm and soon it became quieter outside our house. The wind was still strong but now it was more like the normal kind of northerly wind that comes in December. By the morning we had forgotten all about the possibility of a typhoon.

A few days later, on returning to our room after the evening meeting, I tried in vain to undo the door lock and then the whole lock mechanism fell out. I wasn't having a very good relationship with Mamburao door locks – I had already broken a lock three times before.

I went back to the reception of the hotel and woke up the man who was asleep there, to ask if he could repair my lock because now I couldn't open the door at all. He sleepily mumbled, "Where on earth can I get a new one at this time of night?"

As I waited for him to fix the door, I noticed a newspaper thrown away in a waste bin in the corridor. Newspapers are very seldom available in this area, so I picked it up and started reading. The headline already announced the answer to our prayer of a few days earlier and I got excited, "Wow! A miracle had really happened!"

The article described the path of Typhoon Thomas which had been heading towards the Philippines from the South China Sea on 20 December. There had been lots of fishing boats, both large and small, at sea when a giant wave stirred up by the typhoon crashed in and sank them, in an area of the sea off Occidental Mindoro. It had been totally calm when the

126. Fishing boat

fishermen set sail in their boats, but suddenly the wind had grown very strong. The locals call these winds "Nortada" as they come from the north. It is not unusual for them to cause massive damage and to kill fishermen who happen to be out at the sea in their small boats.

The typhoon had whipped up waves to mountainous proportions, and smaller boats were crushed to pieces in the coastal area. The little boats do not venture far out to sea as they are not strong enough. Normally they are very well balanced as they have a bamboo frame around them on both sides acting as supports, but most of these fragile structures had no chance against these huge waves. Bigger boats capsized and sank. Over 70 fishermen had died but the fatality count might grow even bigger, said the newspaper report: many fishermen had disappeared, according to the Santa Cruz police who were investigating the tragedy caused by the typhoon. Some of the fishermen had been lucky enough to row and find safety in the Scarborough shoal, a group of islands consisting of atolls and reefs about 30 sea miles away.

The newspaper article said that the typhoon had been approaching the Philippines, but mysteriously there had appeared a cold air mass acting as a shield in front of the islands. It was a shallow low pressure area estimated to be 940 km east of Luzon, based on satellite and surface data. This air mass was huge. Typhoon Thomas was like a small leaf in this mighty river and was tossed away back towards Japan. As a result, Mindoro only received a strong north easterly wind and very rough seas. The report said that observers had expressed alarm when Thomas entered the Philippines area as a tropical storm: the last such storm had created a super typhoon that destroyed several areas including Catanduanesia, Camarines Provinces and Albayn, just when the same places were recovering from another super typhoon known as "Reming". But the low pressure air deflected Thomas away from the Philippines.

> **this event was a miracle that saved the Philippines**

The article was emphasizing that this event was a miracle that saved the Philippines – this very rare appearance of the air mass rescued the country from the typhoon by sitting there as shield for the archipelago. This was on 21 December – timing that matched precisely when Lea and I had been asking God for a miracle to turn the typhoon away from the Island.

God hears prayers that come from the heart. The Word of God says that He is the same yesterday, today and forever (Hebrews 13:8). Believers can underestimate the power of prayer and the Word of God, but it was Jesus Himself who calmed the storm by His word:

> **Jesus answered, "Why are you afraid? You don't have enough faith." Then Jesus got up and gave a command to the wind and the waves, and it became completely calm. (Matthew 8:26).**

The authority of the voice of Jesus made the storm obey. Now I was happy that my door lock had broken – otherwise I would not have found the newspaper in the bin. Next day I was walking down the corridor past other hotel rooms and noticed that one door was missing a lock … ah, so that was the one that was moved to my door! Now someone else was without a lock.

127. View from the shore

128. Pastor Sonio leaving the Mangyan village

CHAPTER 25
FAITH & WORKS

BALANSAY CHURCH IS PLANTED

On the same trip I planted a congregation in an outlying part of Mamburao called Balansay. I had heard that there was no church there, even though it was a village of 5,000 people. So on 24 December we travelled to Balansay by motor bike and started looking around the rice fields and other places where people might be.

We asked the local people whether they would come to church if there was one and we told them about the meeting that we were arranging in that area. There was one believer who offered his house for the meetings, or rather its yard. The houses were far too small for such gatherings but the yards were big, having enough room for crowds of people.

129. *Preaching at Balansay*

We went around from hut to hut, knocking on the doors and asking if there was anyone at home. Plenty of people came out, mothers and fathers, uncles and aunts, grandmothers and so on … the families were big. I asked if there were any sick people in the family, knowing that almost everyone in these communities had some sort of illness or health problem. After this it was easy to tell them about the healer, Jesus, and how He had already healed the sick in Mamburao. Many of them seemed to know about it already.

We asked people to stand in a row and started praying for healing, knowing that Jesus would show that His word was true. There were eleven people in our first meeting and the second gathered thirty. Edwin Sonio's stepson Jonathan initially took on the responsibility as pastor for the fledgeling congregation.

There are many young people in the Philippines who have graduated from Bible school but who don't have a job. So there is no shortage of pastors available who know the language and the culture. A foreign organisation can work as a starter and catalyst, as a guest and teacher, and it can give funds for the work, but the work itself must be left to the local people themselves. Brother Boy, whom I had already got to know in Sablayan, had been a leader in a Bible school and he promised to come and teach in Balansay as often as possible. Everything seemed to be falling into place.

130. *Mealtime at the Sonios'*

We returned to the Sonios' house, and sat in the yard under the hay roof to eat our rice portion for the day. We paid for the food as there was no restaurant close to our accommodation. Pastor Nena complained that she had to cook 6kg of rice every day, as a lot of the hungry people tended to visit when it was food time.

Hospitality is a Filipino trait and it means that guests must be fed. The Sonio family's house was so small that the kitchen table wouldn't fit inside. So the kitchen was out in the yard and hence there was nowhere to hide when you wanted to have your meal. As well as the extra people there were also hens, cats and stray dogs … all of them (as the Syrophoenician woman said in Mark chapter 7) wanting to get the crumbs falling from the table.

I often wondered where our school teacher Nheng slept, as there was no room in the house. One morning I arrived at the hut a bit earlier than usual, wanting to talk with her. I first saw Frances who went to wake Nheng up. She opened the door of a small clothes cupboard and there was Nheng asleep sit-

ting on a cloth sack. I found this sight heart-breaking and I decided we had to find proper lodgings for our teachers. Because of the big hospital in Mamburao, the Pastor always had visitors from other localities. They had to sleep on the wooden benches in the church as there was no other accommodation for poor people. All these extra guests were making the place jam-packed.

131. Balansay children

CHILDLIKE FAITH

Then Jesus said to her, "Didn't I tell you that if you believed you would see the glory of God?" (John 11:40)

Miracles are manifestations of the glory of God. Often we feel the presence of God's glory in a meeting, but it is a totally different thing to make it manifest. Many believers want to stay in the presence of the Lord but are less willing to have His presence demonstrated in their own lives, even though it is this very same glory that makes miracles happen.

Once I was having a discussion in a church with a 19 year old young man about miracles. He had just recently come to Christ and was enthusiastic about manifestations of the power of God. He asked many questions and told me that he couldn't understand why his hands felt like they were on fire.

"It's the healing power of the Lord, so use it!" I told him. The boy got excited and said in a loud voice: "Wow, does that mean that I have the gift of healing?" There was an old believer passing by at the time and he overheard what the boy saying. He was annoyed, and commented, "If you had the gift of healing, I would not need to live with these pains."

The boy asked him what ailments he was suffering from and he was told the story. "My neck doesn't move and I have pain there all the time. It has been like this for five years and the doctors can't do anything for me." The boy laid his

175

hand on the man's neck and said: "In Jesus' name your neck is now healthy." The old believer got cross and pulled himself away from the young man's hand. "Don't get so excited! Your hand feels like a hot poker." But then he tried bending and rolled his neck around and was embarrassed: "Where did the pain go? My neck works fine now." He was totally healed from his neck problems.

This old believer didn't have faith for a miracle but the young man wasn't infected with his unbelief. He functioned with a childlike faith and through that he pulled down the miracle out of the glory that was present. The question is not how much faith we have, but rather who has told us to do the job – namely Jesus Himself. Soon after this healing, another believer came over to ask us what had happened. He had seen a big crowd of angels standing around the young man. Where the glory of God is, there you will find angels.

The same young man told me about his mother, who was not a believer and really doubted the miraculous. She had hurt her hand and her son asked if he could pray for healing. His mother laughed scornfully but he took her by the hand and commanded the pain to go away. In that moment the woman was healed, and she admitted, "That Jesus of yours certainly seems to be doing something."

'Do whatever He tells you'

"Do whatever he tells you" (John 2:5). With these words Mary, Jesus' mother, gave directions to the servants at the wedding in Cana and the water in the jars was changed into wine. The servants probably didn't have any faith to believe that the water would change into wine, but they trusted and obeyed the person who gave the order and that birthed a miracle.

Perhaps a modern day believer would have behaved differently than those servants. Maybe he would have looked at these stone jars full of water for the ceremonial washing and said to himself, "Hmmm, I expect dirty feet have been soaked in this water and we don't want any fungus infections to be spreading." Or maybe he would say, "Water has never before changed to wine, so it will not happen now either." Or again, "These jars are part of our washing tradition, and it is not possible to drink out of them. My father did not drink out of them, nor my grandfather, so I'm not going to either."

The servants didn't have time to clean out the water jars in the way that ritual would have demanded, nor to sterilise them with hot water, nor time to think that infectious diseases might be passed on. They just did what they were told to do, and Mary herself had faith for a miracle.

In that place there were six stone water jars that the Jews used in their washing ceremony. Each jar held about twenty or thirty gallons. (John 2:6)

The wedding in question was a big one, judging by the size of the jars and the amount of water needed. The measures of that time were "metretas", one of which equals 39.5 litres or 9 gallons, and each jar contained 2-3 such measures of water. After this there was more than enough wine for everybody.

Our own faith might be microscopic in size but when our own faith is finished, then the faith of Jesus steps in instead. No miracle is impossible for God; the only restriction is the unbelief of an old believer.

God has made us what we are. In Christ Jesus, God made us to do good works, which God planned in advance for us to live our lives doing. (Eph. 2:10).

| when our own faith is finished, then the faith of Jesus steps in |

God's job for you may be unusual, but it has been prepared especially for you in advance, so that you would carry out the good works just as the Bible says. Maybe it is not the kind of work that you personally would have planned for yourself, but it is a fact that you will only succeed in work if it is what God has planned for you.

ANGELS ON THE DOOR

On the evening of our Balansay visit, I preached at a church pastored by a man called Eddy Macgalayo. He complained that not many people had been coming to his church, but tonight it was certainly full.

One lady testified with tears how she had been healed in Pastor Sonio's church: she said that she had stood in the line where I prayed for the sick and she had felt a burning sensation in her stomach. There had been a tumour there but when she received prayer it was healed and immediately vanished.

Later Lea told me about a strange happening near the open entrance door, close to where she had been standing during the meeting. A mentally disturbed man had come from outside the door and tried to get in, but for some reason he just couldn't manage to step through the open door. He tried several times to enter but every time he seemed to bump into an invisible wall filling the doorway, and each time he had to back off. People sitting at the back of the church were amazed as they saw this going on and his peculiar antics.

177

Lea showed me the digital pictures that she had taken during the meeting. The open doorway was filled by two bright circles of light. Was it these that the man hit every time he tried to step in? We couldn't find any other explanation for this phenomenon but that heavenly guardian angels had blocked the doorway, to guard us from a troublemaker trying to get in to disturb the meeting.

My other vivid memory from this meeting was of a boy about 10 years old who fell under the power of the Holy Spirit and wept: God seemed to be touching him powerfully and doing significant inner healing deep inside.

HAIR ON FIRE

When I arrived outside Edwin and Nena's church for the next meeting, I heard such amazing singing over the PA system that it brought tears to my eyes. The singer was this same 10 year old boy. His voice was fabulous, and tears were running down his face as he sang the Tagalog language song. I did not

132. *The wonderful singer*

understand the words but I knew that the song was telling about Jesus. It was totally incomprehensible to me that such a small boy could have such an amazing voice, the equal of which I have never heard before. It was like an echo from heaven itself.

Later in the meeting a young lady brought forward an older grandmother to meet me and she fumbled around touching my hair. This dear granny was half blind and explained to the younger woman that she had seen from the distance how my hair had flames of fire in it and she wanted to come closer to see why it was burning. She wouldn't believe that it wasn't actually on fire until she touched my hair to make sure for herself.

I said to the young lady: "Maybe she is seeing blonde hair for the first time in her life and that's why she thinks it's on fire?" But the older lady categorically denied such illusions and said that the flames were still there. The younger lady said that granny had the gift of revelation and was seeing by the eyes of the spirit how there really was fire around my head.

178

Because Lea knew sign language, she would always gather the children at the front of the church and teach them our worship songs, together with her daughter Princess, in sign language. That breaks down all language barriers and dialects. For children, sign language is like play, and they learn very quickly. I aimed my preaching at the kids in this meeting and again danced with them around the church, pretending that we were a railway train that I was pulling as the engine. The worship group sang until they were hoarse, and now and then they burst out laughing in mid-song as they watched even the adults joining in the comical dance line.

133. Letka-jenkka dance

As a result of this visit, Pastor Macgalayo's congregation gained twenty or thirty new members and when the next meeting was held at the Sonios' church, they sent a busload of their own people along too. The children especially had wanted to go because they got so excited about the previous meeting, and they were hoping for more marching and dancing.

179

134. Enjoying the meal

135. With the Mangyans

CHAPTER 26
SLUM VILLAGE

THE SLUM VILLAGE OPENS UP

We also received an invitation to go right inside the slum village near Mamburao. Until then we had only been allowed to visit areas on the edge of the village but never to go inside. We were the first white people who had been allowed to do so, because our school had broken through social class divisions.

There I met a mother whose husband was one of the fishermen who had drowned in the recent freak waves from the typhoon. She had been left alone with their children and she wept in misery. One of her children was studying at our school. We prayed for her and I quietly pushed a small amount of money into her hand.

We blessed homes and their inhabitants, and prayed for sick people. I felt like the Pied Piper of Hamelin because about a hundred slum kids were following me in a line everywhere; when I stopped, they stopped too and stared quietly and watchfully. In the fairy tale I would play the flute and would guide the children out of misery. In real life, I felt that the school was the flute, and would bring them to the start of a better life.

I saw small beggar children around the narrow paths of the village, with clothes in tatters and carrying bundles of twigs or cloth rags on their heads. In their bundles they had collected all sorts of thrown away things, hoping that somebody would buy something from them.

I asked a lonely mother why her children hadn't been at the school celebration. She answered, "I heard that we had to bring something on a plate and we didn't have anything to bring." Nheng explained to her that it was not any kind of rule, but if somebody had something that they wanted to take along, they could have done so. Anyway, the school was offering food for everybody, and other contributions would have been just a bonus.

> **Nico was gaining strength every day**

I also met Nico's mother, who told me how his heart was now healthy, his breathing was normal and he was gaining strength every day. The whole family now attended church together. I reminded her about God's promise that He was going to heal her son totally and not just some part of him. As I talked with her, I repeated my request for her to tell me what Nico would like from Australia, so that I could send something to him.

Nico's mother confirmed to me the story of how the other children had heard that there were two "kanas" on the beach. She also gave me a more detailed explanation of where that word actually came from. During the Second World War there had been American troops on these islands and since then all foreigners tend to be called Americans, which in the Tagalog language was ameri**kana**. The people were not familiar with international geography as their life and world was the here and now.

On the clay floor of one hut was lying a thin, paralysed boy of about 10 years old. Beside his head there was a bowl of food, put down as if for a dog. The boy tried to move it with his head, which was the only part of his body that he could move. A couple of younger kids wandered around in the one-room hut but nobody seemed to give any attention at all to the attempts of the boy. Surely somebody had to feed him now and then? Here, before my eyes, was a clear example of the desperate situation of a paralysed person in this country. On the other hand, what else could they do in a place where there were no wheel chairs or other equipment designed for helping disabled people in their lives? I could not go in and pray for this child as understandably the local people do not like strangers looking or coming inside their homes without invitation. But this home was a very rudimentary shack with no door and open for all to see.

The school children were very excited about my visit to the village – everyone wanted to show me their own hut. It was difficult to recognise them without their school clothes, which were hung carefully on the wall of the huts, cleaned and prepared beautifully, waiting for the new school day. It felt strange that in this abject poverty the school uniforms could be kept in such great condition, but they were treated like treasures. The uniform was a key to a better future, it lifted its wearer to the same social class as others and it had a tremendous impact on the child's self image.

Just as valuable were their notebooks and pencils. I had at first been worried whether we should distribute them before the Christmas holiday, thinking they would get messed up even before the new school term had started. But Nheng assured me with a smile that such a thing would never happen because they were the childrens' only property and they would guard them as carefully as they did their plastic chairs. She was right.

136. *Slum children*

Next day the ladies from Edwin and Nena's church were again preparing food, this time for 600 children. We planned to feed them with a local delicacy known as **piko** – sticky rice sweetened with syrup. In addition, the kids would also be getting chicken. Preparing the piko was a long process which had started already the day before, as the rice was first jellied and then cut into pieces. This dish was really loved by the kids, as there were no other sweets available. This time we had enough food for everybody and we could even give about 25 portions to the poor members of Pastor Eddy Macgalayo's church, where I had preached a few days earlier.

When the feeding and evangelising of the kids was over, I returned to my accommodation for the afternoon to meet another pastor couple. I had not met them before but the man had asked prayer for his wife who had a goitre and was suffering from heavy metal poisoning. They had also asked me to come and preach in their church that same evening. While talking with these people I recognised that my surname Miettinen, which was very difficult for the Filipinos to pronounce, had now changed into a local version *Pitimini*, which meant rose. "Who cares?" I thought to myself, "It's OK with me to be called Mrs Pitimini."

On the Saturday morning we again visited Pastor Macgalayo's church, this time for a special meeting held at the sea shore, where they baptised 12 new believers, mainly young people. This church had grown as a result of our visit and so they had more people to baptise than usual.

NEW YEAR IN MAMBURAO

During the early hours of the morning I woke up to a strange bump. I switched on the lights and saw that Lea had disappeared – there was only Princess fast asleep, lying crossways on the bed. Then Lea crawled up from the floor where she had fallen and muttered, "I wonder when we can have a wider bed, so there will be room for all of us?" After a moment the lights died – it was brown time again. The next power cut came later that same day when I was in the internet cafe in town, and once again I lost everything that I had managed to write. Not the best of starts to our New Year's Eve.

At midnight a few firework rockets whizzed into the air and one lonely biker went back and forth on the street, dragging behind his bike a string on which some empty tins had been tied. They made a wonderful clanking noise as they bounced over the road surface. It was a cheap and ingenious way of having fun for the new year; the poor could not afford anything else.

NEW YEAR'S DAY

We certainly spent New Year's Day 2007 in a rather different way than most other westerners, as we went to preach the Gospel to the Mangyan tribes. Pastor Daniel again interpreted for me and he gathered the villagers together from the surrounding area into an old decayed building with only its walls left standing. The roof had collapsed ages ago, and seating arrangements were planks that had been placed upon some termite-eaten tree stumps. But there it was, the church ready to receive the congregation.

The old building filled up with people who looked really sick with all sorts of complaints – scabies, rashes, tuberculosis, Dengue fever, malaria, mental illnesses … There were about 25 families in this village, and not one of them looked healthy. I felt such pity for these people and we gave them food, while to the children we gave a bag of sweets each.

Young girls carried babies in their arms. Amongst the Mangyans, girls normally get married between the ages of 10 and 12 years, when they themselves are still children and have not even had their first periods. Often they are made to marry even close relatives, as the respective parents arrange the marriages without letting the girls have any say in the matter. The spirit of apathy and depression hung over everything. Everyone seemed to have some sort of lung problem and very many were infested with vermin.

I prayed for these dear folk and hugged some of them. Others usually do not want to even touch the tribes people for fear of infection, but I didn't have any problems, and maybe the Lord just blocked my nose from any bad smells. Dirty they were, but they looked so pitiful that my natural instinct was one of love towards them. Either I am slow to learn about infectious diseases or my memory was giving me trouble: in these sort of situations you just can't think of yourself. Real pity towards these poor people and the state of their lives totally overwhelmed any human reservations or reasoning. How great is God's love towards each one of them.

137. *Mother & child*

GOAL ACCOMPLISHED

Back in Mamburao, we planned the final session of outreach to the local children. Our goal was to get the new ones to church. So we decided that this time the kids would be brought from three new areas to the church and we would feed them there. We arranged the transport and the church soon filled up with children, brought from everywhere.

All possible means of transportation that we could mobilise cheaply had been brought into use: the three-wheeled bikes were full, the jeep was full and children were even lying on the roofs of the vehicles. We played, sang and danced with the kids, many of whom had brought their younger brothers and sisters with them. There were some very young ones, even two year olds, who danced along with us and had fun. Many of the children were dressed in their very best frills.

They all had great fun, and everyone jumped along with us in the games - I'm sure some wondered if this was really a church! Again I explained about heaven and told stories about what Jesus does, and all the kids seemed to live through the stories, at one moment listening as quietly as mice, and at the next moment laughing with joy as the story continued. I told them that there is a huge flower garden in heaven with such big flowers that babies can lie inside of them just like in a cradle. One kid wanted to know, "Are the babies allowed to do anything else or do they have to just stay inside those flowers?"

138. Flower garden in 'My Heaven'

A Muslim boy asked, "Are my parents allowed to go to heaven, as they believe in another God?"

About 250 children in total had crowded into the church, just about fitting in as they were so small. Again many of these little ones were born into the Kingdom of Heaven … and church became familiar to them. Several asked when they were allowed to come again – tomorrow maybe?

I did some quick calculations. There were 250 children in the church, 600 slum kids on the beach, and 100 kids from other communities - we had fed almost a thousand children and preached the gospel to all. Every little soul is important to Jesus.

In many churches perhaps 80% of the audience are children but sermons are not preached to them but to adults instead. No wonder that kids are lost and so the whole coming generation is lost.

When we reached out to the children, it also brought in adults to listen to us too. As a result, many adults and teenagers came to Christ. They came to observe and to listen to what was going on and they saw the Living God working and physical pains disappearing. Healing is not an insignificant matter; if it had been, Jesus would not have spent so much time doing it.

CHAPTER *27*
WITH THE TERRORISTS

INTO THE TERRORISTS' DEN

There was one trip that I especially wanted to make and that was to Abra, to the area where the terrorists had now settled in. I had got to know a lady who told me that she had run a Sunday School there some years before. She had also acted as a guide into the Mindoro mountains in another part of the island for some travellers who wanted to get to know the Mangyan villages: on those trips she had got acquainted with the NPA army and she now supported their political propaganda. Subsequently the government had banned such trips because they were too dangerous.

139. The road there

We talked over this idea with Pastor Sonio and he was not exactly captivated with it. He told me it was far too dangerous a journey for a white lady. But I pleaded over and over again, and finally he gave in. So we planned the best possible timing for our outward journey, which would be as early in the morning as possible. We would go by jeep and motorbike as the road was in poor condition.

NPA men are also fishermen, because like everybody else their families need something to eat. So the men fish at night and come home very tired in the morning for some much needed sleep. We aimed to reach their families and children.

We followed the jungle road that wound along the coast line. When we came close to the village that was our destination, we stopped the vehicles a short distance away from the road leading into the village and walked the last part. It was better this way, not to draw so much attention to ourselves by driving a noisy and rattling old car inside the village. Some of the people were sleeping but we saw a few women going about their morning housework. The pastor went over and explained to one lady why we were there, and this lady, who probably was one of the eldest in the village, nodded and sent children to call people to come together. The kids went through the village hut by hut and people started to gather around us.

140. *On the way to the village*

Our audience was made up of women and children, as we had planned; only a couple of older men came with them. They shook the coconut palm tree with a long pole, to make some coconuts fall down, then cut them in half and gave them to us to drink as their guests. Soon we had a small group gathered, 32 people in all, and we preached to them the gospel of the love of Jesus and then we prayed for them.

The village women knew the lady who was with us and that is why they accepted us too. The lady said that they used to normally come by boat at the time of high tide because the journey by road was too dangerous. "Ahah," I thought to myself, "now she tells us!"

No wonder that Edwin had been so nervous as we drove towards the village. The area was totally ruled by the terrorist militia: we would have only ourselves to blame if something happened. The women told us that nobody had dared to come to their area for the two last years, and they looked at us in a strange and meaningful way.

The result of our visit was 32 new believers being brought into the Kingdom of God. The village women wept and begged us to come again, wanting to hear more about Jesus and asking if we would establish a church in their village. Rev. Sonio started to relax his watchfulness only after we had managed to get well away from the area. He reiterated that it was too dangerous to travel there in the daytime and it certainly should never be done in the evening.

I also got from him some more detailed information about how the terrorist militia operated – for example, when we were in Sablayan, the NPA had killed three outsiders. Oh well, ignorance is bliss, as they say. I noticed that my adult hosts had a tendency not to supply the whole picture on such matters, but the kids would often tell me more about the actual happenings in their towns and villages.

141. *Preparing coconut drink*

MAKING A DIFFERENCE

This journey had been important because Jesus wanted to save these people. After the trip, I heard of a warning that was meant for us: "If you think you are safe in this town, we can get to wherever you stay and kill you. You are not safe in Abra, nor in Mamburao, nowhere." We might have pushed our noses into the wolf's den, but they still left us alone afterwards.

I believe that we have fed the kids of terrorists, and maybe even taken them into our school. This is our weapon. The terrorists may spread their propaganda in the poor areas but they do not practice what they preach and the local people do not see any changes in their everyday lives. The NPA, the state, the army, the politicians and the presidents may change, but the people's misery just stays the same. We walk the talk, we live like we preach and we give help to the poor. That is the big difference.

The combination of a living gospel and practical aid causes the enemy to flee. The gospel drives away fear, village communities are saved and the lies of the enemy are revealed. The terrorists start to see in their own children how

God changes lives and brings hope for the future: results that they have been unable to achieve with their own weapons and propaganda. Providing what we are doing is what God wants us to do, then He will stretch out His mighty hand to help, and that means that we will succeed in our task.

142. Chatting with the villagers

143. New believers

PART FIVE.
INTERLUDE IN
AUSTRALIA

144. *Outside the school in Mamburao*

145. Children from our school in Mamburao

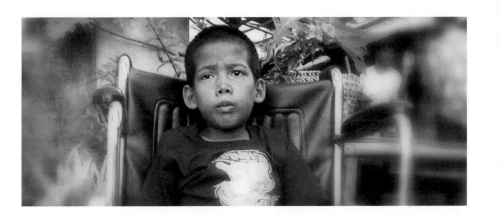

CHAPTER 28
NEWS ABOUT NICO

WHEELCHAIR WANTED

I had been back in Australia for just a few weeks when I received an email from Nheng saying that Nico's mother wanted a wheelchair for her son, as he was now too heavy to be carried around. I stared at the text for a while, quite embarrassed by this request. "A wheelchair?" I wondered, "Lord, why is this happening and what should I do?"

Of course I could send money for the wheelchair, as I had promised to help in whatever way I could, but God had promised to heal Nico. Now if I sent a wheelchair, what would that do for people's faith levels and especially Nico's? But if I refused to do so, wasn't it breaking my promise to send whatever they asked for? I asked the Lord to give me wisdom and a clear answer – expecting Him to tell me how I could politely refuse the request for a wheelchair and substitute something else instead. But the Lord's answer about what to send really surprised me, "It's the wheelchair – send Nico a wheelchair."

I wrote back to Nheng telling her that money for the wheelchair would be forthcoming and asking her to find out how much it would cost. But I felt disappointed, and a rebellious feeling was brewing deep inside of me ... "Lord, I do not understand what is going on, why did You first say 'yes' and then 'no'? At what point did I misunderstand You?" But this time I did not get any answer to my whingeing. Everything seemed to be heading in the wrong direction.

After a week the money for the wheelchair was sent to Mamburao, and soon the new transportation was proudly brought from faraway Manila with appropriate fanfares to Mamburao. The chair and Nico were photographed and soon I was staring at the photos on my computer screen: it was an adult's wheelchair! In the photo Nico almost disappeared inside it.

This was even more humiliating; do they really not believe that the boy will ever start to walk if they go and buy a chair big enough for him to sit in even when he's grown up? I felt like the prophet Jonah must have been feeling as he sat under the vine outside Nineveh; I was deeply offended that things did not go the way that I thought they should.

146. Edwin, Nena, Nico & his mother

Jonah went out and sat down at a place east of the city. There he made himself a shelter, sat in its shade and waited to see what would happen to the city. (Jonah 4:5)

But as I struggled with my own reactions and feelings there in Australia, the wheelchair was becoming very famous in Mamburao town. It was the very first wheelchair in the whole town and people looked on in amazement as this novel transportation carried the little paralysed boy.

Nico became well known because of his chair, and many people were very touched that someone had given this child such a wonderful gift. People were drawn to the church and some relatives of Nico's from another locality even became believers because of this donation. This wheelchair really caused a chain reaction. I could not understand how one wheelchair could bring such results – did the Lord mean that this was the miracle?

Nico was so enthusiastic about his chair that he made his parents come to church three times per week. And for the local kids the wheelchair was a wonderful attraction too – they all wanted to push it all the time and so Nico got to ride everywhere.

A Mail from Nheng

Nheng wrote to me again.

> The church has grown to over 200 members and the building will soon be too small. We are so happy that God's anointing has come to the church and what you prophesied has actually happened. People bring their sick ones here and God has healed many. Even politicians have heard what is happening and come to our church to ask Pastor Edwin Sonio to bless them.

147. *Our youngsters*

> Many have been amazed to see how quickly the church is growing: last time we had 30 young people in the meeting, but today there were 52 of them and we have decided to split into three sessions on Sundays so they can all fit in. The first meeting is at 7:00 for the adults, the second at 9:30 for the youngsters and then the children's meeting is at 12:00.

> We have also held a meeting at school for the close relatives of our school kids. The Bible school now has 60 students and the Balansay church that you founded on your last visit has grown to 30 members."

The widow of the fisherman who you prayed for in the slum village has told us that it helped her a lot; your prayer touched her heart and she has received many blessings since then.

Her small daughter is in Sharon's class and now also her youngest one is at school in Frances' class. In the beginning Sharon had problems with the girl: when she bent over to help another pupil, the girl would bite her in the bottom. She was always seeking attention and was a real troublemaker in the class. At home too her mother had difficult problems with her. Now God has answered prayer and the girl is behaving very well, and is calm and polite. Her mother says that it is a miracle from the Lord.

I was overjoyed to read Nheng's letter but the Lord had an even bigger surprise in store for us later.

NICO'S MIRACLE

I was with Lea in Tonga, one of the Pacific islands, on a visit to preach the gospel when we heard the latest part of Nico's wheelchair story.

The miracle happened in a Sunday morning church meeting, when Nico's family were also there. After the meeting people were standing around talking in front of the church building, and Nico was waiting in his wheelchair

148. Nico & Pastor Sonio

as he always did. Suddenly he got up and started walking just like it would have been the most natural thing for him to do! The glory went totally to Jesus: no one could claim any part of this miracle as nobody had even prayed for him. From that time on Nico has been walking – he is completely healed! Lea and I had a good laugh about it, wondering whether he just got fed up with listening to the adults' boring conversation and decided to walk home on his own!

God's wise plan about the wheelchair now became clear. By now the whole town of Mamburao knew Nico because of his amazing wheelchair, whereas previously he had just been one of the many disabled kids to whom nobody paid any attention at all. If he had started walking without this phase in his wheelchair, that would not have caused such a commotion. But now the miracle became public in the whole town and also the surrounding areas. The coming of the wheelchair had put spotlights on Nico and what Jesus did.

Nico believed Jesus' promise that he would walk one day, but the wheelchair made his life much easier as he waited for that time. After this, his other hope came true too, as he was able to start at our school in the next intake. I asked Minda, a believer lady, to massage Nico's legs once a week to ensure that his muscles would get stronger. She did this faithfully and prayerfully for some weeks, and at the same time we sent Nico some multivitamin and calcium tablets to strengthen his bones so that normal growth would start.

Many of our school kids had vitamin deficiency diseases but we could not help all of them. Their usual food was a cup of white rice. In the rainy season the rice was rationed and not boiled in the normal way but soaked in water first and then made into a thin soup, which the families then ate. The children were always hungry.

During the fishing season the price of a fish was 30-35 pesos per kilo. The mothers tried to sell at least 2 kilos of fish to get 60 pesos to buy food, as this amount of money got them 2 kg of rice. If the rice season was poor, the price went up and the rice had to be imported from elsewhere. But this year a miracle had happened and the rice crop was exceeding all expectations. It was as if the Lord had blessed the crops from the earth because there was a revival in the town.

Chain Reaction to Nico's Healing

Nico's miraculous healing brought more sick people to the church. One man came with partial paralysis and having lost his ability to speak but when Rev. Sonio prayed for him, he regained his speech. The faith level of all the people grew because they saw what had happened to Nico. Also the Sunday school group increased so much that it had to be divided in two, one taught by Sharon and Nheng and a group for the smaller ones taught by Frances.

Nheng wrote to us about a lady called Jane, for whom I had prayed. She had lived in Lebanon during the war there and the shock from an explosion had caused her to lose her ability to talk. After prayer she was healed and started to speak again, and this miracle brought her whole family to Christ and they joined the congregation.

The last two chapters of the Book of Acts tell about Paul's sea journey to Rome. The ship that was taking him there sailed into a storm, and in the resulting shipwreck Paul and his companions found themselves on the island of Malta. In Acts 28 we read about a man called Publius, whose father was sick. Publius is described as the chief man of the island, so he was probably the highest ruling person there under Roman rule. Paul went to Publius' father, laid his hands on the man and he was healed.

> **Publius' father was sick with a fever and dysentery. Paul went to him, prayed, and put his hands on the man and healed him. After this, all the other sick people on the island came to Paul, and he healed them, too. (Acts 28:8,9)**

The healing of one man caused a chain reaction on the island, and it resulted in healing for all the other sick people there too. That very same thing was now happening in 2007 in Occidental Mindoro in the town of Mamburao.

INTERCESSORS' VISIONS

On my previous trip, my Finnish intercessors Hilja and Paula had visions of various situations that exactly paralleled my schedule. They had seen me visiting a slum village, before it even happened. It is the Lord who opens doors and

149. Mamburao school children

makes things to happen and it is He who sets the intercessors at their posts as watchmen.

In one vision, Hilja was walking along a path and on the right hand side was a white birch tree trunk lying on the ground. The branches had been pruned from the tree trunk and it was strong, not rotten. Hilja saw light-coloured arrows fired into the trunk, that sank into the timber and remained attached there diagonal to the trunk. Tied to the ends of the arrow shafts were kites. The arrows hit the trunk in sequence and for some reason the trunk resembled a backbone with ribs.

The path continued, and on the left hand side there were little shacks or booths side by side creating a fence. In each of them there was a person. The first occupant was dark-skinned and had their mouth closed with tape, with a scarf around their head like a sweatband or a bandage covering a head wound. He looked out of his shack casting furtive glances around, as if mentally disturbed.

In the next booth was a totally normal person but seemingly quiet and fearful. Hilja could not tell whether these people were men or women. From that point onwards the people in the shacks looked normal, but everyone had a white scarf around their heads resembling an Arab headdress.

Then came a whirlwind in Hilja's vision, bringing light to all of them. Hilja was wondering what it meant, when the Lord said to her, "What are you trying to figure out? Don't you understand that these are bound people, who will now see what I am doing. Wherever Anne goes, there will come freedom – she is preaching freedom to the bound ones …"

Hilja had also seen handwriting, but not clearly enough to be able to read it. There was quite a lot of writing already in notebooks. Although Hilja did not know it, I tend to write down what happens on my travels in notebooks, and eventually I collected the material together for this book. She also saw fields where rice had been planted.

The slum village in Mamburao looked exactly as Hilja had seen it, with shacks bordering the lanes like fences and with bamboo fencing around them. When I walked along the lane, people stood in front of their huts staring at this weird wanderer. Men often wear a scarf around their heads, sometimes as a sweatband, a cover against the sun or sometimes around the neck like a bandana.

Hilja and Paula understood that the white birch trunk symbolised the nature of my ministry and my Finnishness. The trunk was strong because it was on the ground. The ministry is at the grass roots level and what had preceded this work was pruning of the dry branches from my life. Nobody is scared to approach a trunk lying on the ground, in contrast to one that is standing up proudly.

The slums and the tips and the people rejected by others belong at the grass roots level, and bringing the gospel to such as these doesn't win you any earthly medals. They are the people that western society considers a burden and saving such people doesn't make the columns of the gossip magazines. Nor are they welcomed as generous givers in churches, but they are the same poor and weak ones to whom Jesus went.

the same poor and weak ones to whom Jesus went

Paula had seen orange-coloured butterflies fluttering upwards – beautiful and shining, resembling a firework display. Their main colour was orange, but there was also blue, turquoise, and red. What Hilja saw supported this vision of Paula's … Clouds were rolling across the sky, glistening with different shades of colour. They then floated down into a valley in rounded shapes like balls.

When looked at more closely the clouds were made up of bundles of string or cotton which glowed like fiery filaments. Their fire burned up everything that needed to be burnt and left the valley looking clean and tidy. Above was a clear sky and then another cloud that grew and grew bigger.

199

The Lord gave these words from chapter 9 of Isaiah:

Before those people lived in darkness, but now they have seen a great light. They lived in a dark land, but a light has shined on them.... Like the time you defeated Midian, you have taken away their heavy load and the heavy pole from their backs and the rod the enemy used to punish them. (Isaiah 9:2,4)

SYMBOLIC PICTURES

God was speaking through symbolic pictures in these visions:

CLOUD means heavenly protection, guidance and care. Gen. 13:21-22, Ps. 18:11, Isa.19:1

ORANGE, amber = the glory of God. Ezek.1:4, 8:2

BLUE = heaven, heavenly, authority, the Holy Spirit. Num.15:38 ("Tie several pieces of thread together and attach them to the corners of your clothes. Put a blue thread in each one of these tassels")

PURPLE = royalty. Judges 8:26

ARROW = speed, piercing. Ps.18:15, 2Kgs.13:17 (the arrow of victory)

TREE(S) = nation, nations, single person, church, Jesus. Isa. 55:13, Ps.104:16, Nebuchadnezzar's dream about the tree Dan. 4:17-23

The vision has been accurate and it has been amazing to see the change that has come to the "people living in the shadows of death" as they have come to know Christ. Not only has their inner being been cleansed but also their whole appearance improves and the blessing of God spreads through the saved children to relatives, to the town and even to the surrounding areas. The picture of the rice fields probably meant that God was blessing the crops as well as the people: earlier the rice yields had been miserable, but now the earth was producing a record amount of rice.

CHAPTER *29*
THE SCHOOL GROWS

THE NEW SCHOOL YEAR

The first group of our pre-school pupils "graduated" and they were all accepted into the local catholic school. Some parents and close relatives had been hoping until the last moment that I would start further classes so that their children could go through the whole of their primary education in our Christian school. But sadly I did not have money for that, nor the building.

One day back in Australia as I was driving home in my car I clearly heard the voice of the Lord saying, "You now have more than 100 pupils." This shocked me for a moment and I wondered what on earth it meant, as I knew the building didn't have enough room for that many. I had agreed with the teachers that they would accept the same number of pupils as before and even then we knew it would be tight.

> **'You now have more than 100 pupils'**

When I arrived home I immediately picked up the phone and called Mamburao, as I knew that they were registering new pupils at that very moment. I asked Nheng how many pupils she had now taken in. The line went quiet for a moment and then she said, "Anne please don't be angry but we now have 105 pupils. The poor people came and cried, wanting their kids to enter the school and I just could not say no. Many of our kids that have just graduated have younger brothers and sisters."

I told Nheng what the Lord had said to me and she relaxed a bit. But I still wanted to know how they managed to fit 105 children in, as the inspector had already warned us the year before that there were too many children in one classroom. The Department of Education stipulated that the maximum class size is 20. I knew for a fact that state schools in practice didn't follow this rule, but private schools had to keep in line because they were subject to stricter inspections. And I certainly didn't want to lose our permission to run the school.

150. Three of our schoolgirls

But Nheng had already solved the problem creatively: the school would start working in two shifts, mornings and afternoons. Classes were already divided into three age groups: Nursery for 3-4 year olds, Kindergarten for 4-5s and Pre-school for 6-7s. The first two groups would study in the mornings and Pre-school in the afternoons. When the school year officially started, I noticed that the total number of pupils had mysteriously increased still further, this time to 120!

We also agreed that the children would get food at school every Friday and that their close relatives or single mothers would be given a sack of rice every month. I could not afford to give food every day, but I still had faith that the Lord would provide money for that too.

So many parents and relatives had become believers that they now made up an intercessory group for the school as well as being keen on doing voluntary jobs.

The pupils that we had sent onto the first class of state school turned out to be academically outstanding. They behaved well and could already write, count and read – facts that amazed the education authorities. Of course our pupils had received good teaching during the year but their becoming believers was a more significant factor in the process.

ANOTHER MAIL FROM NHENG

Nheng kept me in touch with the latest news by email:

> Do you know, Anne, that our school is now really famous in Mamburao? The mother of one of our pupils got a job in the local radio station as an announcer, and now she is giving us free advertising by talking about our school every day over the radio. Now everyone knows what is happening at the school.
>
> The celebration marking the end of the school year was a big thing in the town. Ours is the first private school giving free education to kids living below subsistence levels. There are other private Christian schools in the Philippines but they all collect fees from their pupils. The level of our teaching is high and it is grounded in our Christian faith: the good results are visible to all. Parents and close relatives have to come once a week to Bible class as their only "payment" to the school, and this is a totally revolutionary idea.
>
> As the Philippines is a catholic country and very religious, the state's catholic school doesn't consider us as competitors in the area, because our kids go on to study under their roof when they leave our school.
>
> We received surprise guests at our own end of school year celebration: the Honourable Ver Cascalla and the Minister of Education graced our ceremony by their presence and made speeches. The state school wondered why such important guests did not go to them but instead visited the celebration of our small school.

151. Innocence

> The church where the ceremony was held was so full that many had to stay outside. The mayor of Mamburao promised that next time he would reserve the town square for us, so that everyone can fit in to watch the performances of the children and to celebrate together.

We subsequently got an even better offer from the mayor: he now lets us use the auditorium of the catholic school, a large venue nicely central in the city, and it's free.

Thank you and God bless you, Nheng

God had promised us, "I will help" (*autan*). I believe He despatched His angels to help us in very practical ways to found this school in Mamburao. Many of us are totally unaware of the invisible spiritual world that surrounds us, even though it is as real as our visible world. The Hebrew word for an angel, *mal'ak*, emphasizes the fact that angels are God's messengers, agents of God representing the Almighty as His ambassadors. I am convinced that God has positioned angels in Mamburao and its surroundings as Heaven's Diplomats, who are there to make this school go ahead, to protect us and to enable us to accomplish our goal.

MAMBURAO UPDATE

Lea visited the Philippines next summer, while I went round Europe preaching and doing seminars. She sent me an email with fresh news from Mamburao and the area. I read that Pastor Sonio now had six Bible study groups in addition to the Sunday meetings and the Tuesday and Thursday Bible teaching sessions.

152. I love to work

Journeys from the town to the wooded areas outside had become more dangerous. The NPA terrorists had had to withdraw from the island and had lost control of several areas, creating a vacuum that the enemy was beginning to fill with other sorts of evil. Muslim terrorists had started to move into the island, much to the dismay of the Philippines government who sent out public warnings and offered two million pesos (about €30,000) as a reward for information on where they were based. These terrorists disguised themselves as mango farmers and settled among the local people. They pressurised some into joining them, especially from the young poor; some villages were terrorised by fear and some villagers were even killed.

Lea and I wondered if the cycle would ever end – after getting rid of one wicked group, another even worse comes along in its place. We felt that the only way of suppressing terrorism was to spread our work among children everywhere we could – not just in Mamburao town but beyond and to the rest of Mindoro island.

But there was some encouraging news too. The Department of Education sent me a letter asking if I could establish a private secondary school and high school in the town since the results from my existing school were so amazing. They would send a hundred pupils to my high school and these students could make a small weekly payment. In the state school in the town there were a thousand secondary school level students, and the sizes of the classes were huge – around 80-100 students in each. Such a size made the class impossible to control, so getting even a hundred pupils to another school would be of help to them.

It was a lovely thought – 100 young people for the gospel – but I answered, "Not possible," as I did not have the funds for such an enterprise. When a school becomes "official", it has to pay all the social payments and those were impossibly high for me. State schools take a payment from high school students, for example for every test that they have to do, and many other payments as well. In theory the school is free but in practice it is not. This is why many poor people cannot go to high school, as they normally do not have enough money for their everyday food let alone such fees. This is why the poor always stays poor and are not able to disentangle themselves from the poverty trap.

I felt that, rather than following the Education Department's request, it would be better to establish pre-schools in different places and to reach the kids and their families that way. There was massive potential for the future.

My dream was to go to the real hornets' nest – to the islands where the inhabitants are mainly Muslims and also to the northern parts of the Philippines where NPA troops and the Mafia rule. Also Palawan Island was on my mind and I thought that one day I could make it a stepping stone to slip into Burma or Borneo, or to make contact with Mindanao which is the Islamic terrorists' area. Yes, these were just my dreams – but I had stepped in through a door that God had opened for me, and I was following His call to a destination that I could only dream of at this point.

> **God takes care of the preparatory training**

God gives us the motivation for the task He sets us and He also takes care of the preparatory training. Many believers fail to fulfill their tasks because they do not have a balanced perspective of what God can do. They tend to trust their own understanding and the practical circumstances, what they can see with their natural eyes. But in the military arena, when the general gives the order to a soldier in wartime, the soldier does not ask the general why it should be done, but he just obeys. God is our General who has a much bigger war strategy than we are able to understand. Our task is to obey, and to trust in the written Word of God, that promises that we will not fight alone:

> **I am sending an angel ahead of you, who will protect you as you travel. He will lead you to the place I have prepared. (Exodus 23:20)**

153. Preparing food in a dangerous village

PART SIX.
NEW CHALLENGES

154. Palawan from the air

155. Christmas angels

156. Cooking for Mangingisda kids

Chapter 30
Invitation to the Northern Philippines

Pastor Ron Lozano

In the autumn of 2007, I received an invitation to visit the Pangasinan area, in the Northern Philippines. Lea and I decided to travel with a friend from Youth With A Mission (YWAM), who we had got to know while working in Fiji. We'll call her Lucy.

This YWAM lady knew a pastor who lived in the area where we were now heading – let's refer to him as Ron Lozano. This sort of trip would be far too dangerous for an individual missionary on their own so we formed a group. Lucy wanted to visit Pastor Lozano's church in a place called Balungao and asked us to add that church to our itinerary for this coming trip.

159. Pangasinan

Pastor Lozano had built a Christian School for 100 pupils in Balungao, covering primary education up to high school. The school pupils had to pay fees

209

each term, so only the wealthiest families could send their kids there. He had also founded twelve churches during the twenty years of his ministry: he is a real pioneer in an area where other people do not want to go.

160. Children at Ron's school

The pastor told us that no foreigner had ever visited his congregation. A foreign pastor had some time earlier promised to support the mission but his level of interest had not developed any further: no financial help had materialised and a commitment to visit the area had remained as just a promise.

Lucy wrote to this foreign pastor telling him about our forthcoming trip and asking if his congregation could send some monetary gift that we could bring with us to this Filipino church. She received a letter containing a cheque for the equivalent of €150 for Pastor Lozano. It seemed rather a small amount of money in the light of all the promises given down the years. Lea and I wondered why a big foreign church, that seemed to take pride in its mission work, could not be more true to its commitments. God doesn't bless empty promises. I feel that such undertakings are a covenant before the Lord, a voluntary agreement to actually carry out what you have promised.

If you make a promise to God, don't be slow to keep it. God is not happy with fools, so give God what you promised. (Eccl. 5:4)

TRAVEL PLANS

The Pangasinan area is controlled by the NPA army and by the Mafia. Both these organisations sustain themselves by criminal activities, in particular by kidnapping wealthy businessmen and foreigners and then demanding high ransoms for their release. The NPA has also suffered internal wrangles and divisions which resulted in the existence of several terrorist groups operating in the area. Through the pioneering work of Pastor Ron Lozano, some NPA men had become believers and that guaranteed protection for his work from the regular NPA, but not of course from splinter groups.

When Pastor Lozano heard of our plans to take a flight by local plane to the airport closest to his church in Balungao, he sent us a very firm "No". He said that instead he would come and pick us up from Manila by car, if we would pay for the petrol. I on the other hand felt that a flight would be both easier and cheaper than the prospect of a ten hour drive through a Mafia area on local roads.

Also, finding accommodation for the pastor and his wife in Manila would be difficult. The Mount Moriah mission centre was currently full of Norwegian guests so we could not go there, but Israel Forbes had ordered us a motel room. Our own team (Lea, Princess, Lucy and I) would fit in that one room but Pastor Lozano and his wife would need a room of their own, as well as food and rest. After such a long journey they really would need some time to recover before driving the same route back.

Later I understood why Pastor Lozano had blocked our plan to fly to Balungao – it was simply impossible. The nearest local airport was abandoned, with its air traffic control tower standing rejected and forgotten in the middle of high grass. There had been no planes flying into or out of that airport in the past ten years, even though the guide book claimed it was operational. So we would have stood with our luggage at Manila airport, waiting for a flight to Balungao that was never going to come.

Ron told us that we would be safe with him. He was widely known among the NPA troops, whereas of course no one knew who we were. The NPA had even promised to guard the church and other places where we planned to visit, deep inside the area controlled by the NPA. The caretaker of one of Pastor Lozano's churches, as well as some of the church members, belonged to the NPA. They would give physical protection, but otherwise we were told not to trust them.

The pastor also warned us not to say anything about monetary gifts, because as soon as the NPA heard about it, they would take the money for themselves. Honesty and trust didn't belong in their vocabulary. The message of Christ had reached some of them, but fear and loyalty towards this terrorist army was stronger than their trust in Jesus.

The presence of the NPA was advantageous to the pastor because it gave him a free hand to preach the gospel. He told us his story: the Lord had called him to this area long ago when he was a young Christian. He had just got married and they didn't have any money or any belongings other than a Bible, but God had fulfilled His part of the deal. The Lord had protected him many times from death and He had healed many sick people through Ron's prayers.

This had had a big impact on the terrorist and criminal groups that controlled the area: they respected the pastor and had made it clear that nobody should touch either him or his wife. It was very useful to get this background information from Pastor Lozano before we set off on the trip.

ANIMAL TROUBLE

A couple of weeks before we were due to fly out, I got a feeling that I should warn Lea not to ride her horse. She was a keen rider and had her own horse. So I told her about this feeling, but she didn't really take it very seriously, telling me that anyway she was planning to sell the animal since it had become increasingly difficult to look after it because of our overseas trips. She didn't have enough money for the flight tickets either, so selling her horse would help.

I could not pay for her tickets, as I only had enough money for my own flights and for food and accommodation in the Philippines for the three of us during our visit. Also the Lord had told me to keep back a certain amount of money that we were going to take with us, for a reason that He would reveal later.

Lea had placed a 'Horse For Sale' advertisement in the local newspaper and she told me that a possible buyer was coming to see the horse. That's why she would be arriving a bit late for an information and training session that was arranged at church with some pastors from Vanuatu, a Pacific island north east of Brisbane.

I waited for Lea and when she finally arrived, I could see that something was wrong. She walked in slowly and sat down very stiffly. "Anne, I should have listened to you," she said, "something horrible happened."

The potential buyer had been enthusiastic about the horse but had asked Lea to ride it so he could watch. So Lea had put a helmet on and climbed into the saddle. But without warning the horse had gone crazy, bucked and thrown her off. Apparently she felt everything go dark for a while and pain shot through her body, but soon she staggered to her feet, very thankful for her last minute decision to wear a helmet. Naturally the incident scared off the possible buyer and he said he would not dare to buy this sort of wild horse. "There went my travel money," murmured Lea.

But it was very strange because this sort of behaviour was totally out of character for her horse – never before had it acted like this. Interesting that the Lord had given a prophetic warning beforehand, "Do not ride the horse."

Probably the enemy didn't like the prospect of our coming trip. Before that, the only animals that had given us any trouble were the stray dogs we found in Filipino villages – you had to be careful as some carried rabies. Human beings of course were a different matter … in fact in some villages in Asian Pacific countries the dogs were more clear-headed than the villagers if they had been drinking too much "*kava*". This is an intoxicating drink consumed quite widely in the Pacific islands and made from the root of the pepper plant.

Lea thought that some of her ribs must be broken, as she was suffering from a lot of chest pain and finding it difficult to breathe, let alone walk. She could not move one arm and one side of her body felt like she had been run over by a bulldozer, so badly bruised was she. Only by Finnish *sisu* could she make it to the church to be prayed for. We could not afford to be sick, as the time to leave was approaching fast. The pastors from Vanuatu had given all of us some anointing oil to take home, so we all prayed for her to be healed and anointed her. After a short

> **We could not afford to be sick**

while she said that the pains had eased off. I urged her to go to hospital for x-rays to get a clear diagnosis of her situation – real healing stands up to tests and doctors' reports. So off she went and came back with the great news that the medics had been amazed that she had no broken bones after such a fall from the back of a horse, and that they had pronounced her fit to travel.

Another answer to prayer was that she managed to sell the horse before we left too. Lea anointed the horse with the same oil that we had used on her, feeling that if God has used it to bring healing to her, it would probably calm down the wild horse as well. After its anointing the horse behaved so well that even a total stranger could ride it. Through this sale Lea received more money than the first buyer would have offered, so the finances for the trip were in hand. The buyer was happy too: he had brought a horse trainer with him to assess the animal and both of them considered that it had a lot of future potential.

THE START OF THE JOURNEY

I have lost count of the number of times that I have been through Brisbane Airport coming or going somewhere but when the staff start asking me which airport department it is that I am working in, that's the time to ease back a bit.

So there I was at the airport, on 6 December 2007, waiting for my travelling companions. It was getting late so I duly checked the date and time on my flight tickets again and even went over to ask at the desk whether I was in the wrong place, as I saw that other passengers were already boarding the plane. Finally I saw Lucy running towards me with Lea's daughter, but still Lea herself was not to be seen. Lucy explained that Lea couldn't find her tickets and the flight staff were trying to figure out what to do.

Lucy, Princess and I boarded the plane and sat there with all the rest of the passengers in that packed cabin, as the plane remained stationary on the tarmac. Finally Lea ran up the steps and into the cabin holding the missing travel documents in her hands. Many pairs of eyes were glued to her as she made her way down the aisle to her seat next to us. "So **she** is the one that we have been waiting here for," was the unspoken chorus.

On a separate occasion when we were again off on a trip together, Lea lost both passport and tickets while moving from one apartment to another. She had searched desperately in both apartments but without success. When it got to the day that we were due to leave, Lea phoned me and said, "Please pray, Anne, that the tickets and the passport will be found soon!"

> **send an angel to collect the missing tickets**

Yes, I really did pray, as Lea had my tickets too, and there were now only a few hours before the plane was due to leave. I asked the Lord to send an angel to collect the missing tickets and passport and put them in a **visible place**. Lea's brother, who had helped her move to the new apartment, was adamant that there was no possibility at all that the tickets could still be in the old apartment, as he and Lea had both checked it and it was absolutely empty.

I phoned Lea to tell her about the impression that I had received in prayer. I urged her to go one last time to the old house, as I had a feeling that the tickets would now be there, positioned by an angel in a visible place.

So Lea sent her very reluctant brother to her former home, while she continued to dig miserably through huge piles of her stuff, which were already in a complete mess as a result of her previous frantic searching. A short time later her brother reappeared looking both embarrassed and astonished. "Right there in the middle of the room was this old bag," he explained. "How could it possibly have ended up there – I'm sure it wasn't there before!? I almost fell over it as I walked into the living room, and when I looked inside the bag, there were the tickets and passport. This just can't be possible!"

He was still shaking his head and muttering to himself an hour later, as we sped down the highway towards the airport.

CHAPTER 31
NORTHERN HAPPENINGS

JOURNEY TO PANGASINAN

Israel Forbes had booked us rooms in a cheap hotel in Manila, next to a main road, and Manila is a city that never sleeps. The three-wheelers putt-putted up and down the street without a break, together with ambulances, jeepneys and anything else with wheels and an engine. The windows rattled and the beds shook because of the traffic. When I finally managed to slumber a while, I felt I had fallen asleep in the middle of a roundabout.

161. Three-wheelers

Unusually for hotel rooms that I slept in, this time even the AC system worked, but it only blew onto one of the beds. So the occupier of that bed shivered as if they had been dropped inside a deep freeze, while the person in the bed on the other side of the room got baked in microwave-level heat.

215

Lea and I decided to sleep in rotation: first we would freeze next to the AC unit, then defrost and quickly bake in the microwave, then back to the deep freeze again. Princess was fast asleep but she got hauled around after

162. *Enforced rest break*

her mother in the same rotation from bed to bed … rather like a Finnish sauna followed by a cold plunge, on and on right through the night. Lucy slept with earplugs in and her bed enjoyed a happy medium temperature – in the middle of the room halfway between freezer and microwave.

After a not very restful night, we set off on our journey towards Pangasinan, a district on the far north west coast of Luzon Island, from which there still would be some hours to our final destination. The old four wheel drive car managed alright on the first part of the trip but then the oil warning light started flashing and so we had to give the car a little rest by the side of the road. A forced refreshment break for us all.

Close to where we were parked I saw a young woman sitting on a bench with a small child of about two years old, and I went over to take a photo of them. That was a mistake … Suddenly, out of nowhere there appeared a wall of big men surrounding the child, and they speedily escorted both mother and child into an expensive-looking car standing nearby, and then accelerated away. I stood staring into the distance after the disappearing vehicle, completely dumbfounded. I could not understand what had just happened.

Pastor Lozano's wife came over to me and explained that the entourage were actually bodyguards, as the little one was the child of a local millionaire. They probably thought I was taking a photo in preparation for a kidnap attempt by the mafia, by whom that area was controlled.

The wisdom of travelling with the pastor began to dawn on me. He had managed to get his old car driveable again by adding a full can of oil and doing some mysterious mechanical stuff under the bonnet. But he explained that we should do our best not to stop at all again during the rest of the journey, but just keep driving, or else the car probably wouldn't start again. So the last leg of the trip was quite peculiar: when we drove through villages or small towns, the pastor would speed along side streets to avoid halts and traffic jams, and sometimes he even used the pavements.

Balungao

As we got close to the pastor's home town of Balungao, I suddenly developed a horrible back ache, probably because of the draught and the endless sitting down. The previous day we had been on an airplane for eight hours and the following night we had had the sauna therapy, courtesy of our hotel room's AC unit. My back just said, "No more, thank you" and it locked: I could not bend in any direction at all and pain shot through my back all the time. "Oh well, this is really what I needed," I complained to myself.

After we had reached our accommodation, the other ladies told Pastor Lozano what had happened to me, and he immediately came to ask if he could pray for me. I tried to explain politely how I would be fine after a decent night's sleep and that I would manage … A Finnish woman with *sisu* does not complain but just stands and copes with whatever pains and difficulties may come along.

163. Pangasinan church

The pastor ignored my Finnish stubbornness, laid his hand on my lower back and prayed. I felt heat coming in the place where the pain was worst, and something there eased … Soon the pain was gone, as Jesus once again healed this 'jar of clay'. We were quite a bunch of wounded soldiers – first Lea's ribs, now my back and finally Lucy suffered twice from kidney stones. But God doesn't focus on our ailments and weaknesses – He has promised to be strong when we feel weak (2 Corinthians 12:9-11).

One night after returning to our room when the evening meeting was over, I went to take something out of my suitcase. I bent down and was just about to open the case when, out of the corner of my eye, I saw something move. With an instant reflex I shot my foot sideways and stepped upon the little intruder with an unpleasant scrunch.

On examining the result I found a large, black flat blot, being the remains of a funnel-web spider. This creature, the size of someone's palm, is one of the most dangerous spider species, and its poison can kill a child in 15 minutes. I had learned to identify it in New South Wales and also learned this reflex action: react to everything that moves, by hitting first and only later investigating what it is. This one had come in through the open window, as there wasn't any netting to prevent unwanted guests.

Funnel-web spiders live especially in mountain areas, where we now were, and they like to make their nests among clothes. This fellow didn't quite manage to make its way into my suitcase, and from that time onwards I made sure that the zip stayed well closed.

164. Children at Ron's church

During the night I woke up as I felt someone with many legs making its way up my leg. Again like a lightning I was up, jumping up and down in the bed, waving and flapping the sheets – but I found nothing. In the morning I woke up beside a flat lizard as my extra bed-mate: he appeared to have suffered an accident.

Pastor Lozano had arranged a good programme of meetings and he divided us into three groups to allow more congregations to have the unusual benefit of hearing a foreign preacher. I went in one direction and Lucy in the other. We also held ad hoc meetings in different places, mainly in the evenings but also during the daytime.

BARACBAC

In a village called Baracbac many of the inhabitants belonged to the NPA. We decided to visit there without any advance warning so that nobody could prepare an ambush to kidnap these foreigners coming to visit.

Wherever we went, it was always the kids who were the first ones to gather around us, in their natural curiosity over new things. This village wasn't any exception and soon there were more and more children around us coming to listen to the music and singing. I told them the message of Jesus, and

Lea and Princess sang songs and taught them singing games. The local kids were thrilled and soon there were also adults there too – more than a hundred listeners, who all answered the call for salvation. I also got to know some of the NPA men and it felt surrealistic to be finally fulfilling my dream of preaching the gospel to the terrorists. Once again the kids had opened the way for us and softened the hearts of the adults.

> **finally fulfilling my dream of preaching the gospel to the terrorists**

On our journey back we drove in the dark along the sandy road, often totally covered by grass or disappearing in the middle of vegetation, or changing to a muddy pot-holed track full of holes. I asked Pastor Ron if he had ever had dangerous situations on such journeys as this. He told me how his life had many times been on a knife edge when gunmen had come out of the bushes and stopped his car, intending to rob and kill him.

On one occasion when he was ambushed, Pastor Lozano told the NPA men that he was only a local pastor on a preaching trip and the men recognised his name. They had heard of healings that had happened in that area through this pastor's work, so what was the point in killing him? Maybe he might be of help to them one day if they or their families fell sick. So they let him keep his life and freedom … but that very same night someone else had become their victim. A body was found next morning by the side of the road at exactly the same spot where the pastor was stopped the evening before.

Pastor Lozano explained to us that he was always careful to be very alert on this road, as it was always possible that somebody might attack you from the bushes. There was a lot of witchcraft in the area too and the local people were very superstitious: they took particular care in showing us the exact spots on the road where murdered people had been found. Whatever the reason was behind the killings, whether ritual murders by occultists or robberies by terrorists, the local people didn't want to travel after dark, so we tried to arrange the meetings mainly in the daytime.

THE LORD OPENED A WELL

We also visited a church founded by Pastor Lozano, next to which we could see a well-watered and productive rice field. At the back of the church there was a pump on top of a well and water was constantly running from it, supplying plenty of irrigation for the paddy field. I knew that during rainy seasons many parts of the Philippines suffered from floods but in the dry season there were often water shortages in this area, and sometimes not even enough for drinking. So why on earth were they wasting precious water by letting it run like this? I asked the pastor if the well pump was broken or why it was that the water was just running out to the field.

He answered that this was "The Miracle Well", given by God in a totally waterless area. When the church was built, they couldn't find any water at all anywhere and the congregation decided to gather together and pray that the Lord would do a miracle by giving them plenty of water for drinking and for the

165. The Miracle Well

rice fields. A paddy field needs enormous amounts of water to yield a good crop of rice. God did exactly that and water started to bubble from the ground exactly in the place where the believers had prayed. The only problem was that they could not stop the water from flowing – so they channelled it into the fields, and that's why it looked so fruitful and productive.

It's difficult enough to find any underground water for wells and when you do, the water coming out can often be undrinkable, but the output from this miracle well was absolutely clear, clean drinking water.

Even though the NPA had officially granted safety to the pastor, there were still some unpleasant surprises now and then. There were men in the area who either pretended to be NPA or who had been expelled from it because of territorial disputes and the like. These violent men operated at night and wore the familiar camouflage uniforms, so you could never be sure if they were real NPA, a fringe group or soldiers of the Philippines army. In the beginning NPA men tried to demand 30,000 pesos (€450) of 'safety money' from the pastor but it soon became obvious that he didn't have that sort of money, so the problem was solved in a different way. Each of his congregations was obliged to give the terrorists sacks of rice and to feed them, to show that they were on the NPA side and not against them. Many villages and small towns too had to buy their freedom through such 'donations' whether they wanted to or not.

CHAPTER *32*
RETURN TO MAMBURAO

BACK TO MANILA

After our visit to the north of the Philippines, we travelled back to Manila in the pastor's car. To make sure I would manage this time without my back seizing up, I claimed the back seat to myself and lay down for part of the journey.

But we didn't stay in the capital for long. Pastor Lozano and his wife wanted to come with us and visit Occidental Mindoro and the Mamburao school, and this suited us fine. We shared the travel costs with Lucy but in Mindoro she ran out of money, so I then paid for her motel room. Our financial resources were starting to get low, except for the amount that the Lord had told me to keep back for something special – even though we had no clue what that might be.

> **our financial resources were starting to get low**

Pastor Lozano's wife fell sick while we were in Mindoro with a stomach complaint and had to rest in bed. I often wondered how it was that these illnesses, aches and pains seemed to circulate around our group. Well, at least it wasn't just us foreigners who were getting ill in the tropics! Stomach problems were always close by, and just drinking bottled water didn't prevent it because the food was prepared in

221

unboiled water and it was the same for the water used for washing the dishes. Whatever we did, at least once on every journey we got a good internal clean out …

AROMA VILLAGE

Back in Mamburao, we decided to feed the children and hold meetings in three new areas, so we formed a plan of who would do what and where. The idea was to feed hundreds of children in different areas of the countryside. Once again the ladies of the congregation were mobilised for preparing the meals and Pastor Sonio travelled around telling people about the times of the meetings. Pastor Lozano and his wife were excellent in playing games with the kids and preaching the gospel. Of course they had a lot of experience from running their own school of 100 kids.

One of the new places we went to was a village known as Aroma, which is part of Mamburao but is separated from the rest of the town by a river. This

166. Feeding children in Aroma

time there were around two hundred excited kids present and Pastor Sonio got them to sing and play games, and we went through our usual programme. Lea's daughter sang and I preached: every one of the children wanted to belong to Jesus, so we prayed for them and Sonio carefully explained to them what it means to be saved.

There were also adults who had come along to listen to the message of the Cross, and they too joined the queue to be prayed for: many had sicknesses and sorrows burdening them. Pastor Sonio agreed with the village chief about opening a new Bible group in the village and how meetings would be arranged in the future. This meant that the kids would be taken care of too.

We closed with the food distribution and then played some more games. The children really didn't want to let us go – they ran around us and begged us to stay, while the darkness of the evening started to descend. But the mosquitoes were getting very busy around us and our Autan repellent didn't seem to be having any effect at all on this species. As the dark evening pulls in, so the dengue and malaria flies get more active. It was wisest to escape quickly, because neither Lea nor myself can take anti-malarial preventative medication.

After another trip a lot later, I fell ill with Ross River fever – another tropical disease that is spread by mosquitoes. I suffered from the symptoms for about five months afterwards, but nothing could prevent me from continuing to travel. I seemed to get more pain at night and this was often accompanied by a high fever. But I continued to press forward with Finnish *sisu*, determined that I wasn't going to let it get the better of me. I refused to give up, and bit by bit the disease gave up on me.

167. *Boys from Aroma*

During that time, for some strange sort of reason, I was always completely fine when I stood up in the pulpit to preach, even though just beforehand as I sat in my seat waiting for my turn to come, I felt that I was going to die. After a couple of minutes of reeling around in the pulpit, I suddenly would feel absolutely fine … until I went back to my accommodation after the meeting and the fever hit again. Probably it was the anointing from God that kept me up.

Later in Australia I visited my dentist, who is an unbeliever. She said she had also fallen ill with Ross River fever at the same time as I did. She wondered how on earth I recovered from it so quickly and so well, as she had had to go to hospital twice during the half year that she was recuperating. I told her that I have recovered three times from cancer, once from fibromyalgia and once from paralysis, not to mention many other diseases: so a dose of Ross River is a minor ailment in comparison! We might have different weaknesses but when we let God be our strength, we always win through in everything. It is important to hang on to Jesus' completed victory and to shout to Satan, the father of sicknesses: "It is finished!"

NEW OPPORTUNITIES

I also spent some time going around Mamburao trying to find a new building for the school as our current place had become too small for 110 kids. The children didn't complain but the Ministry of Education had issued a warning that the building was unsuitable for such a big group. So far they had let us continue in these small premises, mainly because of our friendly school inspector who was a believer, but now it was urgent that we find a bigger building.

168. Mamburao school

Pastor Sonio told me that Santa Cruz town had asked for help as they had seen how fruitful our project in Mamburao had been and how the town was getting free from the influence of the terrorists.

There was a large garbage dump community in Santa Cruz and a slum area full of children with no chance at all of going to school. The newly elected senator of Santa Cruz was a believer and he really wanted to get both a school and a church established in his town. He had been a pastor before he had been elected to the senate, but now he was excluded from holding both offices simultaneously as his church's rules said that church and politics could not fit together.

This believing politician felt that spiritual work was vital in the area, even though he himself could no longer play a part in it. He wanted us to set up a church where kids and slum inhabitants could come after they had become believers, and he asked me to found a school with a similar programme to the one in Mamburao.

> **Palawan Island had been very much in my thoughts**

I asked the Lord what I should do. Was this the new project that the Lord meant? I did not get a clear answer, so I resolved to decide later, maybe back in Australia. But the Lord had something else in mind. Palawan Island had been very much in my thoughts but it felt like the way there was blocked. These thoughts wouldn't leave me and it was the same for Lea. We gazed at the map of the Philippines and saw that it was only possible to travel to Palawan through Manila. But the most important thing was to find a contact person.

I knew that I would establish a new school but where? Was it going to be on Palawan Island? From a human perspective, starting a new school was a foolish idea, but my view is that if you never step out of your boat and onto the waves, you'll never get to know whether they'll hold you up.

Santa Cruz wasn't a green light right now, maybe it would be later. There was absolutely no money for the new school – but that was the same as when we founded Mamburao school. When the Lord sets us a task, He takes care of the resources if we open the door and start doing the job. This time I was sure that the door was going to open to a much bigger task. We usually don't see our destiny puzzle ready made – more often than not we take it just one piece at a time, with every piece being a step of faith.

169. A full church

This was the first trip on which we had all been ill one after another, but the hardships just make me push forward with even more *sisu*. If there's no hassle in front of me and around me, I start asking the Lord if I am on a detour from the main route He has for me. Is the enemy taking a rest and agreeing with me? God certainly does grant us times of rest and blessing, but before we can undertake any substantial task we'll probably need to break through some pretty tough obstacles.

SCHOOL KIDS CELEBRATE CHRISTMAS

The children's Christmas celebration in Mamburao was a real victory. People couldn't fit into the church and had to stay outside. That is why the Mayor promised that the town would let us have a bigger place for free for next Christmas' celebration, as he promised the year before. The whole town wanted to see the children's performance as it meant so much to them to see what amazing progress these poor small children had made. At the same time the celebration gave us a good opportunity to preach the gospel to everybody.

The kids had made a drama of the birth of Jesus, and each and everyone had a part to play in it. Most of them were angels, with wings made

tears in the eyes of many adults

of cardboard and covered by cotton wool. The floor of the church was soon covered by bits of cotton wool which flew in the air like snow after every flapping of the little wings. There were tears in the eyes of many of the adults as

225

they watched the children's performance. The transformation of these rejected slum kids into school pupils was so striking. Probably the most touching moment was the prayer of a small child at the beginning of the feast, where he burst into tears when giving thanks to Jesus from the bottom of his heart for the chance to go to school. This prayer was a complete inspiration – not only the child cried but so did the audience.

170. *The boy who prayed*

NEW AREA AND NEW KIDS

Again we met with a new group of children, in another slum area. The whole coastline is full of such villages where families of fishermen live at a subsistence level. There we sang, played games and preached about the saving power of Jesus Christ.

Mrs Lozano taught the children a new game, which involved putting them in teams and having a race to see which team could sprint from where they left their sandals to over the finishing line on the other side. The team that was fastest to regroup into a long line got the prize. Some of the children stripped down to the bare essentials, so keen were they to win the competition.

Mrs Lozano had also worked in an orphanage which had specialised in twins. In the Philippines some primitive tribes still believe that when a mother gives birth to twins, then one of them has an evil spirit and the other one is free from it. After the decision of who is the cursed one, that child is then abandoned in the forest or killed. The pastor's wife and her fellow workers tried to locate these rejected kids from the mountains and bring them to their orphanage. Occasionally mothers would leave one of their twin babies at the orphanage. The workers visited families if they heard that twins had been born, and tried to persuade the parents to let them both live.

The custom was that if the mother died in childbirth while delivering twins, then both babies were killed because it was thought to be their fault. The orphanage was full of twins, children who were from twins or even triplets. I wondered what kind of criteria the people used to decide which baby was good and which one bad, but I never was given any explanation. On the other hand it became clear to me why I had never seen twins in the countryside. Just once I saw triplets and that was in Mamburao town.

BACK AGAIN TO MANILA

On the following day we held a morning meeting and then started our journey again back towards Manila. The wind was very heavy on the sea crossing and the ship was tossed around more than usual, so much so that Princess got sea-sick and also I felt quite queasy. The wind gusted through the whole ferry and we hadn't thought to take warm clothes with us, as it had been so hot and sultry in the harbour. Sea winds are so very unpredictable in the archipelago area – they can arise without any warning at all.

When we finally got to our familiar accommodation in the mission centre of Mount Moriah, after a couple hours crawling through the city traffic jams, it felt like heaven to us. The only thing that spoiled my joy was a sore feeling in my throat caused by the sea wind and the draughts through the car windows. Happily I had antibiotics in my bag.

In the Philippines you can freely buy as many antibiotics as you want, as they are available to everybody over the counter in each pharmacy. So I normally kept some in my bag, ready for use. The people living in the tip areas and slums were always in need of them, as they never had enough money for food and definitely could not afford medicines. Often mothers would beg us for medicines for their sick children or relatives, with tears streaming from their eyes. The children suffered from severe infections, malaria, or TB and this was the least I could do. Now the antibiotics came in useful for me also.

WHERE NEXT?

The accommodation at Mount Moriah was full, and there was not enough room for all of us, so Pastor Lozano and his wife slept in their car. Lucy's flight to Australia was due to leave in the morning but Lea and I had a few days longer. The pastor would have wanted us to come back up north with him to evangelise the mountain tribes, but Lea and I had decided to do something else. We were going to Palawan.

Palawan Island is shaped like a sword, the point of which is towards Borneo. That was a place where I certainly wanted to go, but first we would need to conquer Palawan. The only problem was that we did not know anybody from there. Lea had met a Filipino teacher called Julie in Japan and she understood that her relatives lived in Palawan. Lea had occasionally written to Julie, so we wondered if she would become our contact point and a gateway to the island.

Lea had this lady's email address written in her note book, so she sent her an email and included our mobile number just to make it even easier for her to contact us. Then the only thing we could do was to wait. If this initiative was from the Lord, then the way would open up, if it wasn't then we would go to North Luzon again.

171. Beleni

The answer came straight back: Julie was so happy that somebody wanted to go to Palawan. Her sister Beleni, also a believer, was a social worker in the capital city, Puerto Princesa, and offered to meet us at the airport if we would let her know which flight we were taking.

Julie also sent us Beleni's mobile number. We quickly agreed about flight times, ordered the tickets and eagerly awaited the start of this new adventure. Beleni promised to arrange a tour through the tip areas of the city where she worked among the children, and if we wanted, we could also visit the surrounding islands.

She made it clear that we were very welcome and that people were really looking forward to our visit.

God was opening the door to Palawan.

CHAPTER *33*
PALAWAN

GOD'S PLAN

Because Palawan was opening up so quickly to us, I knew that this was the place that the Lord had arranged for us. It also became clear why He had told me to keep aside some extra money – it would be enough to pay for a few feeding operations and trips on the island. However the amount of money was so small that we felt compelled to eat only rice in this last part of our trip. This is what almost always happened on our journeys: very often in the last week we had to use our imaginations to fill our stomachs.

172. Palawan

PUERTO PRINCESA

Palawan Island looked so beautiful as we gazed out from the windows of the airplane as it approached Puerto Princesa. The island was like a green diamond inlaid into the azure sea. At last we were coming to the island that God had placed on my heart.

Owwww! A flashing pain stabbed my left ear. The small plane had to wait for permission to land and it circled around the airport for maybe another fifteen long minutes, while the fall in the air pressure in the cabin was causing me ear ache at totally new levels. The throat infection I had managed to kick off but this ear infection, or whatever it was, had crept in secretly. I pressed a pillow against my face and shouted. Lea passed me another pillow, saying, "You scream so loudly!" Owww, if only this plane would land **nowww**! Owww, owwww!!

But all the pain disappeared as soon as we landed, and we were delighted to find Beleni waiting for us at Palawan airport with some young people from her church.

173. *Welcoming band*

There was even a brass band there that the city had hired to welcome everyone coming to visit the island. The city was trying to attract tourists to the island and had renovated the area of the city bordering the seashore into a beautiful boulevard. They were also very proud of having the biggest Christmas tree in the whole of the Philippines.

We were really surprised to see that there was no litter in the city of Puerto Princesa. The Mayor was a real character … he had introduced waste-bins and the collection of rubbish really worked well. But how on earth had he managed to persuade the citizens to put their litter in the bins? The answer was very simple: every litter-dropper was punished so severely that nobody wanted to throw anything down on the streets. If somebody dropped litter they were fined and it increased for every offence. On the third time the fine was 5000 pesos (€80) which was more than a poor worker earned during the whole year … and on the fourth time the person would go to jail. That worked so well that the city was much cleaner than many western cities are.

I suggested the same system should be adopted in Manila but my friends told me that it really wouldn't work there, as there are millions of poor people who do not have a home. The litter bins would immediately be taken to be used as shelters by the poor. What an amazing plastic home it would make, with even a lid for a roof – much better than just a piece of metal over your head. In Manila the garbage collection trucks visited areas on certain days of the week but there was so much rubbish on the streets that the task was impossible. As they emptied one pile, so new mountains of plastic bags would appear within seconds.

The boulevard in Puerto Princesa had been built in place of the former slum area, which had caught fire and burnt down. Instead of letting the slum-dwellers reconstruct their shacks and sheds in the same place, the city built them flats somewhere else. So the city centre area became clean and relatively crime-free at a stroke, and people dared once again to walk along the sea shore.

Further away from the city, the shore was still covered by long rows of squatters' shacks but the Mayor's plan was to get rid of those that were close to the centre and to give their inhabitants better homes to live in. I do not know how well that had worked, but at least the rubbish and effluent had disappeared from the city.

John Wimber used to tell of how he had been brought up in a slum area that had subsequently been pulled down and new better homes built for the poor people. His family had moved away from the area and years later, when he happened to be passing through, he was astonished to see the new area looking as miserable as before. He commented that a person can be given a new place to live, but if their mind has not been renewed, the new will quickly become similar to the old. It's the person that has to change first.

174. *Puerto Princesa boulevard*

Street children were still wandering around on the boulevard. Beleni knew almost all of them and urged them to go home or to their shacks or wherever it was they slept, as it was so late already. Some other social workers were also out on the streets, as their task was to gather these kids off the streets. The system seemed to work. Many of the kids had some sort of home but a violent one, so they were forced to beg on the streets for their food.

Beleni promised to take us to the worst areas, and also to the city tip area to see the community where a lot of children and adults lived. Also we

231

would visit a collection centre where they gathered kids that had been thrown out onto the streets, raped or otherwise mistreated. We had made contact with exactly the right person – the Lord is such a wonderful arranger of people and timetables.

> **Christians on Mindanao had systematically been killed**

The terrorists had caused disturbances even here, and there were also many Muslims and people who had fled the disorder on Mindanao Island, the closest island to Palawan. Mindanao was controlled by Muslim terrorists and the majority of the inhabitants were Muslims. Any Christians on Mindanao had systematically been killed or they had fled.

BELENI'S STORY

Beleni was a beautiful woman but later she showed me several scars around her body and even on her head, that she took care to cover. She explained that her family had been very poor and lived on Mindanao Island. The parents had to leave their two daughters at home alone when they went to try and find food for the family.

Once when Beleni was two years old and Julie five, they were cooking food over an open fire. Julie had put oil in the hot pan and Beleni was

175. *Island houses*

bending under the table when the hot oil pan fell from Julie's hands and the oil ran all over Beleni, covering her whole body and burning her skin so severely that she passed out. The neighbours heard the screaming and ran to help.

The family couldn't afford doctors, there was no hospital and no real medicines. But by sheer coincidence a military paramedic was visiting one of the neighbours and he was able to administer good first aid. However Beleni was burnt so severely that no one believed that she would survive.

Eventually Beleni came round from a deep coma and her mother nursed her with banana leaf dressings for over six months. The small children accepted her as she was, but when she went to school the bigger kids teased her saying how ugly she was and calling her names. Nobody wanted to play with her.

Beleni recounted to me how she became bitter because her older sister became more beautiful, and during High School the boys just laughed and mocked her own looks. She started to blame Julie for all her misery. Several years later Beleni sought comfort from church and became a believer, but she still had to go through her own struggle to be able to forgive. Yet God was faithful, and even though she was poor she somehow got enough money to study. Life was difficult with an ongoing battle with poverty, but she passed her final exams and graduated to be a social worker, deciding to dedicate her life to helping poor kids and families, as the Lord had been so merciful to her.

176. Local children

She didn't use her salary just for herself. The city had given her a small piece of land on a nearby island and she built a bamboo hut there for her parents and paid for their move from Mindanao to Palawan Island. She continued to pay her parents living expenses from her own salary.

Beleni's aunt and her children also lived in the same bamboo hut as her parents. The aunt herself had a horrific background. When she was a child and lived in Mindanao in a Christian village, Muslim terrorists had attacked the village and killed everybody, cutting their throats with swords. Some villagers tried to escape by boat but they were shot as they tried to get aboard. Her father and mother and her brothers and sisters were all murdered that night and she alone survived. Her mother had been breast feeding her when the terrorists attacked – they cut her throat and at the same time hit the baby on the head. Mother collapsed over the baby and the terrorists believed that their task was complete with everyone slaughtered, so they left.

Some of the villagers had hidden in the mountains, not daring to sleep in their homes and when they returned to the place of the massacre they found Beleni's aunt still alive under the corpse of her mother and they took her to safety. The Muslim terrorists systematically slaughtered all the Christians village by village as part of their jihad.

The villagers were simple farmers and poor fishermen, who knew nothing of politics let alone of a religion that sought to execute those who did not follow it. Nobody understood the horrendous rage that the Muslims had against the Christian minority, who posed no threat to them economically or politically. People lived in anguish and fear, and those who could fled to Palawan Island, away from the violence and terrorism.

Beleni's aunt, who now was an adult, never recovered from the trauma. Her head constantly ached, she had suffered a nervous breakdown and she behaved weirdly. She could not manage without help from other people. I heard many similar stories in Palawan from people that had escaped from Mindanao.

Before my work in the Philippines started, the Lord had shown me some islands, one of which was Mindanao as the last point in the archipelago. At that time I didn't know its history, nor its current situation or how dangerous the island is even today. Yet I knew that the Lord had a plan for it.

MANGINGISDA

Beleni had arranged us a trip to the little island where her parents lived, where we would feed poor kids and preach the gospel to them. This time we would all be taking part in preparing the food.

177. Boat trip to Mangingisda

We caught a small ferry to this island, called Mangingisda, and it should not have been a very long crossing, but this time it took longer than we expected as a storm suddenly rose up on the sea. Princess started to get scared as the waves seemed to be getting mountainous and after every climb up there was the very scary drop down the other side. To distract Princess I created a game: when the boat climbed up to the top of a wave, Princess and I would shout "WoooOOOO!" and when it crashed down we screamed "WOOOOooo … Bang!" There were about fifty passengers altogether on board and eventually everyone ended up joining us in the game. The full boat-load of people were shouting with us as if it were a competition to see who could shout the loudest.

234

When we finally reached the harbour, the local passengers laughingly explained to the people on the small ferry going in the opposite direction what great fun they had had with these funny foreigners, pointing at us. In reality the trip hadn't been fun at all and our stomachs were still very shaken up, with all the "woooos" up and "bangs" down, but at least Princess had enjoyed it.

We bought the ingredients to make the meal for the kids and set to work. Lea and I shelled more than one hundred boiled eggs and from time to time went out to stir the big pots boil-

178. Mass food preparation

ing on open fires outside the building, containing some sort of thin rice porridge, which to my mind looked suspiciously like mucus. Mixed in it was lemongrass herbs and sugar to make it more tasty, and when it was ready, the eggs were mashed and mixed in. I wondered who would possibly want to eat that sort of

mixture, but unfortunately we didn't have the money for any better food. Beleni said this was a common local food and many of the kids would not get even this basic meal every day, and often went hungry.

About 200 kids and plenty of adults gathered to listen to us and we preached the gospel. This was the first time that anything like this had happened in the area and once again the Word of God was well received, with even the adults wanting to become believers. Beleni's testimony was particularly moving – she really knew how to speak to these people because she herself had been brought up in a slum.

After this we started to distribute the food. Everyone received a paper mug

179. This tastes good

filled with the rice-and-egg mixture and the kids came back to ask for more. One little boy plucked my T-shirt, held out his mug and said: "This is **soooo** good,

235

can I have some more?" I wondered if I was getting too fussy about food so I plucked up courage and tasted it. I was amazed because it really **was** good!

The kids almost fought over the pieces of egg because there were not enough for every mug. They followed very carefully the distribution of the food to see who got some pieces in their mugs.

Batantay Centre

Next morning back on the mainland of Palawan, we visited an orphanage with boxes of food for the children. The Batantay Centre was a temporary shelter for

street kids, consisting of a building with a few rooms and a shed outside, where kids were collected from the streets. Their ages varied from 3 years up to 13. The city tried to relocate them to foster homes or worked as an intermediary between the parents and bigger kids to try and place them back in their own homes.

That year there had been altogether 72 children, out of whom 30 were still in that temporary shelter home and of course new ones would appear when brought in from the streets. We distributed food to these thirty and again I talked about Jesus.

These kids were different from the ones on the day before – many of them were traumatized and joyless. A small flicker of hope was kindled in the eyes of the small-

180. Boys at Batantay

est ones when I read the "My Heaven" book to them. Some of the older boys made the sign of the cross on their chests according to catholic tradition when we prayed, and they wept silently and assured us that they wanted to know Jesus as their Saviour.

The City Dump

From the Batantay home for street kids we continued our journey towards the rubbish tip outside the city. On our way we popped in to the YWAM centre to meet the people working there. I really honour these young YWAM workers who trek into the mountain areas, walking as much as nine hours to reach and preach the gospel to the Mangyan tribes.

In the YWAM center we also met two young Mangyans who had become believers and wanted to go to Bible school. One of them, a young woman, was in difficulties because her tribe wanted her back in their Mangyan village, as they had found her a husband and were telling her to stop studying at Bible school. The girl didn't want to get married but the word of the tribe is law and she knew she would never be able to return to her village if she did not obey. At the same time it was a big problem for the YWAM organisation if they wanted to continue to do outreach in the girl's village.

The tip community area surrounded a massive rubbish hole, in an area known as Red Mountain because of the red sand there. The local kids started to gather around us and we had kept a hundred food portions for them. They wore dirty ripped T-shirts, found from among the rubbish, and often their clothes were so ragged that they hardly stayed on their shoulders.

Some adults also came to meet us and we could see that many of the mothers were actually young but looked untimely old, and carried in their arms children many

181. Mother & baby at the dump

of whom looked ill. One of the babies looked like a couple of months old, with such a tiny little head and limbs, but actually the child was already two years old. Everyone was dirty and some of the mothers begged us to give them antibiotics for their children, so of course I handed out the small amount that I had with me.

Beleni whispered that many of the kids were victims of incest but it was best not to ask any more, as the most important thing was that the children dared to come to the meeting. Beleni spoke to them about her own childhood and I preached to the kids and any adults who had come to listen. We were in a shed that the AOG Church had built there, with a sign on one side of the roof saying: "Tip Church"

The shed was filled with kids and as so often happened they really lived along with the stories that I told them of Jesus and of heaven. I explained to

237

them the message of salvation and asked them to place their hands over their hearts if they wanted to be owned by Jesus. All of them did and so did the adults and they prayed with me the sinner's prayer, with tears running down their dirty cheeks. The Holy Spirit moved among them and as I watched I thought how much Jesus must love these little ones.

One small boy wouldn't take his hand away from his heart even when we had finished and I asked him why. He looked at me in a serious way, saying, "I am keeping hold of my heart so that Jesus will stay there and won't escape." I had told them that Jesus comes to live in their hearts. This same boy had sat right in front of me and stared at me all the time that I preached, sucking in my every word.

Later Beleni asked the kids if they had understood the teaching and urged them to ask us anything they wanted to know about heaven and about

182. Good food at the dump church

the story in the book. A small boy asked me a serious question: "Did you see my friend Joel there?" I answered, "There were so many children and I do not know what Joel looks like!" This answer seemed to satisfy the boy.

Other questions followed quickly, such as: "Do children fight with each other in heaven?" and "Do my teeth get holes in heaven?" The children wanted to keep looking at the pictures of the "My Heaven" book, and more questions kept coming up.

In the end we distributed the food. Some children were so astonished to see the food, that they didn't dare to touch it ... they just stared at the food box. One tiny little three year old just looked so embarrassed at the food box that had arrived in her lap, until it slipped onto the ground. Even then she didn't cry about the accident. The boy next to her carefully collected her box from the ground, gathered the chicken pieces and rice back into it with some pieces of soil and placed it back in her lap. What did it matter what the food looked like when they were used to digging their daily food out from among the rubbish?

The portions in the boxes were a banquet meal to them, even if there was a bit of soil there too. When we left the place this same little girl was still standing there with the box in her hand, staring at us as if she were in a trance. Maybe we were the first white people that she had ever seen.

STREET CHILDREN

On one of our sea trips our small boat wasn't able to come right in to the shore, so we rolled up the legs of our trousers and waded with our bundles to the beach. Such paddling was an interesting experience as the island was famous for its tame fish that would immediately swim around your legs and even let you touch them. Princess got excited and ran in the water trying to catch them. Suddenly there was a scream and she started crying, for she had stepped on a sharp coral, and now her foot was bleeding.

There was no doctor on the island so we just tried to clean the wound as well as we could and then took turns to carry her on our backs. Next day she was hopping around on one leg as the foot had become infected during the night. For the moment, prayer together with local first aid had to be enough.

183. Getting on board again

Finally we found out where there was a doctor's surgery in the city of Puerto Princesa. We found the building but when we went in, the receptionist told us that the doctor was on holiday. Lea wanted to have her daughter's foot examined as sometimes coral can be like a piece of glass and you can have a tiny splinter of it in the wound without realizing it. Suddenly the doctor walked into reception as he had forgotten some papers and had come back to pick them up. When he heard why we were there, he examined Princess's foot and gave her a rabies injection.

Within a couple of days the foot was better but then Princess got an ear infection, probably the same that I had suffered from. This was the first trip where all of us suffered time and again, one after another, from all sorts of pains and infections. But we had decided that nothing was going to stop us – we would press forward even if we had to crawl, or maybe even hop like Princess.

239

Beleni belonged to a small church called Christlife, mainly composed of young people like herself. One of the members, Daniel Lebante, was a school teacher and he was very gifted in interacting with poor children, as he came from a very poor background himself. He told me how he had had to sell coal by the roadside to pay his way through high school.

184. Daniel Lebante

Daniel helped us get ready for the last meeting that we were going to hold for the street kids. This time the group of children that gathered were quite wild and restless, and it took us a little while before we managed to gather them together in one place and get them to stay there. Daniel got the kids to play games and sing together until all their extra energy had been run and jumped out of them, so they finally quietened down and listened to my message.

Again it was eagerly received – the children asked about Jesus and wanted to become believers. In the end we again gave them food. Now we had spent all the money that we had, and nothing was left. We had our tickets for the flight back to Manila and from there to Australia, but there were no pesos left to live on in Manila or to buy food for ourselves.

Chapter 34
A New School

Free?

Beleni invited us to talk through the school situation with a group of young people from Christlife Church, including social workers and a couple of teachers.

At first they seemed suspicious and not at all enthusiastic about the prospect of a new school, and I didn't understand why. I later learned that they had experienced problems with another church organisation that had tried to take them over and bring them into line with their own teachings and doctrines. This left them naturally reticent of other potential take-overs.

185. Christlife church

So once again I went through the whole thing with this group of young professionals and emphasised that this was nothing insidious, but I just wanted there to be a **free school** aimed at children of the tip area and the slums. Next morning things had changed – they told me that they had finally grasped the concept and were now so excited that they had found it almost impossible to sleep. Their earlier stumbling block was that they found it so very difficult to understand that somebody was actually offering something without requiring payment. There was already a private Christian school in the city but it was an expensive one, so no poor child could possibly attend it.

Now the school issue was agreed on, and the next step would be to find a suitable building for the school.

A BUILDING

This group of about fifteen or so young people had for some time been gathering to hold meetings in an old building owned by a believer. That house was on the market, it had a good big yard with fences around it and there was also play park equipment ready for use. An American missionary had given the equipment to the owner of the plot as a gift when he left the country. There were no

playgrounds for kids in the area, so local children had come to ask when this park would be opened, thinking it was a public one. "Now this would be a good place for a school," I thought.

The building itself was in such poor condition that it was of no use as a school. Small larvae had eaten the bamboo walls soft and the hay roof let the water in. Chadwick Abdullah, one of the pastors at Christlife Church, went to negotiate with the owner, asking if he would rent the building and the piece of land to us. The man wanted to sell it but it was far too expensive, and I didn't have the funds for that.

186. Pastor Chadwick

I was just about to give up the whole idea when the man suddenly sent a message to me, "You can use this land and the building free, without any rent at all." I asked if we could build a new building instead of the old decaying one, as the owner would get more benefit from such a deal than we would. The plot had been on the market for a long time, but nobody in the city seemed to have enough money (a few million pesos) to buy it, and neither did we.

We came to an agreement that we would make the new building the same size as the old one. I decided that, even if the land would be sold after some years, I would still have paid less than if I had been renting, because rentals on big buildings in the city area were expensive. I believed that the Lord would do a miracle before the land would be sold and we would get our very own piece of land for the school, as the Lord always works things through to the right conclusion when He assigns a task.

My young friends asked if we could accept Muslim children to the school if they were poor enough or fatherless. Religion doesn't mean anything in those circumstances, the only thing that matters is to be able to go to school. Wow! This was more than I could hope for. All kids were welcome, we would have only one criteria for entry – the child had to be poor, miserable and homeless, or they could be in a home if it was in the rubbish tip or in the slum.

I understood that the Lord was about to open a totally new avenue for us and new challenges, as I talked with these young people. They told that a couple of them had just left for a mission trip to Burma! That got me excited! I was approaching my goals and Burma had been one of them for quite some time. Innocently I asked if I could accompany them on their next trip. They looked at me rather weirdly, as if they were evaluating me, so I interrupted: "Well, OK, how about the time after that?"

I don't believe that they were wondering what this Granny was going to do on such a trip … but the situation was very complicated. I looked far too different from the Burmese local population. Burma is a closed country for the gospel and my white skin would endanger even their lives. Filipinos do not physically differ from Burmese people so they would find it much easier to move around inside the country without anyone noticing them. I do believe that one day God will mess up Burma and that the door will open. Everything is possible for Him.

We started the school business immediately. Unfortunately I didn't have any money left for the registration fees of the school so that I could pay it there and then. But I promised to send it through soon, as well as money for the new school building, providing they would estimate how much it would cost when using old materials as far as possible in the building work.

Money Miracle

Lea looked at me doubtfully but didn't say anything until we were back in our accommodation. "This school thing is wonderful," she said, "but tell me where we are going to get the money for the building from, as we don't even have money for food?" Building up a school really was a huge task and for a while I wondered

about the wisdom of what I had just promised. But I knew that the Lord had everything ready. I was not giving empty commitments: I promise only when I am absolutely sure that God is behind it. Of course I didn't have any written document in my hand, signed with His seal, but only faith. But faith builds a bridge between heavenly and earthly things, and if one never starts walking along that bridge into God's possibilities, then nothing ever gets achieved.

> **where are we going to get the money from?**

While at our accommodation we received a text message on Lea's mobile, from Manila where someone I didn't know wanted to meet me. Lea asked me how she should answer. I said, "Tell the truth, maybe he is a tourist … say that we will be living next to the rubbish tip in Manila, and we have no money even to eat. Anyway, that is the truth." Lea sent the text message and soon the answer came: "I will provide the food, just tell me where and when we can meet." We started to laugh – at least we would get something to eat and this person certainly had a good sense of humour.

Next morning we flew back to Manila and went to meet this man. He offered us a meal and also for the two men that had given us a lift – Israel Forbes and another pastor from Mount Moriah mission centre, who had been going in the same direction. We looked a bit war-torn and weary after our long tour, and the second pastor was walking with a stick as he had just had a leg operation. Our group of soldiers didn't appear terribly noble, but at least we managed to stand up, and there was of course a big incentive in front of us: a good square meal.

Our new friend was a businessman who had lived in Manila for the past five years. He was a believer and had heard about our work in the Philippines. When he had looked up my mission schedule on our website, he realised that we were in Manila at the same time as he was. Through the website he had asked for and got our contact mobile number.

He asked us how much we were in need of money and how we were managing there. Immediately we both replied, "We don't need anything, thank you" That of course was not in line with our text message to his mobile – something which we totally forgot in that situation. But even though we looked miserable, we were not beggars.

At the end of the meal he gave me an envelope which I opened when I got back to Mount Moriah. How amazing, it contained exactly the sum of money that I needed to register the Palawan school! This gentleman was God's courier and the school project could now officially start.

Back Home

When I arrived back home in Brisbane, I sat down and drew up a budget for building the school in Palawan, as I had promised. I soon realised that without a miracle from God I would be up to my neck in debt.

I had received a small inheritance from my parents, so I decided to use that, if nothing else would show up. The inheritance wasn't very big, and I wanted to keep it for travelling costs and accommodation, since poor people often could not afford to accommodate us and we didn't want to be a burden to them.

Mount Moriah accommodation was not free either, as the school and Mission Center functioned out of donations, and every guest was expected to donate something. Its location suited us very well for our work. But at the end of our last trip we really didn't look (or even smell) much like the other guests: we do tend to get a bit squalid on these trips.

187. *Inside the old building*

I asked the Lord to give me wisdom and assurance if it was His will for me to pay for the school from my own money. If the plan to start the school was from the Lord, then of course there would also be the right money available.

Finance at the Right Time

Soon after my return from the Philippines I received a surprise guest – an old friend that I had not seen for a long time came to my house meeting. He passed over a small packet to me, saying that it was for the kids in the Philippines. Many people give me small gifts to bring to the children there, so I didn't pay any more attention to it and simply thanked him.

In the morning I opened my emails and there was a message from the Palawan group with a budget for the building. The amount of money needed

> **the Lord told him the exact sum of money**

felt really big and many anxious thoughts rushed through my mind. How would I ever manage this project? Anne Miettinen's personal funds would really not be enough for it. As I thought over the situation, I turned to the small packet that the previous day's visitor had given me, and opened it. Inside was a large amount of money piled in tidy bunches. I calculated how much in Australian dollars the building budget sent from Palawan would be, and recognised that it was **exactly** the same amount of money that was now lying on the table in front of me.

I called the donor, told him what had happened, and asked how he had got the idea to give me this sum of money. He told me that he had been praying, when the Lord told him the exact amount of money, to what purpose it should go, and that it should be given personally to me. This was how the Lord assured me that the Palawan project was His idea.

As the building project continued, a problem arose. About 80% of the building was complete but now the funds were used up. We had planned to use old materials as far as possible, but most of them turned out to be good for nothing or decayed. The sewage pipes too had corroded away and need-

188. School construction

ed to be totally renewed. Funds were also required for school tables, painting, and all the school equipment. The building group had really done a good job and everyone was volunteering in the project.

It was important to link together the church and the school for registration purposes, because according to the law in the Philippines the church is a charitable organisation. If the school were linked to it, that also would be handled as a charity. I needed to explain to Chad and his group why this approach was necessary, but at the same time wanted to assure them that I was not going to try and take over their church in the process: the church would stay independent and I would just look after the school organisation. A separate school would have to pay the state a large amount of taxes and also would have

246

to follow the rules obligatory for state schools – ones which these schools do not even follow themselves, because of lack of funds. Still the government makes draconian demands from foreign organisations, as they assume that all of them are rich.

The people in Christlife church had understandable reservations about linking the school with the church itself. After their bad experience with another Christian organisation, they were naturally reticent of anything that resembled a take over.

AGREEMENT IS REACHED

I wanted to be wise in the use of our funds: as the piece of land was not mine, I was wary about putting a lot of money into a building that I could lose at any time if the owner decided to sell the land. Also I was not able to pay the teachers the minimum salary demanded by the state, so their salaries needed to be smaller. All the teachers in Christian schools work as missionaries and with a smaller salary. Yet other private Christian schools still take fees from their pupils, in contrast to my schools which are totally free, as they are not meant for elite kids but for the poor ones, who have no other chance of going to school.

I wrote an email to the Christlife group explaining these matters, and shortly afterwards I received the following reply, "Anne, we will do what you want, we'll link the church and the school, we'll do whatever you need us to do, providing this project can go ahead."

So now the matter was clear and all was understood. Now the only problem was, where and how to meet the shortfall of funding. I prayed, asking God to arrange it so that I could send the funds to Palawan during the same week. Almost immediately after praying, I received a phone call from a friend who was on his way to Brisbane city for some reason, and wanted to meet me

189. Palawan mums & children

urgently. We exchanged greetings and our respective news and then my friend passed me an envelope, saying, "The Lord told me to give you this sum of

247

money to be used in your ministry. He told me it was urgent and I had to come over straightaway to meet you."

There it was again, the amount of money that I needed to meet our budget, and not a small amount either. I sent it off immediately to Palawan, as there were only two months left before the school was due to start. The Lord had now made it absolutely clear that the idea of starting the school in Palawan was from Him and that it was He who was taking care of all the needs. And indeed the building and all the school facilities were ready in time for the start of the term.

190. Visiting families

The young teachers of my school were eagerly at work – they contacted the city council office, asking what catchment area would be best for this project. The officials suggested the nearest area, so that the small children would not need to travel very far. When I was in Palawan, I had been observing this very same poor area, which was called Bagong Sikat (in English: Arise Anew).

We received favour from the leader of this village area, who happened to be a half Muslim but willingly allowed our teachers to visit his village, calling from hut to hut making evaluations, interviewing and deciding which of the kids and families were most in need of schooling. At the same time many other slum inhabitants were asking for a place for their kids in our school – the rumour about the new school was spreading fast.

Faith means being sure of the things we hope for and knowing that something is real even if we do not see it. (Heb.11:1)

248

PART SEVEN.
THREE SCHOOLS

191. Enjoying a school workbook

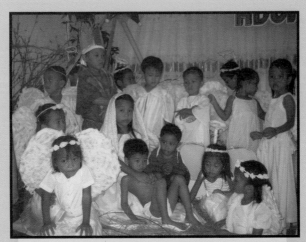

192. *Christmas celebration at Mamburao school*

193. *The new school building at Mamburao*

CHAPTER 35
GETTING TO MAMBURAO AGAIN

EXCITING NEWS

2008 was a busy year for me, but the work in the Philippines was never far from my thoughts, and I was longing to go back and see for myself what God was doing. In an email I received from Chad, he told me about the exciting changes that he and his team had seen in just the first three weeks of term at our school in Puerto Princesa:

> Hello Anne, how are you?
>
> I'm happy to share with you some latest updates regarding the school ministry.
>
> "I almost cried when I finally saw my son joining the line. I can't believe he is already in school." This was what a mother of one of the students shared with us.
>
> "My daughter reminded us when we didn't pray before we ate dinner. She insisted that we pray because her teachers told her to pray before meals." Another mother who happily shared an embarrassing yet funny moment during mealtime.
>
> "We want to know more about Jesus Christ." An answer when we

asked the parents what they expect from the meetings we require them to attend.

"We want to know how to become good parents to our children". Another answer from a parent during the parents' orientation program.

These words from the parents really give us encouragement and inspire all of us. These parents came from one of the most depressed and impoverished villages in Puerto Princesa. They live in shanties along the coastline. Their income averages $100 per month and is not regular. This is why we are so thankful that God has allowed this church, through your generosity, to provide free education for their children.

The school is approaching its 3rd week now and we are really seeing how the Lord has been orchestrating everything to bring glory to His name. You will see in the photos how the school is running. The children are learning both in academics and in their proper behaviour. They are taught how to be independent and yet submissive to authority. See how they set up their own place mats, spoons and forks. They are also receiving nutritious feeding. We thought it wise to provide snacks for the children since the parents cannot afford to provide healthy ones. We also find it wise to have a uniform snack for everyone to avoid comparing theirs with each other.

196. Our new school building at Palawan

You will also see that they are wearing uniforms already. The money you sent for the uniforms was surprisingly enough to produce for all of them. Thank you.

We thank you very much for all of your help and prayers. I will continue to update you as often as I can.

God bless you and stay blessed. Chadwick

ACCIDENTS CAN HAPPEN

The next opportunity to visit the Philippines came in December 2008. Once again I travelled with Lea and Princess and on 5th December our Qantas flight landed at Manila. The route had become very familiar to us and inside the airport I felt like I had never actually left the country: the same heat, same crowd … how weird, had I really been away from here at all?

I tried to manage my suitcases with only one hand because my left arm was out of action, following an accident that had occurred on my European trip of just a few weeks earlier. I had been praying for an elderly lady in a meeting, when she suddenly fell down and grabbed my left arm to try and steady herself. Down she went, and she pulled my arm so strongly downwards that some joints and muscles in my arm were injured. I couldn't raise my arm or use my hand even though the bones were not broken. After returning home to Australia the arm slowly started getting better, bit by bit, but that improvement didn't last long.

My husband Erno was renovating our old house and building a new terrace on one side of it. But the work was a long way from completion. Erno had built a structure with boards which would be supported in an upright position by four pillars. So far there were four deep round holes where the pillars were going to go. While I was busy outside I happened to step backwards and my right leg went straight down into one of these holes. I was well and truly stuck and, since there was nobody else at home to help me, I had to somehow find a way of pulling myself out on my own. The only hand hold available was on my left hand side, so my left arm took all my weight as I levered myself out of the hole. As a result the arm was wrecked again.

> **I was well and truly stuck**

I was like a wounded soldier who drags himself to the medical tent from the battlefield. My right leg quickly went black and blue and swelled to over twice its normal size, while my left arm got its revenge by sending pains like flashes of lightning through my body. But I am not one to give up. I determined that I was going to get on that plane to the Philippines, even if I had to crawl up the steps.

A couple of weeks after my fall, I was wandering around a shopping centre in Brisbane, along with all the other people who had crowded in to do their Christmas shopping. An older lady who was walking towards me suddenly stumbled – even though there was absolutely nothing on the ground for her to fall over – and she fell towards me hitting her head against my ribs and, would you believe it, grabbing my left hand in an attempt to keep up. For the third time my left arm was maimed, causing me such excruciating pain that it was very difficult to grit my teeth and give a sweet smile to the poor lady. She was so apologetic and wondered how on earth she could have stumbled like that on such an even floor. I wondered if there was some sort of glue on my left hand, as everyone seemed to grab it.

Because the arm wasn't fractured, it didn't prevent my journey, and at least one hand was still in use. I reminded myself that even coal can change into a diamond if put under a heavy pressure, so maybe I was now in the coal phase …

Fun in Manila

Good old Manila! We stayed there just one night and the next morning Lea woke up around 5 am and immediately wanted to get a taxi to Batangas harbour, from where the ferry would take us to Occidental Mindoro. I was hopelessly

197. *Loading the ferry to Mindoro Island*

tired after several nights of hardly any sleep, and my arm ached so much that I didn't want to move anywhere yet. But Lea pleaded with me, explaining that if we left now we would catch the morning ferry, which was leaving at 8am. I gave in and by six o'clock we were ready to go. Lea had found an old man to drive us to the harbour in his van, which was much easier for us than trying to get to the bus station with our seven suitcases. Lea had extra luggage with her as she planned to continue on to Japan straight from the Philippines, and she was needing winter clothes there. I wasn't of much help because a one-handed person could only cope with one small suitcase and a couple of hand bags.

When I saw the driver, I couldn't help thinking it was quite possible that he might die before we got to the harbour. Was he really the only one available? Weren't there any younger van owners around who could give us a lift?

Getting on the move this early was a big mistake, as everyone else had the same idea: we got stuck in the rush hour traffic while the heavens opened and rain poured down on us. Only a rally driver or someone with suicidal tendencies can manage in Manila traffic and our driver fitted neither category – he got stuck at every single road crossing. The city council had also decided to close a couple of the lanes on the road to Batangas, and half of Manila was trying to get into the only remaining lane, from every possible side road or street. Why had they started doing roadworks right now?

The trip became a real nightmare. Lea lay down on the back seat to try and sleep but complained that the air ventilation blew her hair up. I sat in front where there was no ventilation whatsoever – not even a breath of fresh, cool air. But someone had to sit there and sweat, to keep the driver awake as he told us he hadn't slept on the previous night.

The only thing that was travelling anywhere in that traffic jam was the exhaust fumes, and the noxious stuff forced its way in through all the possible cracks of the old car. The driver had tuberculosis, or at least it sounded like that. He coughed like his insides were coming out and then gathered the outputs in the handkerchief provided by nature – the palm of his hand, opened the window which was wet from the rain, and then wiped the mucus there. Quite useful as the rain would wash it slowly away without any effort. I tried to look in another direction, wondering which would kill me quicker, the tuberculosis or the exhaust fumes. My feelings were a mixture of pity and anger, as he would doze off when the van got stuck in traffic, then bark Tagalog swear words at the drivers jumping the queue, and at the same time cut in on other vehicles.

Of course the morning ferry left without us for Mindoro Island and we learned never again to try and get anywhere in the morning rush hour traffic in Manila. But we still had enough time to make our way to the next ferry leaving at noon. On our previous trip, that ferry had been cancelled, so there was an element of excitement as we waited for it. The ticket office was of no help either as they knew

> **the morning ferry left without us**

no more than we did. We called it a guessing centre: is the ferry coming – yes it is – oh no it isn't – maybe the evening one – oh look here it is!

FIRST MEETING

After almost three hours drive to the harbour, three hours wait for the ferry, more than two hours on the ferry crossing and then a further hour's driving we finally arrived in Mamburao town. When the minibus turned in to the yard of our accommodation, we saw the teachers waiting for us with ten children who had been chosen to be the reception committee. The small ones had prepared flower garlands for us and one of the children was already crying as the flowers had started to wither in the heat of the day. They had expected us to come on the morning ferry.

A meeting had been arranged in the church, starting immediately after our arrival. The church building itself had been totally renovated after the congregation had grown out of its previous limited space. It was now jammed full with the new mothers and relatives, whose children had started at the school that

198. *Inside our new school*

year. This meeting was arranged especially for them and Pastor Sonio said to me that 80% of the audience were newcomers. As I looked around the congregation I felt that they were a really representative sample of the people with whom we had worked.

This meeting was going to be an evangelistic one because most of these people were not saved. Before we really managed to get going, the lights went off. Brown time, I should have guessed it. Happily, one looks younger in the darkness.

The journey from Manila had taken such a long time and it had rained so much that my hair had been ruined by the dust, rain and sea winds. But there was no time available for either washing my hair or changing my

clothes before the meeting. I looked at myself in a mirror and saw that my hair was hanging hopelessly in tangled lumps around my face. I decided to use a loose hair bun that I had with me, created for just this sort of situation. I tied it as well as I could to my ponytail as I could not find any hairpins. It looked good, or at least much better than before – and behold, now I had an orthodox Pentecostal hair bun!

At a fitting time just before my sermon started, the brown time ended and there was enough light to step onto the platform, with my hair combed into a nicely artistic bun. As a child I had assumed that God had created the Finnish people's white skin colour as a protection against wolves – we would not be seen amongst the snow. I also felt that He didn't care much for our hair – as the few thin hairs that we had would easily stay underneath a fur hat. This time I needed some extra help for my hair.

As I preached I got a strange sensation and I didn't think it was the Holy Spirit this time. I felt something heavy sliding slowly downwards along my ponytail. The audience observed it with interest, wondering how a light coloured lump came to be creeping down my neck; the children were especially keen to observe its progress, until … plop! The furry bun fell on the floor right beside the pulpit. My once beautiful hair bun now lay on the floor like a killed albino rat. I tried to kick it away where it wouldn't be seen, and I noticed one child watching me in an admiring way, "Wow! Auntie killed that thing with her shoe – is she sure that it's dead?"

However disturbing and humiliating this incident was for me, the message of my sermon still seemed to touch my hearers. I preached about the miracles done by God and afterwards sick people were brought forward to be blessed.

A crowd gathered in front and everyone wanted to be prayed for as they had so many

199. *The Sonios' renovated church*

needs: some young people asked me to pray for them to find a job; an elderly lady who had been almost blind spoke of how she could see much more clearly after the prayer; and a woman with TB, heart problems and other pains was totally healed.

ANSWERS TO PRAYER

A paralysed boy was also carried to the front and placed on a table, his limbs limply hanging down like boiled spaghetti. His family had heard about Nico's healing and of course wanted their son to receive the same miracle. I prayed for this beautiful bright-eyed boy, and as I touched his hand, it stood up straight and stayed there as if some invisible person was holding it up. I didn't understand what was happening and the boy wasn't healed at that moment, but Nico himself had been healed months afterwards. Many people came to testify to the pastor that they were healed in that meeting.

Afterwards Sharon, one of our school teachers, came up to me, pushed a little bundle in my hand and whispered shyly, "Umm, you forgot this!" It was my

257

hair bun which had been rolling on the floor and collecting some extra add-ons along the way. Sharon comforted me, "You still look alright, never mind!"

Two weeks later when we were back in Manila, I met up with Nheng and she enthusiastically brought me up-to-date on further outcomes of the prayer time in Mamburao church. Many people had received answers to the prayers immediately and they were so keen on telling what the Lord had done for them during the week, that the next Sunday meeting at church ended up being totally taken up with such testimonies.

> **Your blessings are only a step away from home**

Both physical and inner healings had taken place and some amazing job miracles: in that town normally no-one could find a new job however hard they tried, but the young people who had asked for prayer for jobs had found them. Nheng's own brother was one of them. He had been unemployed for a long time, but I gave him a word from the Lord in the prayer queue: "Your blessings are only a step away from home." The next day he got a job at a small travellers' hostel that was on the other side of the road just opposite his home. The young man was so excited that he made a point of counting how many steps he had to take from his home to his new place of work.

In that Sunday meeting Rev. Sonio had had to stop the testifying and ask people to continue on the following week, as the congregation had grown and everyone seemed to have something new to tell about the great works of God.

PROPHECY FULFILLED

Nheng told me that the prophetic words I had given to the congregation in 2007 had come true this year. The Lord was showing His favour on the whole of Mamburao. The town had received blessings and was starting to prosper, as if the Lord had decided to fix its problems and raise it up from its destitute position to a new prosperity.

I could not remember all the details of that prophecy any more, just bits and pieces here and there. The word had come so powerfully in the meeting and was something totally opposite from what the rational mind would have said or what could be seen in the town at that moment.

God had spoken about people's hopes and desires that had been crushed by the difficulties of life. He was going to breathe new life into those hopes and they would become alive again. He would give back those things that the enemy had stolen and would open new doors to new possibilities and tasks. He was going to bless His people and that blessing would benefit the whole town. The favour of the Lord rested upon Pastor Sonio because he was allowing the Holy Spirit to operate freely and because he had looked after the poor and destitute children. That was the secret of the blessing coming to the church and the whole town.

The flame of God's glory would be seen from far away on the island and He will make His name to be known. This was going to be the year of the new beginning, a year to plant and to build up, to be like Nehemiah with a sword in one hand and tools in the other. The Lord was opening up things that have been impossible for man – but totally possible for Him.

All this had happened. Many peo- ple had found work in the town where it had been almost impossible before. A new school had started in Aroma village and a growing church had been birthed in the area too. Our first visit to the Aroma chil- dren at the end of 2007 had resulted in a Bible study group being set up in the area: Pastor Sonio and his wife had come every week to teach the adults and the children to know the Word of God. Now a congre- gation had been set up there and Pastor Jonathan had taken responsibility for it.

200. Teacher Sharon distribut- ing clothes to Mangyans

Mamburao school had moved to a new building which was much more suit- able. It was now not only accepted but val- ued highly within the educational commu- nity, with our results being the best in the area. New Bible study groups had been set up in the surrounding areas and outreach to the Mangyan tribes established, both through the practical donation of clothes and materials and through evan- gelising. Without the Sonios' hard work and diligence, many things that had been achieved would have just been buried in the cemetery of good ideas. We not only preached the gospel but also showed in practice how it works.

Rev. Sonio was now the leader of all the Foursquare churches in the island and he went by motorbike to many different localities to hold meetings there. God's healing power was evident in his congregations and people often travelled long distances to get prayer. News about the schools and what was happening in the congregations was now well known throughout Mindoro and its surrounding islands.

While I was in Mamburao, several pastors from elsewhere came to ask me if I could found a similar school for poor slum children in their towns or villages. They were hoping for the Mamburao school miracle in their own towns, and many of them even promised buildings for the schools. Some of them had travelled from the other end of the island to meet me and their sincerity and enthusiasm was evident, but my own capacity and funds were not yet large enough for such huge projects. They needed more than just good will, and of course the most important thing is to stay in the Lord's timetable, and not jump into our own.

Revival meetings continued every evening in the church. Meetings for the mothers were held during the days, and they soon became counselling sessions as many of them had personal tragedies in their background. Such things as counselling and therapy were not even mentioned here earlier, as people just had to cope with often impossible family situations or to somehow manage to handle the consequences of natural catastrophes. Some of the mothers had been stretched beyond the limits of their mental and emotional capacities, and the effects were now starting to come to the surface.

201. Classroom

CHAPTER 36
AROMA SCHOOL

MY FIRST VISIT

We also visited our schools and got to know the children better as we got involved in their day by day activities. The teachers were working in such a wholehearted way and doing amazing things with the kids.

They even acted as substitute mothers for some of the little ones, 24 hours a day, as some parents were in jail or had just disappeared somewhere, and other relatives either didn't exist or were not able to take on an extra load.

These children are really hungry for love. One small girl hung as an extra weight on my leg wherever I went in the school. Whenever one of the teachers picked her up and placed her on a chair, in a second she was back again clinging to my leg, apparently claiming it for herself. I

202. At Aroma school

felt that the children were *syötävän suloisia* ("edibly cute")! Nheng, Sharon and Frances had done such brilliant work with them.

203. Daisy

Following our outreach work in Aroma village which started in December 2007, scores of children and adults had become believers. Pastor Sonio's Bible study group had met the spiritual needs of the parents in the village but the children had been desperate for a school. Their families were so poor that even the three-wheeler fare to Mamburao was out of their reach. So we did our best to set up a small school in the middle of their slum village so that the children could walk to school from their homes.

A young teacher called Daisy took care of Aroma School. She had recently moved to Mamburao from Santa Cruz, where she had worked as a cashier in a pharmacy. A young believer in the town had persuaded her to attend a youth night at her church and after that Daisy had become an enthusiastic member of the church, regularly attending prayer meetings and Bible studies. But her boss at the pharmacy was not happy about her closing the shop early in the evenings so she could go to church, and so he sacked her. Before moving to Mamburao where her family lived, she visited her pastor in Santa Cruz, and he encouraged her to go to the Foursquare Church which Edwin Sonio led. On her first Sunday there she met Nheng, who really made her feel welcome and she settled in as an active member of the church.

Daisy was excellent with the Aroma children, but because there were so many of them and Daisy could not be cloned, they had to be divided in two groups: the smallest came to school in the morning and the older ones in the afternoon. A scooter had been bought for Nheng so that she could drive between the two schools, teaching first her own class in Mamburao and then going to help Daisy at Aroma school.

A GOOD START BUT ...

During this trip in December 2008, I visited Aroma school for the first time. The Aroma villagers had given the building for the school and I had no idea what it looked like, but if it was anything like the other houses in the village, then my expectations were not high. Just as well …

The school building was in a slightly better state than many of the other native huts but it still was in a miserable condition. Presumably the previous storm in the island had pushed the walls over at the angle at which they now stood, but I felt that it was remarkable that the structure was still standing. The windows were only openings where some sort of shade had been created out of fishing nets, and it was steaming hot inside. Even though the walls were built from bamboo sticks, the wind didn't find its way in. The air hung thick and damp in the hut, glue-ing your clothes to your skin. There were two long tables, an

204. *Aroma school building*

earthen floor, a plastic chair for each of the kids and a blackboard. Every day Daisy had to heave the tables upside down to prevent drunkards from sleeping on them; she told me that she had lost 5 kg in weight in the past year because of this daily exercise.

The hut was full of school children and mothers. In this village nobody had anything to do, so they had plenty of time to listen. The mothers were sweet and many came to thank me for the school, honestly and from the bottom of their hearts. I felt ashamed that I could not offer them anything better, but it was at least a start: without this free school there would not be any kind of education available for these children. The reputation of Aroma village was not very good, as many adults were alcoholics or drug users, and lacked the money to feed their children or to take care of them. Our kids often told their teachers what life was like at home, with violence being common. The school offered them some sort of safety that they otherwise lacked.

I noticed that during lessons the children would often run out and then come back in again after a few minutes. I asked Nheng why, and she laughed: "We do not have any toilets here, so the kids just run … ummm … somewhere." It was only then that I realised, "Oh my, you don't have toilets?" Then I asked if they had running water, and immediately understood what a silly question that was. The whole village was without running water and toilets. The children had

263

few opportunities to wash themselves so the simple rule that we used in Mamburao school, "Everyone needs to wash their hands", didn't work here. They could only use rainwater to wash or go to the sea for a salty bath.

Many of the children would get hungry and run home to see if there was any rice. If there wasn't any, they came to ask Daisy for food or begged her

for just one sweet – they weren't asking for sweets like a western child might, they just wanted something to ease their hunger.

When the rainy season started, the fishing boats could not go to sea and there was no rice either. There was some sort of plant that grew in the area like a weed, and the people pulled it up and ate its roots to fill their stomachs. I looked at this plant growing along the paths in the village and thought that only a cow would have wanted to eat such a thing. But I didn't see any cows in the whole of the island. Because there was such a lack of food in the area, we started to distribute rice to these families during the rainy season.

205. A full school

I heard that the school had been flooded during the monsoon rains, with water so high that it reached Daisy's hips and the small kids would have drowned in it, so Aroma school had had to take an enforced break.

After school each of the kids happily carried their plastic chair back to their home. It was often their only piece of furniture and anyway the chairs could not be left at the school, or they would disappear during the night. "Oh Lord," I sighed, "we can't go on like this! I need a piece of land that I can build on. The kids need to be able to wash themselves and they need toilets and a proper building with a cement floor. It needs to be strong so that it will stand up when the typhoons come, and if the huts of the kids are blown away, then at least the school would provide them shelter."

I knew that the prices of building lots were extremely high. But I really wanted a good place where the children could learn. The local huts built in a proper way are cool but our present building was a real sweat-shop and the children drooped on their chairs. If I couldn't cope with this heat, how could the little ones!

GOD ANSWERS BEFORE I ASK

The next day when I was preaching to the children and their mothers at school, I noticed a man standing outside the hut listening. He looked a bit different from the other men living in Aro-ma – his posture reflected a confidence and energy that people sunk in the hopelessness of the slums often do not have. When I finished preaching I went out and the man introduced himself. He politely said that the preaching had touched his heart. He had heard rumours about Hosea Ministry and that the founder of it was now in Aroma. He had decided to come to the school to see if the stories he had heard had any

206. *Nena, Sharon, Frances & Nheng*

truth in them, and whether the school was free after all. We exchanged some pleasantries and then I told him about my work in more detail.

Out of the blue he suddenly said that he could offer me a free piece of land in the area for the new school! I could hardly believe what I was hearing – how amazing that someone should be offering us a free building plot. And it wasn't as if I had even managed to pray about it yet: all I had done was complain to the Lord about the present state of affairs. And here His answer was! The man told me that he was an official from the town council, whose job it was to decide how land would be allocated in the area. How on earth was it possible that I had bumped into exactly the right person?

a free piece of land in the area for the new school!

By that time, Pastor Sonio had arrived on his motorbike and the children were starting to gather around us. Soon the entire group moved off in a long and noisy queue behind the official, to go and see the piece of land that was being offered us, as it was not far away.

We arrived at the empty plot and I had a good look at it. I asked whether it would get flooded during the monsoon rains, and the man assured me that it would not. I commented that the piece of land was small so we would only be able to build the school on it and we would still need a playground for it. I felt a twinge of guilt at complaining so soon after the man's generous offer, but the

265

fact was that the kids needed a playground area. Anyway, I agreed to accept the official's offer.

I was still wondering how it could be that the town was giving me a piece of its land, since I was a foreigner. Some time before, I had enquired about the possibility of buying land and was given a firm "No", since a foreigner can only acquire a piece of the Philippines if a Filipino owns it jointly with them. I wanted to make absolutely sure that this piece of land would be totally owned by Hosea Ministry and how it would happen in practice.

The officer assured me that it would indeed be 100% mine, and that he would arrange all the necessary papers with official stamps and signatures. He even promised to deliver them to me next day. That felt unbelievable: a piece of land for the school? Free? No charges? No extra hassles? That night I was still asking myself if this could really be true after all.

In the morning Edwin Sonio came to me carrying all the official papers, signed and stamped as promised. But there was another surprise in store for me. Overnight the town official had decided to grant us the building plot adjacent to the school one as well! I commented to Edwin that maybe I should stay in Aroma a while longer: if every day I was given a new piece of land then soon we would own the whole village.

SOUND FOUNDATIONS

Later, in January 2009, we would arrange to send through funds from the Finland end of Hosea Ministry to Aroma for the building work to be carried out, The school will be built from native materials and there will be toilets and also a water pump in the yard.

207. Building work starts in Aroma

Nheng told us that news about the free school in Aroma and its forthcoming new building had spread around the area and the registration list for the next intake of new students would be full. At first people had found it very difficult to believe that something could be offered to them for free. But now that the school year had been running for a while and the pupils were eagerly working, their

266

relatives and mothers grasped that this school really didn't cost them anything. So there were crowds of kids wanting to join us.

I felt that on this trip the Lord showed us the results of the foundational work we had done during earlier years. Before I left for Manila, Edwin Sonio gave me an estimate of the costs of building the new school in Aroma. He also reported that many mothers of the school kids had got saved during our meetings there. The visit to Mindoro had produced a good crop in so many ways.

Out of curiosity I asked Edwin why he thought that the offer of a free piece of land had come up now, considering that it had seemed an impossible dream earlier. I had been amazed to hear from the town official that he had wondered whether I really existed, given that our school had already produced such good results.

208. Aroma girls

FLEECING THE FLOCK

Rev. Sonio replied by telling me a sad story of what had happened in the town of Sablayan a few years earlier. A Korean church leader came to visit there: he contacted the local pastors, hired the biggest auditorium in town and sent out the word about his meetings. He promised that everyone who came would be offered a free meal, that their travel costs to and from the meeting would be paid for and that there would be other funds available too.

Of course lots of people crowded in to the meetings because there was a free meal available and also since they would get money for coming there. Altogether about 6000 people gathered to the auditorium from a wide area around Sablayan. The minister had also invited pastors from different churches in Korea to attend and he arranged the meeting to be videoed as well. The visiting Korean pastors were put in a nice hotel and were kept well away from local people – something that the Filipino pastors couldn't understand at all.

The big meeting started and the video cameras started filming the Korean pastor's opening remarks. He spoke in Korean and his words were not interpreted in this first part of the meeting. For most of the audience it really didn't matter much what was being said from the platform, as they were being paid

267

for coming. But there were some Filipinos there who understood the Korean language. Korean believers had done a lot of good work in the island earlier and many local churches had received support, both financial and practical, from the generosity of some Korean congregations. This visitor was probably not aware of this link. Many Filipinos work in different parts of the world and they have an amazing ability to pick up other languages very quickly. Perhaps it is because there are so many different languages in their home country and they have to learn at least three of them – Tagalog and English in addition to their own tribal language.

This Korean pastor introduced himself in his own language as the leader of this huge church in Sablayan. As the videoing continued, he told of how there were 6000 members in his church and that the growth had been miraculous. To continue this amazing work in the town, he was asking for financial support from Korean believers. The Korean visitors invited to the meeting were truly delighted to see this awesome ministry and promised that their own congregations would be supporting it in future. They said it was a privilege to see such marvelous out-reach work in Sablayan, and were so grateful to be able to witness it with their own eyes. The poor people did not bother about the talks – they just continued to enjoy their free meal, happy to fill their stomachs for once.

But there were Filipino people who understood what was said and they told others. Of course the local pastors were furious about such a betrayal, as this meeting was not any kind of congregation and the numbers had been swelled by offers of food and money. However, this swindler decided to stay and live in Sablayan town. No meetings were held any more, but the funds poured in as a result of his video being distributed widely amongst Korean churches. The so-called minister enjoyed a luxurious lifestyle, complete with big house and expensive car.

> **it requires a considerable time to win local people's trust**

As a result of his deceit, many local people lost all trust in foreign church organisations. Finally the situation around this man became so tense that he had to leave the town. No one knows where he is now, but there are many other such charlatans going around the Philippines, "selling" a so-called gospel like disreputable used car salesmen.

I now understood much better from Edwin's vivid example why it requires considerable time to win local people's trust. They first need to see whether you really are who you say you are.

MOVING ON

The time came for us to say goodbye to our friends in Mamburao, as we were due to travel on to Palawan. As usual, we took the ferry from the port of Abra de Ilog back to Batangas harbour and then took a bus to Manila.

There were big demonstrations going on in the Makati area in Manila and the government had sent in 5000 soldiers to cool down the riot, so we were aiming to get accommodation as close as possible to the airport before our flight to Puerto Princesa on Palawan Island.

The sea journey went quite smoothly and this time we did not even need to fight for seats. I found a padded seat for myself where I could even lie down. The insides of the padded cushions appeared to be trying to escape, and overall the seats looked as if they had been run over with a bulldozer or perhaps

209. Loading the luggage

fed through a mangle. But at least they met my requirements as a flat horizontal surface, and I fell asleep as the ferry made its way through the waves. It felt good to be able to catch up on the sleep that I had missed in Mamburao – there had simply been more work than I had been able to do.

After a pleasant rest on board the ferry, the bus trip from Batangas to Manila was rather a shock to the system. This inside of the vehicle was like an ice cellar and we were wearing very thin T-shirts. In addition, the entertainment wasn't exactly to our taste. Filipinos seem to love horror films and a particularly gruesome one was being shown on the TV monitor of the bus, with volume turned up to maximum, presumably in case any of the passengers were hard of hearing. I calculated that the producers of this film would have had to kill at least ten cows and several pigs to provide the bloody effects in their slaughterhouse story. After three different butchery films and the temperature of a frozen meat cellar, Manila's steamy and hot outside air felt like heaven.

Lea caught a cold and also my throat felt uncomfortable and swollen. Maybe the old man's van had been a better solution for cross-city transportation after all. Princess was so tired that she fell asleep on top of our suitcases that had been summarily offloaded onto the street from the bus. We now needed a taxi with a driver who would agree to load our large pile of suitcases into the car. The normal fare to our accommodation was 100 pesos but the first driver wanted to rob us by charging 500 pesos. Finally a taxi driver promised to take us to the hotel for 200 pesos and we quickly agreed, too tired to fight any more.

We selected our accommodation according to our budget, so Hiltons and Sheratons were quickly passed by, looking only at their photos in the advertisements. Luxury for us meant that we would have more than one bed in the room, and that running water was available. After travelling the whole day we were so tired that even a board would have been good enough to sleep on.

In the morning we went to the airport nice and early, two hours before the flight was due to depart, in order to have a peaceful start to our trip to Palawan. The departure time came and went and we waited and waited … Again there was a further postponement, with 'mechanical problems' being cited as the cause. After drinking coffee and eating some muffins we started to feel a bit more jolly, but we noticed that there was not much else available to eat in the airport. By the time that six hours beyond our departure time had passed, we had run out of sarcastic humour.

Lea's nerves broke first. I watched her take Princess's hand and march over to the information desk. Her arms swung angrily and words came out as from a machine gun. After a few minutes she came

> **Lea's nerves broke first**

back to where I was sitting, and I asked her what she had said to the airport staff. "I barked at them for keeping me and my small child here all day without food, with their interminable delaying," she said. "No normal person can buy these over-priced snacks at the airport café! I demanded that the airline provide proper meals for the passengers that are waiting."

Another hour passed by and then a miracle happened, as a door beside the cafeteria opened and the trays full of food were carried in – hot rice, chicken and Asian salad. Good work, Lea! How good the food tasted after a day of just snacks and coffee. Lea told me that she didn't feel hungry any more, and she pulled two pillows under her head and lay down to sleep on a bench. Princess had filled her stomach with the junk food at the airport and I had to force at least a few spoonfuls of proper food into her mouth. When the darkness came the airplane finally appeared and our journey could at last start.

270

CHAPTER 37
RETURN TO PALAWAN

SCHOOL VISIT

Our friends from Palawan were waiting for us at Puerto Princesa airport, but because our flight was so delayed, they had gone off to the school for a while and then come back again to see if our flight had landed. A special welcome had been arranged for us at school but we were so late in arriving, that there were only a couple of adults left when we got there, and the children had already been taken home. Pastor Chadwick Abdullah had kindly arranged for us to get something to eat.

This was the first time that I had seen the newly constructed school building, and I also had the opportunity to meet some of the teachers. The young people from Christlife church had done an excellent job, all on a voluntary basis. The school had been built out of native materials but it was very well constructed: it had withstood the last typhoon which had hit the area and in fact had served as a shelter for several local families, when their own huts had been destroyed. Chad's sister in law was an artist and some of her marvelous portfolio was displayed on one wall of the school. I saw too that the main hall had been designed very practically, as it could not only be used for school assemblies but also for church gatherings.

The only shadow cast over all this bright news was the fact that our continued use of the building was in question. The rented plot on which the school

> **our continued use of the building was in question**

had been built, together with several other buildings next to our school, had been put up for sale. The landowner was a Christian businessman and he did not have anything against the school, but because of the worldwide recession his businesses were not doing well and the bank was demanding the repayment of his loans. I was told that a couple of potential buyers had already been looking around.

The owner had allowed Chad's family and some of the teachers live rent-free in the adjacent buildings on the same land. The school itself was the newest of the buildings there.

When the school was being planned, I had decided that it should be constructed from local materials because it is cheap and quick to build, and it results in a cool interior with natural ventilation. It would also give us some future flexibility: I reckoned that the thatched roof would last for about three years and then, if the school was growing, we could either remove it and build a second storey or we could just move somewhere else.

Anything could happen in three years – just like in Mamburao. Perhaps someone in the city council would be generous and give us some land, just as we had found in Aroma. If a project is started by God then He is not going to leave it unfinished.

AT THE SLUM VILLAGE

Our school attendance had thinned out somewhat as a result of the typhoon damage: when several families had lost their huts, the city had moved them to Mangingisda Island. It wasn't just the typhoon winds that had done damage in the slum village, but the accompanying floods had washed shacks away and fires had started when the storm affected the DIY electricity supplies in the village. But in spite of this fearsome combination of wind, floods and fire, I was surprised to see many slum dwellings still standing.

Of the shacks constructed on stilts in the water, many had been instantly reduced to a pile of boards and others were washed into the sea. Because all the slum houses are built illegally, they have no utilities such as water supply or sewage. In the stilt houses, rubbish and effluent is simply dropped into the sea. When the tide goes out there are filthy pungent piles beneath the houses and when the tide comes in, it all floats on the water. The same water is used for laundry and for other household purposes and I even saw people fishing in the same all-purpose water.

One mother came to us asking for prayer because her child had a horrible rash. It seemed a very common condition and no wonder in these surroundings – but how could it be explained to them? The children happily went swimming in the polluted water.

The floods had swept the remains of destroyed shacks, together with raw sewage and rubbish, deeper into the slum area. The damage was very recent: paths were covered with mud, our shoes got soaking wet but there was no way that we could take them off because of the filth and effluent there.

Nobody was going to clean the place up, but I saw one brave individual trying to burn up the rubbish left from some demolished huts, probably in preparation for building a new shack on that piece of land. This was despite the fact that the city had explicitly banned the raising of any further squatters huts, as it wanted to get rid of the eyesore that was the slum village from its otherwise beautiful beaches.

After an earlier fire in the slum village, the city mayor, who was a believer, had arranged alternative accommodation to be built for the homeless people in another part of the city. It was an excellent move, but for some reason more squatters huts soon appeared again along the beach.

210. *Our group amidst the destruction*

The new boulevard that had replaced the previous beach slum was alive in the evenings, with a platform for outdoor performances and cinema for the citizens. There were barbecue shelters for picnics and a good family atmosphere. The mayor had designed an open area in the city centre, similar to the boulevard, and there at Christmas we saw a wonderful performance about the nativity. Just like on the boulevard there were plenty of takeaway food shops and cafes where families could relax together and enjoy a meal. The best aspect of all was the cleanliness of it all – the only 100% rubbish-free place we came across in the archipelago.

273

I think that the city authorities had an ongoing struggle against both rubbish and the construction of the slum-dwellers huts. When one area was cleaned up, another one appeared in its place. The people who lived on the streets naturally wanted to be where things were happening, because that's where they could get food or beg for money.

Through Beleni, I got to know several of the city's social workers whose job it was to take care of the children who lived on the streets, and to make sure they went back to their homes. If they didn't have places to go then they were sent into hostels, like the Batantay Centre that we had visited.

We spent some time visiting the villagers together with Chad and several of our schoolteachers – something that earlier would never had been possible. Now they recognised that we genuinely wanted to help them. But the typhoon had left new levels of apathy in its wake – what did anything matter any more? Who cares who is wandering around our wrecked village? There was so much indifference and hopelessness amongst the slum villagers.

When we visited the homes of several of our school children, we were delighted to see the difference that attending school had made in their lives.

211. In the wreckage

There was new hope in their parents that life could change for the better in the midst of their misery. I met many mothers who had attended gospel meetings arranged at the school, and I found that knowledge of us had quickly spread.

In front of one shack an elderly lady was sitting. When she saw me, she begged me to come in because her teenage son was ill. One side of his face was swollen and he had terrible toothache, with no money to pay for a dentist. There would have been a quick and simple solution if this boy lived in the western world, but here their only hope was a miracle from God.

The mothers had told their friends and relatives in this slum community about the meetings at school – everyone seemed to know everyone else in the village. Many of them had started to attend Sunday meetings run by Christlife church and a Bible study had been set up at the school for the parents.

After we left Palawan, Pastor Chad told us that another weekly Bible study was now running within the village itself. Because the school was nearer to the village than the church was, Christlife had decided to run Sunday meetings at the school as well, since many poor villagers could not afford to travel to Sunday morning church services on the other side of the city.

Earlier on the trip, Lea had been bitten badly by fleas She still had little wounds from them all over her legs, and she was doing her best to keep dirt out of the scabs. In the same area there lived a number of street kids, none of whom came to school. They were noisy and aggressive and they followed us everywhere we went. At one point without warning one of the little rascals that followed us jumped into a mud pool right next to Lea, and she was splattered with the filthy substance.

Knowing Lea's disposition I realized that this was a catastrophe for her. In whatever humble conditions we encountered on our travels, she always did her best to be well turned out – clothes, hair, make-up and everything. After a few seconds of practicing extreme self-control, Lea muttered to me through gritted teeth, "I could even catch AIDS from this stuff." After all the hassles that we had been through together. I couldn't help but find it rather amusing.

In the poverty and degradation of the slums, there were a few individuals who still tried to make some money to improve their lot. We came across one woman who had set up a sewing

212. Entrepreneur with her Husqvarna

business in her little shack, and I noticed something very familiar about the sewing machine. It was exactly the same Husqvarna model of pedal-operated machine that my mother had used as a professional dressmaker to sew clothes, in the years following the second world war in Finland. "Was it here that my mum's old machine had disappeared to?" I wondered.

The slum is a self-contained community with its own rules and procedures which an outsider is unable to understand. Another villager had set up a grill house rivaling MacDonalds at a crossroads of some winding paths through the village. On the small barbecue lay several sticks containing somewhat indeterminate meat pieces and tethered to an old lorry nearby was a piglet waiting to offer itself as the next takeaway meal.

Along the pathways there were small shops selling car engine parts and scrap metal. Filipinos are masters at creating working machines out of old pieces of scrap. What to others was just discarded rubbish became useful components in the hands of these master mechanics.

MANGINGISDA VISIT

We had agreed to go to Mangingisda Island on Thursday 18 December – a half hour boat trip from the mainland. Officially Mangingisda is not an island but a promontory of land, but it is almost impossible to reach it overland and hence the only sensible means of transport there is boat. We took a huge amount of foodstuffs with us, and, as well as Beleni, we were accompanied by three ladies who would arrange the feeding programme. Our three companions were from Beleni's workplace and turned out to be trainee social workers who were getting familiar with working practice in the city and its environs. They had planned singing games for the 150 or so children that we expected to be gathering to hear the gospel.

We came together in the yard of a hut beside the road, and local children looking extremely thin soon joined us. They were accompanied by their

213. Games on Mangingisda

mothers, many of whom looked just as starved as they did, carrying smaller ones in their arms. Inside the hut at the back were three men who were preparing fighting cocks for their next tournament. They seemed to have no interest at all in what we were doing right outside their house.

Beleni had a surprise for us: she told us that there was a piece of land some distance away that belonged to her sister Julie, who was working as a teacher in Japan. We listened to her story and made polite comments along the way: "Ah I see." The plot was currently occupied by a water-buffalo, living its happy or perhaps unhappy existence. Beleni

continued: "My sister has married an American and is moving soon to the USA."
"That's interesting," I again politely responded.

"So my sister doesn't need this land any more," said Beleni, "and she has decided to give it away. For example … to you. Perhaps you could, for example, build a school here." It took a little while for me to understand what Beleni was getting at. So … a school on a free piece of land.

I didn't really see why I should start a school here on Mangingisda, but then an idea sprang to mind. I asked Chad that if we were to lose our school in Puerto Princesa, could the building be taken apart and removed, since it was made from native materials? Chad gave it some thought and replied, "Yes that can be done – in fact it should be pretty straightforward."

"OK if that's the case," I said, "because I own the school building but not the land, we're not going to leave the building behind if we are evicted. No, we'll move it here to Mangingisda. And then we'll wait for the Lord to arrange another place for us to have school in Puerto Princesa."

The young people from Christlife church had built up our school in Puerto Princesa under

214. Feeding the Mangingisda kids

the guidance of one professional builder, so why wouldn't it be possible for them to carefully dismantle it and build it again? The only thing we would have to leave behind would be the concrete base – everything else could be taken down and moved to Mangingisda. The water buffalo of course would have to find a new home.

Our young pastor seemed a bit shocked by my innovative approach. He had not yet given up hope of keeping our present school, as the news of its sale had only just broken. I told Beleni, "I accept your sister's gift, providing we can arrange all the necessary paperwork. I don't want to be thrown out again from something that I've just got going!"

The meeting for the kids soon started, and after preaching to them we distributed food. I felt such pity for the young mothers who looked as thin as rakes but we had no spare food to offer to them. One lonely dog wandered

277

around by the children's feet hoping for some little morsels to be dropped. I wished I had something to give it as its ribs were clearly visible through its thin frame and its back legs only moved with difficulty. If only I had a bread bun left over.

Normally in the Philippines these dogs went around in packs and waited until people had gone away before searching for food scraps. Villagers used to throw stones at them to keep them away as some of them carried rabies and other diseases. I wondered why there weren't more dogs than just this lonely individual on the island. Where had this one come from?

After the meeting with the children we spent about an hour with Beleni's parents who lived on the island. Then we retraced our steps along the road towards the harbour. I walked in front, hoping to find a three-wheeler to take us there. Lea was walking behind me and suddenly I heard her shouting for me to come back. I wondered what the matter was, as she looked so shocked. She said, "Look behind the house where we fed the children."

There I saw a man with a bundle of burning sticks in his hand waving it back and forth under something hanging in the tree. I went closer and was horrified to see the same dog that had been scavenging around the children now being itself grilled for food. Its carcase was already black from the fire. No wonder that I hadn't seen any other dogs on Mangingisda. This one had come out of hiding attracted by the smell of the food. It came to the right place but at the wrong time. I knew that local people eat dog – what else can you do if there is nothing to eat? But why this poor creature and why now? Why did I have to witness such a spectacle? Such horrible images tend to stay in my mind for a long time.

I tried to forget the whole thing and to concentrate on the children who were gathering around us wherever we went. They were so wonderful – they came to thank us for the food. One hundred and sixty little ones had come to faith through our visit. "Maybe they really do need a school here," I thought. At least I could offer education to our pupils who had been moved here by the city authorities after the typhoon. Later on Beleni told me that she planned to start a Bible group for the kids and their mothers on the island in the next week, so that these new believers would get support.

> **Maybe they do really need a school here**

During the following week we used the school building to hold meetings every evening and counselling sessions during the day time. There was also a school Christmas celebration in which the children did a performance of all they had learned. God had done so many miracles through the school, in the lives of both children and parents, and the results were so obvious to us all. And yet, our work there had just begun.

CHANGES AT CHURCH

Christlife Church, where Chad was working as one of the pastors, held its meetings in a hotel on the other side of Puerto Princesa. In the beginning of our last week in Palawan, Lea went up to Pastor Chad and asked him in a very straightforward Finnish way: "Can Anne preach in next Sunday's meeting?" However the church had something else arranged as their programme on that Sunday:

we heard that was why they had reserved meetings for me at school. That was good of course, but I needed to show Chad that the gifts of the Holy Spirit really work, and that the most effective ministry happens when Word and Spirit are combined. I did not want to be pushy, but I was only here a short while longer in Palawan, with just one Sunday left before I had to leave to Manila.

215. Meetings at the school

I also understood that they did not know me as a preacher – I was just an Australian lady who had founded the school. So I prayed that the Lord would arrange things and send the other speaker away next Sunday, and also ensure that nobody else would step in.

The following week we had meetings at school, arranged for the close relatives of our school children and the Lord showed the power of the Holy Spirit there. At first, Chad did not know that I was going to give prophecies for the people, and I decided to surprise him. So at the end of one meeting, after I had told the audience about how I had been healed, I asked any people that were sick to come forward for prayer. No one moved at first, apparently lacking the faith.

So I modified my invitation and asked anyone who wanted a blessing to come to the front. One lady plucked up courage and came forward, and I started to pray a fairly 'normal ' starting prayer, in simple language as not many of the audience were believers. Chad had to interpret for me as poor people do not usually understand English. I then started to prophesy and the words just came and came: the whole past life of the lady and into the present. As Chad interpreted he started to gaze in amazement at me.

While I was speaking, Lea moved away the chairs at the front of the school hall so we had room to pray for people. When I finished prophesying the lady wept and wept. Between her tears she said something to Chad, who then turned to me: "Anne, I know this woman and everything you said about her is true. How on earth could it be so accurate?" This was the first time that he had experienced prophetic words, and how like God it was to ensure that he already knew this lady!

I checked with Chad whether I could continue with this, because when the other people heard the prophecy, all of sudden there was a traffic jam at the front. So I got to work and God showed up, revealing many people's hopes, fears, past experiences and secrets. Many cried, many were set free and many became believers. Chad was amazed, shocked and delighted. The news of this meeting spread quickly even among the Christlife congregation and the church members started to ask for the same for themselves. So Chad arranged an extra meeting one evening just for the church staff and the congregation.

216. A meeting at Christlife church

The pressure was heavy. People brought me a chair and Chad sat beside me on another chair with his laptop and a microphone, recording everything. In front of me there were placed two chairs and one after another the couples or individuals came. I didn't know any of them, but I looked at the expressions on their faces and on Chad's face at the end of each session: I saw how they looked at each other and nodded. I ended up prophesying to them until midnight and I was exhausted.

I heard later that God gave to every individual clear and accurate words about their past, their present situation and something about their future. To several people the Lord revealed their occupation clearly and they stared at me totally amazed.

At the end of the meeting I felt like a deflated balloon. So much energy had been going through my body that it sucked me dry – maybe it was also the pressure that everything had to be right, not one single mistake was allowed. I had to concentrate hard and listen to the Lord to make sure I was hearing what He was saying for each person. One mistake and that would have been that story finished!

The meaning of prophecy is to bring souls into the Kingdom of God, and that is what happened there in Puerto Princesa. But it also had a tremendous impact on the members of Christlife church. For the rest of the week my time was taken up in giving counselling sessions or personal prophecies.

SUNDAY SERMON

During that busy week, I heard from Chad that the speaker who was due to preach on Sunday morning had to go away on urgent family business that weekend. There was God's answer to my prayer! Chad had asked the senior pastor whether I could preach instead of that speaker and he was more than happy for me to do so after such good reports from the congregation of the happenings from earlier in the week.

I did not have much time because our plane to Manila was leaving in the afternoon, just after the meeting. I had just one hour to win the people's hearts and to give a moving sermon. Once again I had to trust that God would take care of everything and would give His anointing to the word and to the people ... the pressure was heavy. I knew that I could not afford to fail but I also knew that I have the bad habit of preaching long sermons. But I didn't

> **I had just one hour to win the people's hearts**

need to worry; the Holy Spirit came immediately and, even though I had no idea of what to preach, the words flowed and the audience lived along with my stories: they cried and they laughed, probably finding it rather different from what they were used to hearing on Sunday mornings. It was a victory.

There was no time to pray for people after my sermon, so I returned to my seat exhausted, and turned to Lea saying "OK let's go and eat so we can manage to get to the airport on time." We made our exit as the congregation were singing, left the hotel and made our way to the nearby Pizza Hut.

While we were having our meal, in walked some members of the Christlife congregation and the leader of the YWAM organisation in Palawan. The YWAM lady walked straight to our table, sat down beside me and took my hand, saying, "Anne, your sermon really touched me. It was exactly what I needed to hear and it gave me fresh courage, thank you." This was much more than I could ever wish for, because I knew this lady to be very brave, and one whose word really mattered in that area. I had a great deal of respect for her and these words of encouragement were just what I needed to hear.

Chad came to the airport later and we had a heart to heart talk. Finally a real trust had been established between us and he assured me that he and many of his fellow church leaders would wholeheartedly welcome me if I ever could come to Palawan again. They were so excited about what God had done.

Chad emailed me later to tell me that now he too was operating in words of knowledge sometimes. We had encouraged him to use them. Lea had told him about Pastor Saki from Fiji, who had started to use the same gift right after I had left Fiji. He had been determined to get the anointing and the gifts of the Holy Spirit just as I had been using – and that is what happened. Obviously Chad had taken this to heart because now he was doing the same.

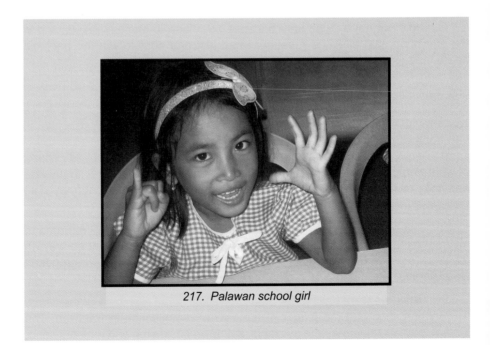
217. Palawan school girl

282

CHAPTER 38
EPILOGUE

ANOTHER UPDATE

Chad sent me a lovely story by email a little while later that really illustrated the changes that were taking place:

> Hello dear Anne, I am sharing with you some wonderful news about the school.
>
> A child could preach! (This story was related to us by the mother of Leslie, one of our students)
>
> One night, Leslie's father and his friends decided to drink alcohol inside their house (as they would always do). As they were happily drinking, they were surprised to hear a loud voice shouting at them. "*Wag kayong maglasing! Bad yan! bad yan!* (Stop drinking! That is bad! That is bad!). The father was astonished because it was his first time to hear his little girl Leslie going on like this. However, they still went on drinking. As if Leslie was endowed with a higher authority that night, she continued to preach at them with ever increasing boldness and said those same words over and over again. Finally, her words got into the heart of her father and he finally decided to end their drinking session. His friends were disappointed. The mother was

so happy. Leslie came to school the next day, as usual. The Spirit of God is moving to push back darkness among the families of the students.

Parents Bible Study

Our Bible study with the parents are really being blessed by God. We are surprised to see and feel how much the parents welcome the word of God. Our schedule is at 2:30 pm but they would all show up almost an hour earlier. The meeting is almost like a second Sunday service for us. We only require the father to come, but they would bring along their wives too. It is also a great encouragement for us to see how these precious souls are hungry for God's word. Almost 90% from them came from the Roman Catholic religion and some of them have not even read a single chapter of the Bible.

> **these precious souls are hungry for God's word**

Brothers Atanoso

Noel (4 yrs) and Christian (6 yrs) Atanoso are brothers. They entered the school with excitement on their faces but one can trace a bit of sadness in their eyes. We were curious for a time but as we observed them daily we found out what was bothering them. First , we noticed that they only come to school every other day. Then we noticed that they wore the same set of clothes every time. They also share one school bag. We started to feel what Noel and Christian are really feeling especially when it's time for the children to get their bags or get their personal grooming boxes. Noel and Christian's boxes were empty. The parents haven't provided their grooming items yet. We discussed these concerns with their parents and found out that they can't afford to send Noel and Christian to school on a daily basis because they are struggling to survive, let alone to provide for their boxes. We then shared this story to some of our church members and we had good response from them. Somebody bought the items Noel and Christian needed for their grooming boxes. Right now, Noel and Christian still skips school a day or two but we have seen a change in their behaviour since the day their grooming items were available. They are active and interested children.

This is all for now. I am happy to share with you these turns of events. I hope this will encourage you. Stay blessed, Chad

284

Heavy Sleeper

On our return flight to Australia I had two missionaries as my travelling companions. One was a Filipina lady and the other an Australian from Cairns, and both worked in Mindanao. We got on very well and the time passed quickly. I told them the story of my left hand and how it magically attracts old ladies to pull it. But if you don't become discouraged you can still travel one-handed.

At one point the lights of the plane were dimmed as it was time for sleeping. I put on my eye shades and drifted off to sleep. I had a strange dream about something heavy coming on me and trapping me so that I could not move. Someone nudged me: "Wake up, Anne – wake up!" My new friend next to me lifted up my eye shades and the light poured in. My brain was still in a state of hibernation and everything felt so horribly heavy. I blinked and wondered whether I was still dreaming, because there in my lap was lying a very large lady! No wonder I felt so heavy – I couldn't move at all under her weight.

She had apparently fainted as she had been walking past my aisle seat and just dropped onto my lap. It needed two strong men to lift her off me. Of all the 360 passengers on that flight, I was the one she chose to give her a soft landing from her swooning! When my companions had made sure that I was alright we all burst out laughing. This was a convincing testimony to them that my left arm really does have a magnetic effect on elderly ladies.

But my arm is still working … and nothing is going to prevent me from embarking on further adventures.

APPENDIX 1: FOREIGN WORDS

Word	Language	Meaning
auta	Finnish	help me
kana	Tagalog	foreigner – short for Amerikana
kana	Finnish	hen
kava	-	an intoxicating drink consumed quite widely by natives of the Pacific islands and made from the root of the pepper plant
letka-jenkka	Finnish	a dance similar to the conga
limbutong	Tagalog	a red scarf worn by the Mangyans
nasira	Tagalog	broken
nga-nga	Tagalog	palm seeds (betel) which when chewed give a narcotic effect. They can also be smoked in a pipe
nipa	Tagalog	a nipa hut is a dwelling with walls made of bamboo tied together and a thatched roof of dried grass.
peso	-	currency unit in the Philippines. In January 2009, €1 = 62.4 pesos
piko	Tagalog	sticky rice – sweet brown rice
sisu	Finnish	determination, guts and stamina to get things done against the odds
syötävän suloisia	Finnish	edibly cute
tamaraw	Tagalog	water buffalo
tau-buid	Tagalog	a pipe used for smoking betel
ulango	Tagalog	a covering made from buri palm leaves worn by Alangan tribes women

LATEST NEWS
APRIL 2009

Aroma School

The new school building in Aroma village is almost finished and will be completely ready to receive the children when the new school year starts in June. At the time of publishing this book, the kids are having their summer holiday, as it is the hottest time of the year in the Philippines.

218. New school building in Aroma

The villagers eagerly helped with the building work and that is why the construction was so quick. We now have great facilities for our children in this nice cool building with its two big rooms. We also have toilets and washing facilities for our pupils. All the villagers are so thankful to God and to those that donated towards this school, as now they have a new hope and future.

Hosea Ministry is also in the process of buying a fishing boat and nets for the villagers in Aroma. This will enable them to get both income and food.

219. A fishing boat for Aroma

Mamburao School

220. *Mamburao School Foundation Day*

Our school in Mamburao is doing excellent work, the pupils are keen on learning new things and are greatly enjoying their new skills. Revival is continuing in the town as the influence of the school spreads wider around the area.

Palawan School

The teachers have done brilliant work with our children at Christlife Preschool in Palawan, and major changes are happening in the lives of so many people in the area where our kids live, as God pours out His love, life and hope in the midst of apathy and hopelessness.

221. *L to R: Juliana, Cherry Ann, and Justine 'graduating' at Palawan*

However, this Palawan school project suffered a bad setback in March 2009, when the owner of the land decided to sell the whole plot, including our school building, after the bank threatened to foreclose on him. Even though we had decided to move the school to Mangingisda in such an eventuality (as described in Chapter 37), we could not do so after all, as the new buyer wanted to buy the piece of land with all the buildings as well. So we were not allowed to disassemble our school building as we had planned.

Pastor Chadwick and his team have found a new location for the school elsewhere in the city of Puerto Princesa. The new building, which we will rent, earlier served as a warehouse, and it will need a certain amount of renovation to make it fit for the children and teachers to use when the new school year starts. The owner of our previous school lot promised to pay for the renovation of this new place, thus compensating our loss. He also promised to pay part of the rent over the next 10 years for which this new building is leased to us.

So this arrangement should be more permanent than the previous one, but we are still waiting for the Lord to give us the piece of land in the city of Puerto Princesa to

222. *Students, parents and teachers at Palawan school*

put up a building of our own, planned and built especially for the use of our precious children. The city has already given us a substantial gift by allocating us a piece of land in Mangingisda, so we will be able to put up a new school there, after we have gathered enough funds for it. This is in addition to the plot on Mangingisda that Beleni's sister Julie kindly offered us.

OTHER SCHOOLS IN THE PACIFIC ISLANDS

I have also started other schools in Tonga and Papua New Guinea during the past few years, and more are either opening during 2009 or waiting for funds to come through so that we can start the construction work.

I want to say a big thank you to all those people who have donated to this ministry. Because of your gifts, many children now have schooling, and a future full of hope. What a joy it is to see these slum children graduating from our school, ready to continue to state school.

I have many more stories to tell of what God has done in other places than the Philippines, so who knows how many more books may be filled with such stories in the future!

For more information on publications by Anne Miettinen
please contact HIMbooks Ltd.

Email: info@himbooks.com
Website: http://www.himbooks.com

Anne Miettinen can be contacted through Hosea Ministry International Ltd.

Email: anne@hoseami.org
Website: http://www.hoseami.org

The Hosea website also contains information on how to donate to Anne's work.